Hindu Gods in an
American Landscape

Hindu Gods in an American Landscape

*Changing Perceptions
of Indian Sacred Images
in the Global Age*

E. ALLEN RICHARDSON

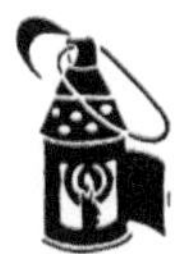

McFarland & Company, Inc., Publishers
Jefferson, North Carolina

ISBN (print) 978-0-7864-9944-1
ISBN (ebook) 978-1-4766-3261-2

Library of Congress cataloguing data are available

British Library cataloguing data are available

Front cover image by Nikhil Patil (iStock)

Printed in the United States of America

*McFarland & Company, Inc., Publishers
Box 611, Jefferson, North Carolina 28640
www.mcfarlandpub.com*

For Betty, Jimmy and Shelly

Table of Contents

Acknowledgments

I am grateful to a number of people who have made this book possible. Dr. Alfreda E. Meyers read drafts of the manuscript sharing her expertise in South Asian history and her insights into Hindu culture. I am also indebted to a number of colleagues at Cedar Crest College including Dr. Micah Sadigh whose insights into psychology and philosophy were invaluable and Chris Duelfer, whose knowledge of economics and globalization were an important asset to my research. Dr. Lindsey Welch collaborated with me, testing *mūrtis* for composition with a scanning electron microscope (SEM) and sharing her considerable expertise. Dr. John Hawley, at Barnard College in New York, provided additional insights into *Vaiṣṇava* iconography. Dr. Anoop Chandola, professor emeritus of the University of Arizona, was an enormous help with the transliteration of terms in North Indian languages as was Anishka Gheewala-Lohiya, who is a Ph.D. candidate at the London School of Economics.

A number of Hindu friends also offered advice and counsel. Kanha Vyas in Jodhpur, India freely shared his expertise in Hindu iconography which was especially illuminating and greatly appreciated. Bhagwat Shah in London offered his considerable knowledge of *Pushtimarg* and also provided both a personal narrative and a number of photos for the text. Kinnari Desai in Allentown, Pennsylvania, provided an extremely insightful narrative about her own devotional experience. Shivana Desai provided personal interviews and also greatly assisted me in gaining access to other second-generation Hindu Americans whose enthusiasm greatly illumined my work. Shree Patel at the *Anoopam Mission* in Coplay, Pennsylvania, shared his many insights about *mūrti* worship, providing an especially valuable contribution to my research.

I am particularly indebted to Rajendran Srinivasan of New Delhi, who facilitated an interview with an image maker, providing detailed responses to my interview questions as well as photographs. Ratnam Krishnamurti Ashok Kumar in Swamimalai (Tamil Nadu, India) graciously described his craft, making it accessible to a Western audience.

I am especially grateful to my *Vaiṣṇava* friends at the *Pushti Margiya Vaishnav Samaj* (*Vraj*) in Schuylkill Haven, Pennsylvania, including Pramod Amin, Hemant Patel, and Manisha Shah. Participants in the *Vraj Youth Organization* participated in the research and helped me understand second-generation perspectives without which this text would be sorely diminished. I also appreciate the advice of *Goswāmī* Shyam Manoharji on *Vaiṣṇava* iconography.

Colleagues in faculty and staff at Cedar Crest College also provided support. Dr. Elizabeth Meade (president of Cedar Crest College) offered suggestions for the discussion of Western philosophy and material culture. I am grateful to Kyle Crimi (lending services coordinator at Cressman Library) whose assistance with inter-library loans was invaluable. Tom Ardizzone (freelance videographer and adjunct instructor in the Communication Department) contributed his considerable skills in photographing images. Seth Rehrig (manager of Printing and Postal Services) worked on many of the photographs, bringing out the best possible result. Patricia Field (administrative assistant for the Social Sciences Department) provided support in numerous areas.

I am grateful to Dr. Margaret Scherrer (associate professor of psychology) and Sam Boss (director of the Samuel Reed Hall Library), both of Northern Vermont University for graciously providing me with library access to finish the book.

Jane Trumbauer of Allentown, Pennsylvania, gave enormous support in indexing, proofreading, and applying diacritical marks in the text. Her attention to detail and support of my work were important parts in bringing this text to fruition.

Finally, I am indebted to my family Betty, Jimmy and Shelly for their support during the research.

Explanation of Diacritical Marks

This text uses terms that stem from a number of Indian languages including *Hindi*, *Braj Bhāsha* (a *Hindi* dialect), *Gujarati*, and *Sanskrit*, and are italicized except for the names of individuals, dieties, places, or terms in common English usage. In order to avoid confusion, diacritical marks have been added only to essential terms and are omitted from the names of persons, deities, places, temples, sectarian organizations and dynasties in Indian history which in popular usage would normally not employ them. Terms that commonly appear in English are also not transliterated.

Introduction

As patterns of immigration from India to the West continue to accelerate, South Asians have rapidly become the fastest growing ethnic group in the United States with a population of over 3.4 million people. Precipitated in the United States by immigration reforms in 1965, this transnational growth has brought numerous forms of Hinduism to North America including classical South Indian temples, North Indian *bhakti* movements, and *guru* led sectarian traditions.

When Hindus have migrated beyond India, a number of important dynamics of religion and culture have changed. American Hindus find themselves separated from caste and the strong relationships that form endogamous *jāti* traditions. In the United States they are part of a secular society where religion is often on the periphery rather than part of the mainstream. As Hindu immigrants have coped with these changes, they have also encountered a confusing array of adaptations of Hindu culture. *Yoga* has been incorporated into the wellness industry. Vegetarianism, once seen as virtually "anti-American," is frequently disassociated from religion and incorporated within social justice and environmental movements. However, a transition that is not as visible is the change in perception about Hindu sacred icons from embodied forms of deity to symbolic objects. In less than fifty years of immigration and accelerated globalization this shift has produced a layered form of Hinduism in the West in which parents and children may hold different interpretations of the icons they worship.

Beyond India

Hinduism beyond India is complicated not only by changes in perceptions about icons but also by the loss of sacred geography. As Diana

Eck has amply demonstrated in *India: A Sacred Geography*,[1] India has been defined by theopanies and the presence of deity in every corner of the subcontinent. From Kashi, the homeland of *Shiva*, to Braj where the childhood of *Krishna* is intimately connected to the terrain around the Yumna River, sacred presence is embedded within the Indian landscape. This presence is defined both through interdependent mythologies from the *Vaiṣṇava, Śaiva,* and *Shakti* traditions and by the land itself.

In the context of such intimate connections between place and the holy, there is significant affinity between perceptions of icons as embodied presence and geography. In India, sacred presence is not an isolated phenomenon. Rather, embodiment is part of India's landscape and is intimately tied to its temple traditions. Pilgrimages often unite the two, enshrining natural phenomenon in temples, marking the sites of theopanies and calling attention to connections between deities and the earth. Examples of this linkage are not difficult to find and form a spectrum of belief ranging from animism to worship of anthropomorphized images. A tree in a modern, highly urbanized section of New Delhi is marked with red ochre and by the signs of repeated worship. In Rajasthan, small bands of pilgrims carrying ochre flags are a common sight as devotees visit temples or shrines where, for them, the sacred has become particularly manifest. In the Trikuta Mountains in Jammu and Kashmir, a cave marks the presence of three forms of the mother goddess, dubbed *Vaishno Devi.* For a *Pushtimarg* devotee on a pilgrimage to Nathdwara, the connections between the town and the resident deity, *Shri Nathji* (an incarnation of *Krishna* as a child) are pervasive,

> Divine presence infuses the entire temple and the temple town. All activities in the temple and the town revolve around the deity. It's difficult to imagine that without being there. This is a feeling that has be to be 'experienced'. The 'mood' of the divine rules the mood of the temple and the town. If ever the God is upset, no matter what the cause, you can 'feel it' in the air. Everything is wrong. Even the air smells wrong.
>
> God's world is suffused with delight—anand. Music, scent, buzz of pilgrims, chants, rituals reverberate through the temple complex and indeed the town. Divine anand flows from the inner sanctum all the way to the market and beyond. It is a subtle thing. Like the quality of air in Paris, buzz of New York or light of Athens, it is ethereal.[2]

In Nathdwara, perceptions of embodiment are not only focused on icons but also permeate the town that has evolved around it. Image and geography are inseparable, symbiotic parts of a larger whole of a unified sacral reality.

Because of the assumption that gods can assume physical form,

Hindu icons are defined as *mūrtis,* a term that connotes a form or embodiment of a deity and implying a living presence. However, there is no English term that conveys this precise meaning since Western perceptions of material culture see objects as things. While the term "icon" is more neutral it still does not reflect presence. Other terms such as "figurine" are often used in the art world but again refer to objects as things. "Statue" is a term sometimes used in Indian literature where *mūrtis* are interpreted as living presence. However, in the West, where "statues" are most often seen as forms of art and as objects, the term fails to suggest life. Because of these constraints, the academic study of Hindu patterns of worship frequently uses the term "image." While still not fully connoting the dynamics of embodiment, images do convey a reflective presence of deity and are the closest synonym for *mūrtis* available in English.

This text asks the question, what happens to perceptions of embodiment in Hindu sacred images when they are removed from sacred geography? How are anthropomorphized forms of gods perceived when they are taken out of context into a globalized, secular environment? The answers to these questions are complex and require familiarity with India's rich history of embodied images, as well as the West's insistence that the material and the spiritual are separate domains.

Embodiment and Hindu Images

The perception of images as embodiments of the gods has been one of the most consistent aspects of Hindu tradition, bridging literature and patterns of temple worship. In his study of the Hindu temple, George Mitchell concludes,

> The willingness of the gods and goddesses of Hinduism to make themselves accessible to man is emphasized everywhere in Hindu literature. That temples are places where the gods make themselves visible is conveyed by the very terms used to convey a temple: a seat or platform of god (*prasada*), a house of god (*devagriham*), a residence of god (*devalaya*) or a waiting and abiding place (*mandiram*). The temple is a receptacle for the gods, who may appear there in the forms imagined by their worshippers. These forms are embodied in the sacred image or symbols of the deities which constitute the most important part of Hindu art.[3]

Assumptions about embodiment in sacred literature are also embedded in Hindu material culture. Complex techniques of lost wax casting with the assistance of priests generated a process called ritual production in which it was assumed that if figures were perfectly created, deities could inhabit them.[4] Detailed descriptions of proportion described in the *Śilpa*

Śāstras present a cultural paradigm so ancient that it is found in the earliest Hindu temples.

However, as cultural patterns of globalization and Hindu transnationalism accelerated in the 1990s, Hindu immigrants and their children encountered a different paradigm in the West that offered another way of interpreting sacred images. The dominant view of Westernized, industrialized societies is that mass-produced objects are utilitarian, transient, and, at the same time symbolic, connoting a variety of consumer responses,

> ... the consumer does not make consumption choices solely from products' utilities but also from their symbolic meanings.... The functions of the symbolic meanings of products operate in two directions, outward in constructing the social world: Social-Symbolism, and inward towards constructing our self-identity....[5]

More durable goods including art, icons, and antiques also convey symbolic meaning, drawing from a paradigm of rationalism with origins in the Enlightenment and the Scientific Revolution.

While the collision between Hindu attitudes about sacred material culture and Western assumptions of symbolic materialism became visible during the accelerated globalization of the 1990s, it was also evident earlier, during the late colonial period in India. Patterns of ritual production of Hindu images were supplanted by a consumer-oriented production system in cottage industries and small factories drawn from the model of European capitalism. Instead of being understood as ritual goods, images became a commodity which can be bought and sold and placed in a market economy, subject to consumer-oriented levels of interpretation.

Later, after the turn of the millennium, globalizing forces created opportunities for image production outside India. This phenomenon no longer emphasized embodiment; instead it marketed their symbolic forms to consumer societies. In China, images were mass-produced for the West by factory workers who had little knowledge of Hindu traditions and were marketed in Europe and the United States. Creating opportunities for expanded markets beyond ritual use, entrepreneurs have blended Hindu iconography with caricatures from popular culture. A *Ganesh* image on Amazon is advertised as a finger puppet and refrigerator magnet.[6] A site called *"Ganesh* Mall," juxtaposes the name of a Hindu god with a term drawn from Western venues of consumption, depicting the deity on a playground slide.[7] A visitor to the internet site, Alibaba, can find dealers who advertise images of *Ganesh* available in quantities of 500. Exhibiting bright colors and lively countenances, these figures stand apart from the craft of traditional image makers or *stapathis* and the strict requirements of proportion used in ritual production. Far more than the Hindu "poster art" that first emerged in colonial India, the emergence of the gods as merchandise in Westernized consumer-oriented societies is a product of a shrinking, globalized world.

Such dramatic variations within religious tradition could be dismissed as part of the adaptive nature of Hinduism and its ability to house a multiplicity of theological and ritual traditions. David Knipe concludes, "Hinduism is rich enough in expression to afford multiple perspectives, not incompatible but interactive ones...."[8] However, while Knipe is correct, within the diversity that he describes there have also been long lasting traditions that have been resistant to change and central to both Hindu civilization and religious identity. This is the case with the perception of divine embodiment which, for over 2,000 years, has been intertwined with the evolution of the Hindu temple, the ritual practices associated with worship (*pūjā*), pilgrimage, and the formation of India's sacred geography.

Globalization

The cumulative effect of increasing contact between paradigms of embodiment and symbolism in the age of accelerated globalization has produced a multi-layered religious environment among Hindus in the West. First-generation immigrants, priests, and temple officials may champion the traditional view of embodiment, venerating the images that reside in temples as sources of divine energy and presence. Second and third generation Hindus, born in Europe and North America, may adopt the prevailing values of the millennial generation, affirming science, technology and a utilitarian view of material culture. For them, while *mūrtis* may point toward deity, they do not contain it.

This layering of tradition can also be found in India where an increasingly urbanized, Westernized middle class is steeped in science and Western perceptions of material culture. In privately run, highly Westernized schools in India, both trajectories can be found among students—many of whom hope to complete their education in the United States. However, while these students have adopted Western views of science and material culture, they are also affected by the influence of India's sacred geography and the premise of embodiment. Schools close for important festivals and families participate in large festivals regularly in which the presence of deity is assumed.

In order to understand the emerging multivalent approach to images among transnational Hindus in the West, this text uses the concept of cultural trajectories found in globalization literature. A cultural trajectory is a dominant paradigm, often molded by an ebb and flow of affirmations and challenges to its claims that has shaped entire civilizations. The term has been used in a number of ways to describe cultural paradigms that have shaped societies. Raymond Brady Williams has employed it in discussions about the fabric of South Asian patterns of immigration.[9] Kamari Maxine Clarke and Deborah A. Thomas have discussed trajectories in black societies.[10] B. Kumaravadivelu has written about trajectories as long standing cultural movements and traditions.[11] Roland Wenzlhuemer has employed the concept in the discussion of the history of technology and globalization.[12] The term is especially applicable to religion, where cultural trajectories reflect the attitudes, beliefs, rituals, and a variety of related practices that have shaped the deepest levels of human experience. The advantage of the concept to transplanted religious traditions is that it is predicated on the processes of globalization, which in the case of religion has propelled traditions once confined to a geographical identity into contact with distant societies and divergent cultural/religious attitudes.

The text demonstrates the antiquity of the trajectory of embodiment which left visible evidence of its influence in the history of the Hindu temple tradition. The trajectory includes both aniconic images such as the *liṅga*, and iconic *mūrtis* which are anthropomorphized. Iconic images may be *achala* which are frequently crafted from stone and are immovable, or *chala* which may be moved.[13] *Chala* images include metal figures in temples that may be moved by priests and smaller *mūrtis* in homes which can be transported by laity. In addition, some images (*utsava mūrtis*) are crafted especially for festival occasions. Some *utsava mūrtis* are made of clay and intended for a single use in large festivals while others can be used repeatedly. While all of these categories reflect the trajectory of embodiment, this text will concentrate on iconic forms of *chala* images in order to demonstrate the trajectory.

Chapters one, two, and three show both trajectories evolved and became resilient, surviving intense counter-reactions in philosophy and practice that challenged their central role. The Hindu trajectory of embodiment found advocates in the long history of image worship in India and in philosophy where the eleventh century reformer, Ramanuja, challenged traditional *Advaitan* perceptions of non-dualism that had removed image worship from the center of Hindu tradition. Western assumptions about material symbolism evolved with the Enlightenment and the industrial revolution, surviving challenges from Jungian psychology and theology.

Chapter four discusses the ways in which Hindu sacred objects have been seen in the art world in the West through the lens of aesthetics and symbolic interpretation. It also demonstrates how they may be seen to possess presence or "agency." Chapter five shows how, among transnational Hindus in the West, competing influences of temple traditions, families, education, and host cultures have created a multi-layered mosaic of ideas and perceptions that redefine religious practice. Within this flux of ideas and practices some devotees may try to affirm conflicting trajectories. On one hand, second- and third-generation Hindu children may view *mūrtis* at home as statues that have symbolic meaning. Yet, they may also hear a contradictory voice as parents discuss temple *mūrtis* as actual presence. As Millennials, they also encapsulate a level of "message confusion"[14] that has been experienced by children of immigrants who frequently experience bi-cultural conflict.

However, this message confusion should not be interpreted to mean that members of the second generation do not see themselves as Hindu. In a number of interviews most students both affirmed the religious identification of their parents and indicated that they had also adopted it. The purpose of this text is neither to question their Hindu self-identification nor to enter a debate about defining Hinduism. Instead, this book hopes to document a generational shift among Hindus in the United States where layered traditions of belief and practice coexist in the same families and ethnic communities.

Finally, chapter five also shows how these changes and the flux of trajectories about sacred material culture have become part of transnational Hindu networks. Through networks of temples, online *pūjās*, intimate religious conversations (*satsaṅgs*), and sectarian discourse, the internet becomes a vehicle through which trajectories of embodiment and symbolism are incorporated within the identity of devotees. Rarely voiced in debate, but assumed in a multiplicity of evolving transnational Hindu identities, first-, second-, and third-generation Hindus are picking and choosing their perspectives about image worship from a rapidly evolving flux of cultural trajectories.

ONE

Globalization and Shifting Cultural Trajectories of Hindu Sacred Objects

After having taught Hinduism for 25 years in a small liberal arts college in eastern Pennsylvania, I began to hear different perspectives about the nature of images (*mūrtis*) from Indian students. Most were second-generation Hindu Americans. Many had been to India for short periods of time and frequently during alternate years with their families. For them, *mūrtis* were not a form of living presence but, instead, symbolic expressions much like a cross or menorah. A second-generation student suggested "*Mūrtis* are only symbols for God so that we can worship (them)."[1] Others added sentiments that suggested that because god was omnipresent a symbolic presence was necessary. What these students experienced was a transition of understanding among second-generation Hindu Americans that prompted me to look at the significance of such shifts in perception. I heard my students saying that the classic doctrinal concepts of image worship embedded in Hindu culture no longer resonated in their understanding of religious practice.

The perception of Hindu images as symbolic was dramatically different from traditional Hindu attitudes that I had experienced in literature and seen firsthand in India where *mūrtis* were understood as living presence. Cast in traditional methods using precise lost wax techniques, bronze anthropomorphic images became vessels for the deities who resided in them. Their eyes, and seven other orifices in their bodies were opened by the artisan (*sthapati*) who made them in preparation for their residence in a temple or home. A priest then brought them to life.

9

I heard my students saying that the traditional concepts of image making and worship no longer resonated in their understanding of Hindu practice. This realization led me to ask not only about the change in perception that I was seeing but how significant these modified views were when compared with traditional views. In *The Lives of Indian Images*, Richard Davis provides an understanding of this confluence of the spiritual and material in classical Hinduism,

> The worship of images became the dominant form of public religious practice in early medieval India, within the theological dispensation of gods who involved themselves actively and repeatedly in the world process while yet remaining transcendentally aloof. For humans who aspired to gain contact with those gods as the best means of attaining happiness and salvation, the material icon—fabricated by humans and inhabited by God—was taken as a primary site of ongoing interaction and exchange between humans and God. It was this interaction, involving initiatives by both parties and bringing them into a relationship that was unequal but fulfilling for both, that animated Hindu images as living, personal deities.[2]

Hindu tradition concluded that the divine energy was within the metal, the wood, clay, or stone before being formed into an image. "Although the image is 'made' by those who carve and anoint it, the god is also, as a devotional poem to Viṣṇu puts it, in the image 'as butter lies hidden in fresh milk.'"[3]

Complex Forces That Affect Transnational Hindus

This text emphasizes the impact of generational change in keeping with studies of second-generation immigrants such as those done by Alejandro Portes and Ruben G. Rumbaut.[4] However, the issue is also far more complex than any single marker could indicate and includes a number of forces that can shape varying perceptions of religious practices in ethnic communities. For example, South Asian families, like other immigrant groups, follow a host of familial alignments. Some families have migrated from India to the United States collectively. Yet, others may be blended as fresh arrivals marry persons who have been in the United States for a number of years. This model was popularly attested, before the 1965 immigration reforms when males, after a number of years living in the United States, would return to India to secure their brides through patterns of arranged marriage.

A host of other alignments are equally complex. Some South Asians who migrate to the United States as children (identified as "1.5s") may retain more traditional values than second-generation Hindu Americans. In addition, location is an important variable. Families in areas of high Asian Indian concentration, such as Flushing, New York or central New Jersey have far more resources to choose from in retaining their culture. A visitor to Edison, New Jersey, for instance, may notice grocery stores that cater to the South Asian community offering fruit and vegetables that are often difficult to find elsewhere. Accoutrements for daily *pūjās* are also readily available in these locations whereas in regions removed from centers of the Indian community across the United States the lack of resources may affect worship practices.

Globalization has also heightened the number of possible family alignments and made any uniform pattern of assimilation unrealistic. This was not the case when immigration patterns were "one way" when assimilation became the only viable option for new Americans. When Milton Gordon wrote *Assimilation in American Life* in 1963, a seven stage process of assimilation from acculturation to "civic assimilation" (in which power struggles between competing values diminished or were eliminated) seemed realistic.[5] However, in a globalized world, where minority communities may retain traditional values through regular infusions of immigrants and bicultural lifestyles, there is no longer any clear pathway to full assimilation.

Yet, despite the level of complexity in the lives of Hindu immigrants, generational change has become an important marker of the diminishment of a traditional Hindu belief—the perception of divine presence in sacred objects. While not all members of the second generation of Hindu Americans may perceive images in the same way, coming from families with varying backgrounds in religion and culture, as a whole they have exhibited a shift in values that will undoubtedly have a profound effect on the nature of Hinduism beyond India.

Embodiment and Hindu Culture

Among other immigrant South Asian populations in parts of the world with less exposure to mainstream Western thought, there may be no change in perception at all. Views of Hindu image embodiment are often traditional, quite unlike the perceptions that my students expressed. Such traditional views were evident in Trinidad, where Hindus have migrated since the mid–nineteenth century. In 2010, Trinidadian Hindus reported that an image of *Ganesh* had consumed milk,

> Murtis of Sri Ganesh "drank" or accepted milk, offered as part of a religious ritual by Hindus yesterday. The "miracle," (sic) as it was called by believers, was first noted at midday on Tuesday at the Om Shanti Mandir (temple), Cunjal Road, Princes Town, where devotees have been observing the holy period of Ganesh Utsav (festival).... "It occurred on September 21, 1995, all over the globe, and again, on August 20–21 in 2006, in almost exactly the same fashion...."[6]

Similar reactions could also be found in India. In New Delhi in 2016, some Hindus claimed to have seen *Ganesh* drink milk. The story was widely reported when a devotee reported a dream in which *Ganesh* wanted milk. When a priest allowed him to offer the deity a spoonful, both were astonished when the milk disappeared. Devotees in New Delhi reacted *en masse* hoping to recreate the miraculous event,

> Within hours news had spread like a brush fire across India that Ganesha was accepting milk offerings. Tens of millions of people of all ages flocked to the nation's temples. The unworldly happening brought worldly New Delhi to a standstill, and its vast stocks of milk—more than a million liters—sold out within hours. Just as suddenly as it started in India, it stopped in just 24 hours.[7]

While miraculous events such as this make news, they are not normative within most Hindu ritual traditions and they are not typical of Hindu perceptions of the manifestation of the sacred. However, the perception that the gods are fully alive *is* well established and may be interpreted both emotionally and ontologically.

This was the case for a middle-aged Hindu American woman who described her experiences of divine presence during *Kumbhābhiṣekam* and *Prāṇ Pratiṣṭhā* ceremonies in the United States. *Kumbhābhiṣekam* is a bathing ritual in which the powers of the deity are enhanced when the divine presence is channeled through holy waters into a sacred pot and then transferred to the deity. *Prāṇ Pratiṣṭhā* is an installation rite in which the *mūrti* is brought to life and enthroned in the temple. Both rituals are times of significant emotion and inspire the repetition of *mantras* by priests. For devotees, they are also a time when the ontological power and presence of the deity can especially be evident. She described her experience,

> Once when I attended a Kumbh Abhishek or new temple opening a divine vision of the Lord appeared to me. As the ritual was taking place mantras were being chanted. Murtis were being brought to life. I saw the divine power being incorporated into the murtis of *Vishnu* and Krishna. Murti worship is important as an outer form of worship of the God in individuals' hearts.

In another instance, she felt the power of the deity directly,

> At a Kumbh Abhishek at a temple in New Jersey a huge ten foot statue of Viṣṇu was being installed. Many men brought the big black stone image (vigraha) to the temple and no one was supposed to go there to see them do it. The door was chained.

> But God was directing me internally to see him (darshan) and I went to the interior of the temple without hindrance. A small gap of ten inches was opened and I saw them bringing in the Lord with exertion. The image gave me an internal message saying now I have come here and you must worship me regularly. It was a revelation.[8]

Embodiment may also be experienced as transcendence by priests who have a unique perspective through performing multiple rituals in which they encounter divine presence firsthand. A case in point is the observations of the high priest at the prestigious Tirumala temple, known for its central deity *Shri Venkateswara*.[9] The priest, Ramana Deekshithulu, is the son of a priest, and was awarded a Ph.D. by *"Sri Venkateswara University"* in molecular biology and was subsequently invited to do cancer research at the University of South Carolina in the United States. In 1974, he became a priest at the *"Shri Vari Temple,"* later becoming the head priest at Tirumala. As a scientist and as a devotee of *Shri Venkateswara* he described his first encounter with the deity, "Believe me.... My whole body shuddered with fear.... The giant Lord appeared to me as big as the Sky.... Then I had quickly closed my eyes...."[10]

Despite his experience of the presence of the deity as *mysterium tremendum*, Deekshithulu was also quick to dismiss popular stories about the miraculous physical attributes or actions of deities, concluding,

> There are many stories circulating on the web about the qualities and appearance of Lord Sri Venkateswara.... A few among them say that He has the same physical body a human being has and we the priests feel the same when we touch Him....
>
> The stories further say that nails also grow on His hands and feet and that He has long curly hair that constantly keeps growing behind His head.... All these are completely baseless stories and there's absolutely no truth in them.
>
> Most importantly, all the above mentioned qualities are the physical qualities of a perishable human body and not the divine qualities of a celestial body.... The devotees should clearly understand this difference in the qualities of man and God and should never view Lord Sri Venkateswara as just a nine and half feet stone deity....[11]

For Deekshithulu, the presence of *Shri Venkateswara* exists in a different plane from human affairs.

In other instances the presence of the deity may be experienced *en masse* through large festivals in which the god "descends" into the natural world. During the festival of *Gangā-Dashamī* in Haridwar (Figure 1), thousands of pilgrims line the river bank, replete with temples, to bathe in the river which becomes the embodied form of the goddess, albeit not in iconographic form.

However, even in India where globalization has empowered an expanding middle class, debates about embodiment have challenged tra-

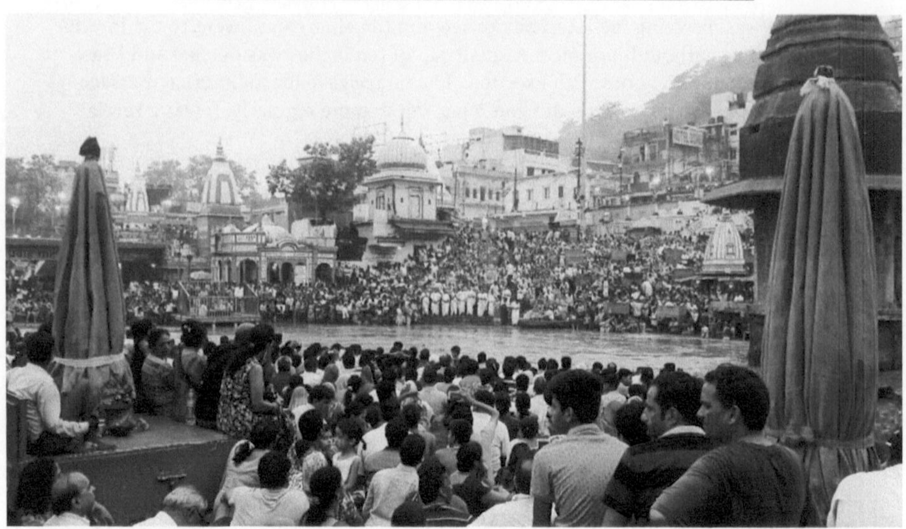

Figure 1: *Gangā-Dashamī* festival in Haridwar, North India, 2015 (courtesy Kanha Vyas).

ditional perceptions. In July 2017 the Indian Supreme Court overruled a lower court decision in Uttarkhand that ruled that the Ganges and Yamuna rivers were "legal persons" with the same rights as human beings. The debated lower court ruling was in harmony with other decisions about Hindu images that had ruled that they were legally persons. In 2010 a god, "*Bhagwan Sri Ram Virajman*," won a 21-year battle when the Lucknow Bench of the Allahabad High Court declared that the deity, through his representative Dceoki Nandan Agarwar, had won ownership rights over the disputed site in Ayodhya.[12] The case was especially significant since Ayodhya was understood to be the birth place of the god *Rama*. In 1992 a communal riot ensued when Hindus claimed that the construction of a mosque on the site had caused the destruction of a temple.

While the Supreme Court decision in 2017 about the Ganges and Yamuna rivers was not influenced by communal tensions, it did show how traditional assumptions of embodiment became the subject of debate. In an odd blend of Western environmentalism and Hindu perceptions of embodiment, the lower court ruling had satisfied both views. By ruling that the rivers were legal persons and subject to the same rights as human beings, the lower court decision seemed to afford a measure of protection to the rivers, both of which are severely polluted. However, in an increasingly globalized India with an expanding Westernized middle class, the Supreme Court decided that the question was not practical and reversed the decision.

For many lay devotees embodiment is also a communal experience in everyday life. Some village traditions endow images with the ability to discuss village problems and to display a range of emotions. June McDaniel describes village traditions in which images of deities are brought together for a *Ṭhākur Pañcāyat,* a council meeting of the gods analogous to village *pañcāyats* in which elders convene to discuss infringements of caste regulations. However, in folk traditions, the presence of the gods goes even further. Images are not only seen as alive but also as having emotions, which can be so threatening that images are sometimes kept behind bars,

> In folk Vaishnavism, we see the statues imbued with a different kind of life. Village Krishna statues are believed by devotees to get upset if treated poorly, and experience the statue equivalent of "anxiety attacks" unless they are a militant form of deity. This is one reason why they are often placed in cages behind bars in larger towns....[13]

While these examples are more extreme than would be found in the majority of sectarian transnational forms of Hinduism, the perception of images as personal forms of divine presence is normative. In classical South Indian traditions this presence is austere and the gods are presented as embodiments of divine energy.

In sectarian traditions that emulate from the Hindu *bhakti* or devotional movement, expressions of presence have been understood as forms of intimacy where devotees establish strong relationships with the images they care for. This was the case for one Hindu in Great Britain, Bhagwat Shah, who remembered acquiring his first images in India when he was a child. Shah's narrative is in the *Pushtimarg* tradition, a 500-year-old *Vaiṣṇava bhakti* faith that venerates *Krishna* as a child. He addresses his images (Figures 2 and 3) as *svarūps* (also transliterated as *swarūps*)—connoting an actual, amplified presence of the deity, or as a *lālan*—a term of endearment—or as *Ṭhākorjī*, indicating supreme reality. He refers to *sevā* which includes the ritualistic care of *swarūps* through daily rites of bathing, feeding, adornment, and entertainment,

> A lalan made of panch-dhatu (five metals) was given to me as a "training" Thakorji so I can (could) get used to nuances of seva and how to do it properly. From old photos, it looks like this might have been as early as 1970.
>
> I took it a step further and insisted on taking him to school with me. School shorts of a 4 year old can't really accommodate a Thakorji of panch-dhatu and there was probably some health and safety assets of having heavy metal objects in class. My headmistress instructed me NOT to bring Thakorji to school. I am sure she was sweet about it. This Thakorji has been in my sevā ever since. He migrated with us to (the) United Kingdom.

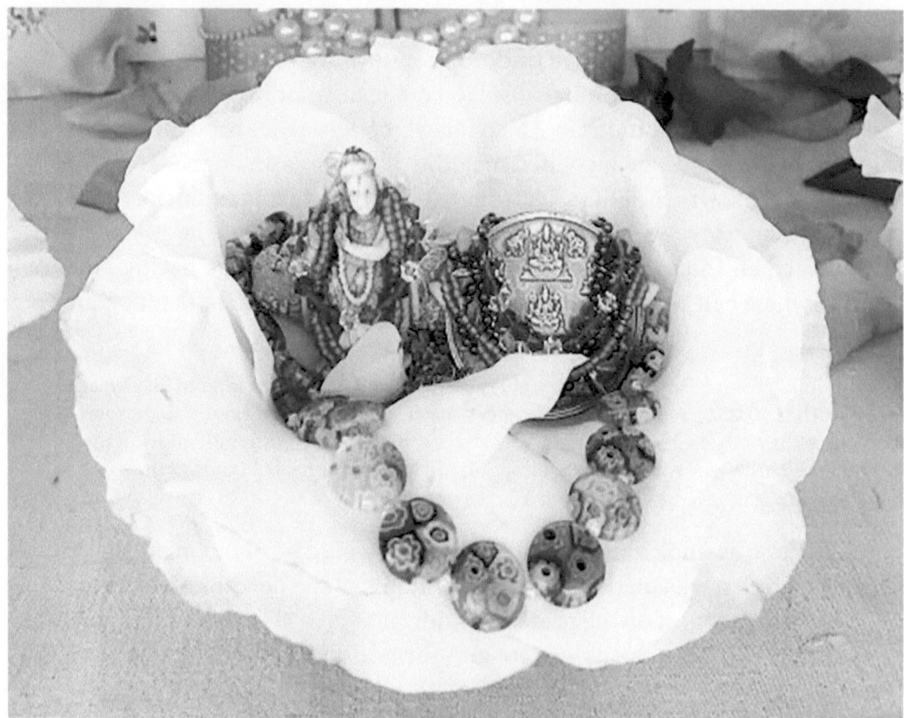

Figure 2: Ivory *Swarūp* of *Krishna* in the company of *Lakshmi* (courtesy Bhagwat Shah).

Soon, Bhagwat acquired other *swarūps*:

My brother was given a similarly small Lalan as his Thakorji. I doubt if he was ever taken to school. He has been in our seva ever since the 1970s. As I have been taking care of both Lalans, when I moved to our house in 2000, both Lalans came with me.

My grandmother (mum's mum) had two small ivory Krushnas (Krishnas). I asked her to give me one of them as my own Thakorji. I used to play with him by taking him for a ride in a toy car and truck my uncle had sent from Germany. My brothers and I used to make Lego houses and place him in there. Thakorji was an integral part of our fun time. After a while I started to take him to my junior school with me. He was with me when I was studying in class and with me when I did homework too. He was in my pocket throughout the rough and tumble of my childhood. Even at night, he would sleep with me by staying inside my pillow case.

Too much love is also not good. My Krushna (sic) suffered much by bouncing around in my pocket. His nimbus and hands broke and over the years, my ceaseless caresses have worn the ivory smooth, wiping out delicate features such as the nose and mouth. By the time I had the maturity to listen to sagely advice and show my love in more measured ways, the damage was already done.

In India, if I accidently lost my Krushna in the school, everyone knew who to return him to. In the United Kingdom, that wasn't going to be possible. So from

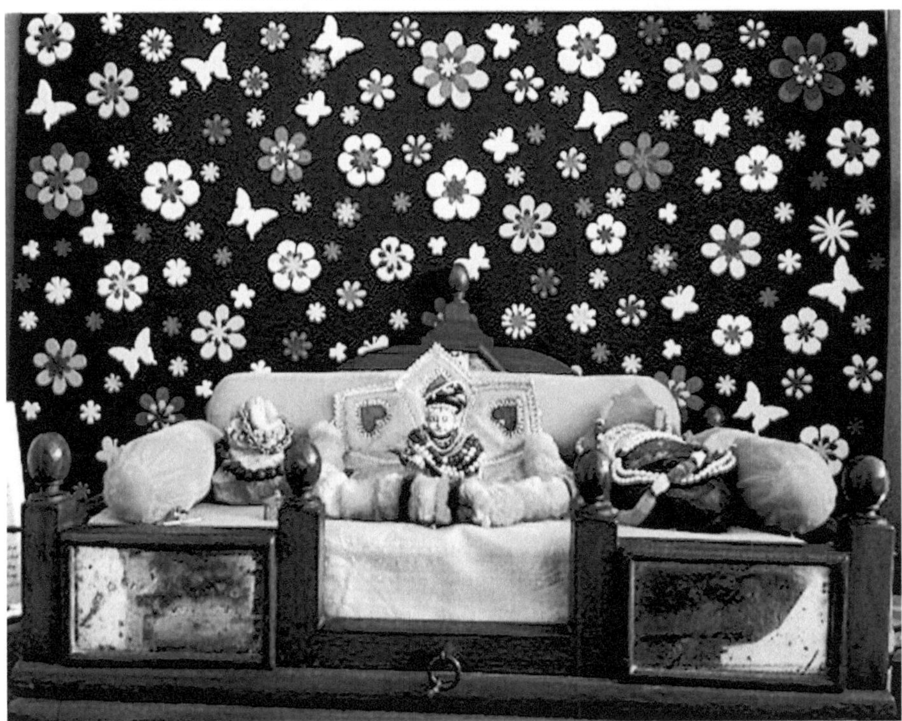

Figure 3: *Krishna* **on a throne made of wood and mirrors (courtesy Bhagwat Shah).**

(the) summer of 1979 as we moved to (the) United Kingdom, Thakorji started to stay at home more and more. He is still the one Thakorji I take with me when I am traveling.[14]

These examples are poignant reminders of traditional Hindu attitudes in which *mūrtis* are understood to be capable of affecting moods and emotions, able to consume the foods that are offered to them, and poised to become the most intimate level of friend or Lord. They are markedly different from sentiments commonly expressed by second-generation Hindu Americans who, like their non–Hindu peers, look at sacred objects as symbols rather than living presence.

Shifting Trajectories

By perceiving *mūrtis* as symbols, what my Hindu American students were describing was a dramatic shift of attitudes, departing from an ancient perspective that flourished in Hindu empires during the *Chola* and *Gupta* periods with origins that may even reach back to the Indus Valley civilization 5,000 years ago and which have persisted for centuries, continuing to the present. This perspective, by virtue of its antiquity and its profound influence on Hindu philosophy and ritual, can appropriately be described as a cultural trajectory—a pattern or pathway that helps define a religion or culture over the course of centuries. It is distinct from the equally important but far more recent cultural trajectory of sacred objects in Western religions and intellectual traditions that were shaped by Enlightenment philosophy and the Scientific Revolution.

Both trajectories remained separate and distinct from the seventeenth to twentieth centuries, separated by the distance between Europe and South Asia compounded by difficulties in communication. Europeans read about Hinduism through the eyes of missionaries, soldiers, and civil servants but embodiment remained a cultural curiosity. In India, which had experienced British presence since the early seventeenth century with the advent of the East India Company, Western observers remained segregated from the indigenous population. While the trajectory of symbolism might be observed in a Christian cross in a church, the wellspring of Enlightenment rationalism from which the trajectory sprang remained distant. However, with rapid globalization in the late twentieth and early twenty first centuries all of this was to change as patterns of travel and communication accelerated. In less than fifty years following the 1965 immigration reforms in the United States, Hinduism became an American religion. A growing cadre of South Asian children entered the millennial generation having adopted the cultural views of their parent society.

The dominance of the perception of *mūrtis* as symbolic among second-generation Hindu Americas was apparent at a temple retreat in 2016. 35 second-generation Hindu American students from colleges and universities on the eastern seaboard met for three days at the *Vraj* temple in Pennsylvania.[15] By virtue of their participation in a temple retreat and their self-identification as Hindus, the group placed value on religion. However, 82 percent, most of whom were in college or graduate school in the northeastern United States, perceived images as representations of deity rather than actual presence. A similar number (80 percent) felt that Hindu devotional art was symbolic rather than a vehicle for a living deity. A minority of students (8 percent) understood images as forms of living presence.

These reactions are consistent with other studies of second-generation Hindu Americans which confirms that many do not perform *pūjā* themselves and are distanced from religion as a regular level of activity. Rather, as Khyati Y. Joshi confirms, to them religion is a family affair and is only celebrated in the context of the home,

> Rituals take on meaning when—often only when—they are performed by and in the presence of family. One might call this a familial adaptation of the concept of *satsang*—the unique power of religious ritual when experienced and performed in the company of other believers....
>
> Put simply, the research participants live religious ritual first and foremost as a connection to family. A large number of research participants, when asked about ritual practice, volunteered a specific type of description; they described going to the house of worship either with their parents or when they came home from college.[16]

Since religion among many Hindu millennials born and raised outside India is tied to family, knowledge of ritual requirements is often scant. In an early study of transnational Hinduism John Fenton found this to be the case early in the post 1965 migration pattern.[17] Writing eighteen years later, Joshi agreed suggesting, "As they passed through adolescence, even those who grew up in the presence of an ethnoreligious community, a temple, or a Sunday school program felt they did not know enough about their home religion to identify with it—or by extension, practice it independently."[18]

The duality for many second-generation Hindus in the West pivots between their life as American Millennials in a competitive, materialistic society and their family obligations. This also helps to explain why some second-generation Hindu Americans have incorporated both trajectories. One student concluded, "The home is considered a place where God resides, and the *mūrtis* are there to personify that presence."[19] However, she also felt that because god is everywhere, *mūrtis* can only *represent* presence and are not necessary for the experience of the divine. Others affirmed that while *mūrtis* at home, online, or in shops and museums are symbolic, the large stone or bronze images in temples can exhibit presence.[20]

The confluence of both trajectories has also sparked polemics when defenders of the trajectory of presence have attempted to convince American Hindus to retain tradition. In *Hinduism Today*, published by the Himalayan Academy in Hawaii and targeted at the Hindu community in the West, one adherent reminded devotees that while "Many people look at the gods as mere symbols, representations of forces or mind areas. Actually, the gods are beings...."[21]

These polemics illustrate the tendency within the complex matrix of Hinduism in the United States for the first generation to hang on to traditional perspectives while their sons and daughters are caught in a nether world, mid-way between established American assumptions about the role of material culture and their parents' belief system. However, shifts in cultural trajectories are not just an issue among generations. They are influenced by a range of other factors including the length of residence in the West, the role of religion in the family, the presence of grandparents in the home, and the role of careers in science, engineering, and medicine, which reinforce the prevailing trajectory in the West.

Understanding the Trajectories

One of the potential dangers of understanding the distinction between the trajectories is the possibility of stereotyping the role of sacred and secular in a postmodern world. The dual trajectories could be misinterpreted to suggest that India is a seat of spirituality while the secular West moves in the opposite direction. This is a dangerous stereotype with a long history.

Jane Naomi Iwamura writes about the evolution of the image of the Oriental monk in American Culture which draws on stereotypes of the "spiritual east."[22] She cites a host of examples of the monk in popular culture ranging from the Dalai Lama, to numerous film portrayals of the serene spiritual guide. In each case, the monk is a composite figure of wisdom, controlled emotion and elevated spirituality.

As the product of Orientalism, the monk carried the stereotypical image of India's spirituality which has frequently been contrasted with the secular West and has been used to invalidate it. This dichotomy was evident among transcendentalist poets who borrowed from the insights that Orientalist scholars found when they translated Hindu scripture. Emerson wrote of the "World-Soul" and the Hindu god *Brahma*. Thoreau, heavily influenced by Emerson's captivation with Indian spirituality, took his insights even further, suggesting that the *yogi* becomes a spiritual being, who was, "Free in this world as the buds in the air, disengaged from every kind of chains...."[23] There was no counterpart to this image in the West which gained further popularity from the presence of Swami Vivekananda in Chicago in 1893 and, later, through the publication of texts such as *The Autobiography of a Yogi*, which drew Americans to a stereotypical image of Eastern spirituality.[24]

More than a century later, during the Vietnam War, Thoreau's interest in a simpler life and the role of spirit in the natural world influenced the American counter culture, evoking the same stereotype. As the Beetles went to India followed by a succession of American *gurus*, the image of the "spiritual East" accelerated the perception of a dichotomy between Indian spirituality and Western materialism.

Conversely, the presence of the trajectories of symbolism and embodiment have a different history and are connected through globalization rather than by stereotypical imagery. Each trajectory has been embedded in the evolution of a civilization with strong historical roots. Perceptions of divine embodiment evolved with the Hindu temple. Much later, in the West, the belief that material culture could reflect the divine, but not contain it, evolved with Enlightenment rationalism. Both trajectories remained separate and distinct through the seventeenth to twentieth centuries while India and the West remained in separate spheres. When colonial expansion brought trading interests and British imperialism to India, most Europeans still only saw India from afar. This separation, coupled with the stereotype of eastern spirituality and Western materialism could create the misimpression that the trajectories are a dichotomy.

The Trajectories Are Not a Dichotomy

A dichotomy is a division of a unified body of thought into two opposing categories in which one helps define the other. Cultural trajectories, on the other hand, are deeply seated, resilient practices and beliefs that the economic forces of globalization have brought together through accelerated patterns of communication, immigration, and travel. Unlike stereotypes, a trajectory does not arise because of an opposing view. Rather, as demonstrated through the context of first- and second-generation Hindu immigrants in the United States, they may coexist among the same population. For instance, at a retreat in 2017 in a temple in rural Pennsylvania, conversations among second-generation Hindus were often more social than religious, focusing on questions related to heritage, marriage, and pressures to succeed. Images were rarely discussed. However, members of the first generation shared stories related to embodiment that had deep personal meaning. A *Pushtimarg* devotee spoke about a man who was so anxious to worship the central deity in a temple that he neglected to bathe and feed his personal god. Both deities were forms of *Krishna*. But that didn't matter. When the devotee neglected to attend his personal god, the deity cried out that he was hungry. This story would never have been told by the second-generation youth at the retreat who saw Hindu images as symbolic rather than as the actual presence of the god. The processes associated with accelerated globalization created an environment in which both perspectives could be shared, not as a dichotomy, but as layers of tradition that in earlier periods had been separated by distance and slower patterns of communication.

Separation Between the Trajectories in the Colonial and Modern Periods

Not only did the Hindu trajectory of sacred presence in religious objects remain intact for millennia, but it also was kept apart from Western material symbolism throughout the colonial and modern periods. While Western intellectual tradition developed, the two parallel traditions existed with minimal cross fertilization and interaction. Throughout the eighteenth and nineteenth centuries, few reports of the Hindu trajectory of presence reached the West. Most were included in missionary tracts which frequently devalued Hinduism and also sought to interpret it through a Christian perspective. As demand in core European nations increased for Indian products, the East India Company relied on civil servants, soldiers, and missionaries to maintain ideological distinctions between core, colonizer European nations and developing countries which were colonies on the "periphery," reinforcing separation. In India, princely states retained strong Hindu identities, reinforcing the cultural distance between religion and the burgeoning British Empire. Hindu and Muslim elites did not challenge the system or the separation which had produced a lucrative economic environment for them. Trade flourished, ensuring the continued movement of goods from periphery to core and at the same time isolated the British Raj from close contact with Indian values and ideas. That system was represented in almost every facet of British life in India.

Hindus and Muslims had limited social interaction with the British. Many became household servants but were never placed on a par with the English *Raj*. When British social clubs were formed, Asian Indians were excluded. The segregation was apparent in modes of travel, in public accommodations, and in the military. In 1857, when the East India Company gave way to direct control of India, empire replaced private industry as a means of continuing this process. Hinduism remained confined to the Indian subcontinent and the trajectories of the faith remained insulated from the West.

However, in a few instances, missionary reports contained nuances that, while still veiled in the stereotypes of "superstition," described the trajectory of presence. A case in point was the Abbe Dubois (1770–1848), a French priest and Sanskrit scholar, whose reports on Hindu *pūjā* were among the first detailed descriptions that Europeans had ever read. Dubois described the rite, suggesting,

> Of all the Hindu rites, puja is the one that occurs most frequently in all their ceremonies, both public and private, in their temples and elsewhere. Every Brahmin is absolutely obliged to offer it at least once a day to his household gods. There are three kinds of pujas—the great, the intermediate, and the small.
>
> The great sacrifice is composed of the following parts:
>
> 1. Avahana. The evocation of the deity.
> 2. Asana. A seat is presented to him to sit on.
> 3. Svagata. He is asked if he has arrived quite safely, and if he met with no accident on the way.
> 4. Padya. Water is offered to him for washing his feet,
> 5. Arghya. Water is presented to him in which flowers, saffron, and sandalwood powder have been placed.
> 6. Achamania. Water is offered that he may wash his mouth and face in the prescribed fashion.
> 7. Madhu-parka. He is offered in a metal vessel a beverage composed of honey, sugar, and milk.
> 8. Snāna Jala. Water for his bath.[25]

While the Abbe's rhetoric continued the European perspective of perceiving Asian Indians as "the other," he was able to capture evidence of a cultural trajectory rarely encountered in the West. Western readers were presented with an image of deity who bathed, washed his face, mouth, and feet, was presented with a seat and assured of his safety. However, as one of the few Western observers who cared to document Hindu practices, the Abbe's writing revealed that the Hindu trajectory of embodiment persisted undisturbed by political and social dominion.

By the time of the World's Parliament of Religions, celebrated in Chicago as part of the World's Fair in 1893, stereotypes about Hindu images had become consuming misconceptions of the two cultural trajectories of embodiment and symbolism. Further, Hinduism was presented in a particular form emphasizing *Vedānta* philosophy and the mystical teachings of the nineteenth-century saint Ramanuja, rather than the stereotypical image of the tradition that missionaries had created. When the assembled Parliament gathered to hear a presentation by a young Hindu monk, Swami Vivekananda, their level of rejection of image worship was so great that the speaker reacted, attempting to unveil their own idolatry,

> Superstition is the enemy of man, bigotry worse. Why does a Christian go to church, why is the cross holy, why is the face turned toward the sky in prayer? Why are there so many images in the Catholic Church, why are there so many images in the minds of Protestants, when they pray? My brethren, we can no more think

about anything without a material image than it is profitable for us to live without breathing. And by the law of association the material image calls the mental idea up and *vice versa*. Omnipotent to almost the whole world means nothing.

As we find that somehow or other, by the laws of our constitution, we have got to associate our ideas of infinity with the ideal of a blue sky, or a sea; the omnipresence covering the idea of holiness with an idol of a church or a mosque, or a cross; so the Hindus have associated the ideas of holiness, purity, omnipresence, and all other ideas with different images and forms. But with this difference: upon certain actions some are drawn their whole lives to their idol of a church and never rise higher, because with them religion means an intellectual assent to certain doctrines and doing good to their fellows. The whole religion of the Hindu is centered in realization. Man is to become divine, realizing the divine, and, therefore, idol or temple or church or books, are only the supports, the helps of his spiritual childhood, but on and on he must progress.[26]

Vivekananda was one of the first Hindus to resist Europe and the United States. While defending the use of images, and undoubtedly offending his audience when he suggested that churches could become idols, he claimed that "...some are drawn their whole lives to their idol of a church and never rise higher,"[27] however, in attempting to rebut stereotypes of Hinduism, he also invoked the trajectory of sacred objects as symbols, suggesting that the use of a church, a cross, fulfilled the same function as a *mūrti*. While Vivekananda was trained in the Hindu system of *Advaita Vedānta*, a non-theistic system that saw images of minimal importance, he was also a product of the British educational system, earning a Bachelor of Art's degree in 1884. No stranger to the Western trajectory of symbolic meaning, he evoked it in his address as a device to help his audience understand *mūrtis* in their own terms. At the same time his presence in Chicago was a reminder of the geographical separation between the trajectories and the difference that expanded patterns of immigration would make a century later when Hindu communities evolved in the West.

Most Americans rarely encountered the trajectory of presence. Hindus who settled in the United States in the early twentieth century were encouraged to assimilate and, in the process, to adopt prevailing views centered in Western scientific and materialistic thought. For most, the journey to the West also marked changes in lifestyles as immigrants took one-way passages with infrequent return visits to South Asia. Patterns of assimilation to Western culture and values were reinforced at entry points to the United States in Ellis Island in New York and Angel Island in San Francisco where immigrants were required to abandon language and dress and to forge new identities as Americans. In New York City, emigration societies met fresh arrivals from Ellis Island, greeting them with Western clothing and enrolling them in language classes. Although South Asian populations were able to form Hindu and Sikh associations and had an increased chance of protecting their culture and heritage, they suffered when states like California passed alien land acts that prevented them from owning the land they worked. Later, in 1923, the Supreme Court denied the application for citizenship of a Sikh, Bhagwat Singh Thind, based on his contention that he was Caucasian.

Following passage of the Immigration Act of 1924 a year later, immigration from the eastern hemisphere was eliminated, maintaining the separation between trajectories of embodiment and symbolism.[28] For Hindus and Sikhs already in the United States, there was little choice but to adopt Western values, forgoing traditional patterns of culture or religion. South Asians who had become farmers in California established relationships with Mexican Americans, a phenomenon that further diluted Hindu practices when families converted to the religion of their mothers, which was frequently Roman Catholicism.

A Rapid Change in an Increasingly Globalized World

In 1965, following an amendment to the Immigration Act of 1924, Asian Indian immigration to the West dramatically increased. With accelerating patterns of global communication and travel, earlier patterns of one-way migration from India to the United States began to wane. What replaced it was a growing Hindu transnational population that moved between large metropolitan areas in India and concentrations of South Asian people in urban areas across the United States.

As the South Asian community began to grow and adapt to life in the United States in the second half of the twentieth century the trajectory of presence began to wane as the children of Hindu immigrants increasingly adopted American values. At the same time perceptions of divine presence and embodiment were retained in temples where priests conducted the same rituals that had been done for millennia in India. As a result, transnational Hindus in the United States came to share a variety of conflicting attitudes about the role of *mūrtis*.

The rapidity of this change is particularly striking when compared with the earliest migration of Hindu tradition between the fourth and eighth centuries, when *Vaiṣṇavas* and *Śaivas* in Southeast Asia continued to see the gods as living presence despite theological changes that accompanied the diaspora. In Cambodia, *Khmer Śaiva* rulers worshipped iconographic forms of *Shiva* as living gods. The connections with Indian *Śaivism* were direct—*Kauṇḍinya Brahmins* migrated from India to what is now Cambodia and helped establish the authority of their tradition by installing a *liṅga*.[29] In the fifth century, a *liṅga* was established at Wat Phu where it became an important center of pilgrimage and repository of divine power.[30] In the ninth-century kingdom of Ankor, King Jayavarman VII was understood to be in direct communication with the *liṅga*, again reinforcing the Hindu cultural trajectory of presence.[31]

While there has been debate about the purposes of Ankor Wat as either a temple or a tomb, there is little doubt that Hindu *Khmer* culture continued to support the trajectory of embodiment.[32] Michael D. Coe concludes,

> Brahmanic Hinduism had been all-pervasive during most of the Classic period, until temporarily (and only partially) eclipsed by Jayavarman VII's Mahayanism. Hinduism is not a congregational religion such as Buddhism or Christianity, but is centered on individual devotion and worship of a god or goddess in a ritual that was always under the care of a Brahmin priest. The temple or shrine was there to provide a house in which the deity could take up temporary residence; there he (or she) would have a place to eat, to be bathed, and even to sleep. If everything was well conducted, the god would then come to life in his/her own stone, wood or metal image.[33]

Perceptions about the presence of the sacred in images were also absorbed in early forms of Buddhism, probably long before the migration of the tradition to Southeast Asia. Donald Swearer has documented rituals, with similarities of purpose to Hindu *Prāṇ Pratiṣṭhā* ceremonies that transform a casting of the Buddha into a living presence.[34] During the ritual, which continues through an entire night, images of the Buddha are linked with cord to the central image in a temple (*wat*). As the awakening rituals proceed in the early morning hours, the Buddha is taught the central tenets of the tradition and instructed to take on the role that he will assume as a living Buddha. The moment of awakening is a crescendo in which the figure assumes power, authority, and presence.

While transplanted Hindu deities in Cambodia and Thailand retained the cultural trajectory of living images, their countenance frequently changed. For example, in Southeast Asia, images of *Ganesh* departed from traditional modes of Indian iconography which represented the god with a large belly and aura of compassion, "...transforming Ganesha into a more naturally proportioned and formalized deity...."[35] Among *Khmer* images of *Ganesh*, the elephant headed god became a fully human representation.[36] The well-known dancing *Ganesh*, ever so familiar in India, was markedly absent in these Southeast Asian adaptations. However, his images continued to express a living presence.

Hybridization and Disembedding as Part of the Globalization of Cultural Trajectories

In the age of globalization, separation between the trajectories of symbolism and presence can no longer be maintained. National borders have become virtually irrelevant since the flow of people, ideas, and goods moves continually in both directions creating a dynamic in which the trajectories have come into contact. These changes are a departure from the colonial period when core and periphery nations were separated not only by distance but through rigid adherence to distinct cultural values, often bolstered by religious dogma and social stratification. European and American Christians looked at India as a land filled with idolatry while Hindus in India saw the West as bemired in ritual pollution, discouraging travel. However, as globalization increased, complete separation between homeland and transnational populations was no longer possible. Trajectories could no longer retain their insulation and isolation.

The blurring of distinctions between homeland and overseas communities has become even more meaningful as the number of overseas Hindus has increased. The Pew Foundation estimates that the number of Hindus in North America will rise from 2.3 million in 2010 to 5.9 in 2050.[37] However, even though this increase in the number of Hindus in the United States is significant, if taken at face value it risks underestimating the effects of transnationalism on Hindus at home and abroad. A number of trends are evident,

- An increasing number of Indian students enroll in American colleges and universities where they are shaped by Western values in the sciences and in business. American colleges are recruiting students in India.
- South Asians living in the United States frequently enter into economic alliances in India, developing small-scale transnational businesses.
- Large corporations in the pharmaceutical and other industries are multinational businesses, connecting the United States and India.

- Indian immigrants in the United States often find returning to South Asia for retirement desirable, economically and psychologically.
- Religious leaders in India frequently market spirituality not only to Hindus in India but also abroad. Many spiritual teachers (*ācāryas*) and *gurus* have become global travelers frequently visiting their devotees abroad.

These levels of interdependence not only connect transnational Hindu communities with the homeland but offer ways of reinforcing traditional lifestyles and conformity for Hindus living in the West who both retain their cultural identities but also adopt patterns of identity of their host society. This in turn creates opportunities in different generations for expressing attitudes of embodiment and symbolism. Together these changes have created a global interdependent religious environment.

Moreover, the "out-of-India" phenomenon is so significant that the Government of India has established a Ministry of Overseas Indian Affairs suggesting,

> In this increasingly inter-dependent and inter-connected world, Overseas Indians are becoming "Global Citizens." Even so, our shared culture and shared values bond all of us together. The Indian Diaspora is a pluralistic community just as India is. It holds within its fold, people of different languages, faiths and regions. The spirit of India transcends the narrow barriers of religion, language, caste or class, both within and outside the Indian nation.[38]

In seeking to maintain connections with this expanding community, the Ministry has established a number of categories including Persons of Indian Origin (PIO), Overseas Citizens of India (OCI), Non-Resident Indians (NRIs), and persons who do not fit into any of these categories.[39]

The rapid growth of the overseas Indian population and its movement back and forth from the homeland has also produced sizable demographic shifts creating the conditions for hybridization—"the mixing of different cultural forms and styles facilitated by global economic and cultural exchanges."[40] This process, which affects all immigrants, mixes elements and styles of the home (originating) culture with those of the host. Among Hindus in the West, hybridization has produced a form of Hinduism that has adopted Western religious values. For example, American Hinduism relies on the denominational system, utilizing well established practices of voluntarism, democratic governance, and the formation of national religious organizations. This process of assimilation creates pathways, especially among second-generation youth, for adopting attitudes toward

Hindu images that stress their symbolic importance in keeping with established American values.

Hybridization has become an increasingly common phenomenon through a process identified as glocalization. Originating from the Japanese practice of *dochakuka*, "...adapting a global institution's practices to local conditions,"[41] transplanted forms of religion adapt to conditions and practices abroad that they had never encountered in the homeland. For example, a *Swaminarayan* Hindu temple in eastern Pennsylvania dresses its deities in clothing appropriate for Valentine's Day while another offers its children an Easter egg hunt. As Hinduism develops a local presence in the United States, examples of hybrid practices that are "glocal" become increasingly common. In the case of the *Swaminarayan* temple the combination of processes could be seen in the deities who were understood as embodied in marble *mūrtis*, but yet displayed strong cultural connections on major holidays, connecting the trajectories of embodiment and symbolism.

Examples of glocalization and hybridization began to emerge in the 1970s when South Asians had established permanent residences in the United States. A woman wearing a *sari* with blue jeans underneath her garment drew attention at a local shopping mall in eastern Pennsylvania. Fusion food became popular, offering seductive blends of Asian cuisine from a wide variety of countries. Hindu temples, utilizing construction patterns that had been in place in India for millennia, were forced to adapt to local building codes, creating hybrid institutions that became part of the American religious landscape. A group of second-generation Hindu college students in the Dallas Fort Worth area, uses a campus celebration of Diwali both to affirm their religious identity and at the same time to demonstrate their "hybrid identity" to their parents.[42]

As hybridized practices began to emerge, theorists also contended that a process called "disembedding" was becoming an increasingly visible part of globalization, including "...all manners through which social life becomes abstracted from its local, spatially fixed context."[43] Hinduism overseas became increasingly disembedded from its Indian context and separated from village contexts, from caste, and, at times, from the dynamics of the extended family. As a consequence of this separation, the focus of the faith outside India often became more transportable, emphasizing scripture, ritual, and an evolving American temple tradition. What remained absent from this configuration were village, animistic practices which theorists had dubbed Hinduism's "Little Tradition."[44]

Both hybridization and disembedding further blurred the paradigm of core nations and those on the periphery, uprooting trajectories of symbolism and presence, and constructing social systems that manifested elements of each trajectory in India and throughout the global Hindu population. Significant parts of Indian society became hybridized, including education. Modeled on the English university system, higher education in India emphasized Western philosophy, religion, and values in an Indian context.

In the late twentieth century, globalization began to accelerate these processes, disembedding trajectories of symbolism and presence not only in the transnational Hindu population in the United States, but also in India where children in the expanding middle class are heavily schooled in the sciences. A student in a privately run high school Mumbai commented that she perceived the *mūrtis* in her home as symbolic representations of deity. Yet, in the fall when *Gaṇesh Chaturthī* was celebrated, and a temporary clay image of *Ganesh* was brought into the home, she concluded that this was a divine presence.[45] As a participant in a culture emphasizing embodiment as the primary manifestation of deity, she nevertheless had also absorbed Western perceptions of symbolism. In many privately run schools in India such as this, the curriculum is profoundly Western, emphasizing Enlightenment rationalism and scientific inquiry, creating opportunities for students to affirm both trajectories.

The internet has accelerated disembedding, removing *pūjās* from their traditional worship settings and offering them online. Commercial internet sites provide opportunities to worship both virtual figures or to participate in temple *pūjās* by proxy. Sites such as Saranam.com help devotees, called "franchisees," make online appointments so worshippers can participate in disembedded *pūjās* as if they were present at the temple in India.[46] The time and place of the *pūjā* are agreed on and the devotee can enter a period of devotion at the very moment that the *pūjā* is conducted. However, in other instances, *pūjās* are more fully disembedded, and offered outside of time constraints in virtual temples.

Sectarian traditions in the United States such as the *Anoopam Mission* (part of the wider *Swaminarayan* tradition) may use a similar process of disembedding, enabling the devotee to participate in a *pūjā* or *satsaṅg* (religious discussion) through virtual means. In these instances the locations of the *pūjā* are real as are the conditions under which they are performed. However, for the participant in cyber space, the *pūjā* is disembedded, offering no direct participation in ritual space and creating a hybridized form of tradition. This is particularly true of the *Swaminarayan* tradition which has expanded into the West rapidly.[47] Phyllis K. Herma concludes that some *Swaminarayan* devotees who were students used this system to considerable advantage,

> As one informant stated, "When I need to pray and establish a connection, I can do so wherever and whenever I need it." He has god posters and calendar art (to let him know about special days in the Swaminarayan festival cycle) in his dorm room, where he can do pūjā the new old-fashioned way, but his electronic access to the deity was available anywhere and anytime (provided the Internet was up). He and other respondents were adamant that the computer allowed them to "make a connection" with god, both literally and spiritually.... While going to temple to perform darśan is always best, many who were interviewed stated that the same or similar feelings arose when accessing online the images and sounds provided by the website.[48]

As a form of disembedding, online *pūjās* offer a number of advantages that have made the rigid requirements of sacred space that are tied to embodiment transplantable or jettisoned them completely. In an astounding adaptation of patterns of sacred space thousands of years old, internet *pūjās* are not tied to environments where water and bathing facilities are available to meet ritual purity requirements. Earlier views of television perceived it as mundane and potentially polluting. However, "A few years ago ... [online *darśan*] would have been rejected as illegitimate and inadequate, quite like watching television, or eating outside, for instance, is seen as 'polluting.'"[49]

The disembedding of *pūjās* from their ritual settings also creates an environment where the trajectories of presence and symbolism can easily be confused. Is the image of the deity in a completely virtual *pūjā* with no reference to existing space, symbolic or is it actual presence? Since the image is entirely visual and is not the product of ritual production, can it have life? This question is complex since on a popular level Hindus frequently claim that wherever god is seen his or her presence is there as well. Yet, beyond this assumption, when the grandchild of a first-generation Hindu immigrant in the West sees this image, will they react to it as presence or in the same way that most virtual images are presented—as symbolic forms?

Mass Marketing of Images and the Trajectory of Symbolism

In a global system of commerce the marketplace is the emissary of the cultural trajectory of symbolism for sacred objects. The advent of the internet coupled with a growing Hindu overseas migration in well over 200 countries, has created a global market for *mūrtis* that are part of a competitive system of international commerce in which the symbolism of material goods is tied to production. Symbolic consumption theory links patterns of acquisition to personal identity in increasingly sophisticated models that tie objects to diverse levels of meaning.[50]

In addition to the power of the internet, the global marketing of goods, including those with religious purposes, has contributed to marked changes in attitudes. Replacing ancient patterns of ritual production is a global manufacturing system that knows little about traditional processes but, instead, sees Hindu images as an expanding international market where the aesthetic is the primary appeal. This change is evident on Chinese websites like "Alibaba" where the casual observer can find images of *Ganesh* offered in virtually any quantity and in a number of postures that are atypical in religious tradition. Websites like "*Ganesh* Mall"[51] sell a wide variety of *Ganesh mūrtis* as well as other "Vedic statues," and a mixture of jewelry, clothing, and ritual statues intended for *pūjā*. Similarly, the "Dolls of India" website[52] offers representations of *Ganesh* that would never be found in the canons of Hindu iconography, creating popular characterizations of the Hindu god of good fortune. Religious objects are divorced from religious meaning. Statues of *Ganesh* are available sitting on a *tabla*, or assuming the position of a musician or priest. Mass production techniques are used for the fabrication process. One manufacturer advertises,

> This Extremely Detailed and Well-Made statue is made with cold cast bronze. The special production process of this piece, originated from Great Britain, uses actual bronze powder mixed in the cold cast resin in order to ensure a richer, more life-like presentation.[53]

Changes in production and advertising techniques also suggests that these images are seen as what anthropologist Michael Thompson calls "transient goods."[54] Thompson distinguishes between commercially manufactured objects that are transient, and durable goods, which have more permanence, including art and antiquities. Transient goods have short life spans and quickly descend to garbage while durable goods re-enter the market place until, again, they become part of personal or public collections in museums and homes. *Mūrtis*, created in conjunction with the trajectory of presence, are durable.

One market site advertises "Ganesh dolls" offering hand-sewn forms of the deity that are marketed in the same way that Barbie would be in the West, clearly departing from any nuance of durable goods.[55] Another, offers "Golu Dolls," for customers in India and abroad. These figures utilize traditional images, often placing them in modern settings. Figures of *Ganesh* are seen sitting behind a desk or relaxing in a claw foot bathtub.[56] The images are cute, painted in bright colors, and freely mix modernity with ancient tradition in a popular art form that is trendy. Separated from cycles of purity and pollution, ritual production, and sometimes even from the mythology that formed them, they are symbolic objects with appeal to a growing cultural trajectory borne in the West and also found in India.

Hindu Temples in the West as Emissaries of the Trajectory of Presence

While second-generation Hindu youth in the United States may see *mūrtis* as primarily symbolic, coupled with an expanding international market for factory produced images devoid of ritual context, so the Hindu temple tradition in the West effectively carried the trajectory of presence abroad. Following the changes in the U.S. 1965 immigration law and the rapid increase in the size of the U.S. Hindu community, Hindu temples gradually became a normative part of the American religious landscape.

The first Hindu temple to be constructed in the United States was southern Indian, erected in Flushing, Queens in 1977. Erected by the Hindu Temple Society of North America on land purchased from a Russian Orthodox Church in 1970 the temple was thrust into an environment where a hybridized presence was necessary.[57] *Sthapatis*, trained in traditional forms of Hindu architecture were brought to the site to erect a temple while, at the same time, building codes in New York City restricted what they could do. Just as those who would worship at the temple, contractors found themselves in between both worlds needing to accommodate and incorporate to survive. For example, "Michael and Thomas Graysing, contractors in Babylon, on Long Island, describe themselves as 'Roman Catholic Boys' who have learned—now that temple building has become one of their specialties—to rattle off Hindu terms in their New York accents, and to harbor a deep respect for places of worship."[58]

Artisans, who had never experienced winter, traveled from India to finish the structure while temple leaders attempted to raise funds, in a way akin to most denominational practices in the United States. In the end, the completed hybridized structure was a faithful representation of classical Hindu architecture but also met the code requirements for the city.

When the temple was completed and deities installed, it established the trajectory of presence, not only in the largest city in the United States, but in the hub of America's business community where the trajectory of symbolism was dominant. Temple leaders insured that the installation and subsequent rededication of the deities were in full accord with ritual requirements of a divine, living presence. This was especially visible during a *Mahā Kumbhābhiṣekam* ceremony of rededication of the images in 2009. The *Shiva-Vishnu Temple* in Livermore, California, which celebrated its first *Mahā Kumbhābhiṣekam* in 1986, and again in 2010, describes the same rite:

> Maha Kumbhabhisekam literally means ritualistic pouring of sacred water from the great vessel. Such abhishekam or ritualistic pouring of water dates back hundreds of years to post-vedic times when temple rituals were formalized. During the Vedic period, deities were invoked and propitiated in great rituals of fire sacrifices such as yagnas and homas, which were performed in the open. After this period, when temples were built for different deities, the divine energy/spirit was invoked ... and transferred into kumbhas—brass or mud vessels containing the water of the holy rivers of Bharatavarsha—by chanting mantras.... (When) the deities were installed, the energy in the water in the kumbhas was transferred to the vigraha in the temple by pouring the water on the gopuram (top of the temple tower) and on the vigraha of the deity. This pouring from the kumbhas was accompanied by the chanting of appropriate mantras derived from the Vedas, considered to be of divine origin.[59]

The *Mahā Kumbhābhiṣekam* ritual is not only used to re-evoke power and presence into a temple's resident deities, but also to give life to the temple itself. In her tour de force on the Hindu temple, Stella Kramrish confirms,

> The temple as house and seat of God in which dwells His Essence is also His body; the temple contains the whole manifestation ... in which he is beheld as Puruṣa, Supernal Man.... The several parts of the temple communicate His living presence.... The door is the mouth, the Āmalaka or the high dome is the head.... The image in the Garbha Gṛha the Life (jīva) of the temple, concealed in the darkness of the cave, enclosed by the mountains of its walls. The outside of the bulwark, teeming with ordered shapes and figures, is its explicit form. The temple is conceived from inside and visualized from outside; the communication between inside and outside is brought about by the radiating power from within which assigns its place to each and every facet of the walls.[60]

This part of the Hindu trajectory of presence is a common point of reference for temple leaders in the United States. A *sādhu* in a Swaminarayan temple in Pennsylvania used an analogy of a nuclear reactor to describe the transforming power within a temple that radiates out through the structure.[61] The inner sanctuary (*garbha gṛha*) of the temple was constructed on an axis, directly over the space that had been consecrated before the temple was erected, and underneath the spires that completed the axis, connecting earth and sky.

In consecration rituals that connect temples both to the life of the deity and at the same time establish the structure as a living, architectural manifestation of spirit, Western temples have relied on the trajectory of presence. Contracting with bronze and stone image makers in India, temples oversee the ritual process of production, inspecting blocks of marble to ensure that they are perfect vessels for god, and orchestrating the rituals in the West which bring them to life.

Conclusion

Studies of South Asian religion have approached Hinduism through a number of lenses including textual studies of canonical and post canonical literature, historical analyses of Hindu traditions, ritual studies, and philosophical explorations into Hindu belief systems. In each of these areas, a number of components of the tradition are often emphasized. These have included the role of caste and the dynamics of *jāti* in addressing purity and pollution. Hindu studies have also emphasized what Robert Redfield termed the Little Tradition, including the role of animism in village studies. Conversely, explorations of the Great Tradition by Redfield, Marriott, and others addressed the structures of textual and belief systems that defined the major tenets of the tradition. Srinivas explored the polemics of a process that he called Sanskritization in which "...the historical processes by which the beliefs and practices of lower castes tend to converge toward those of higher castes, especially Brahmans, as the former try to raise their status by emulating the latter."[62]

As globalization accelerated in the 1990s, shaping the new millennium, each of these elements that had traditionally been used to understand Hinduism became increasingly irrelevant to Hindus abroad. The hierarchy of caste and its connections to ritual purity remained as important components in Hindu temples in the West, but no longer affected patterns of human interaction among devotees. The Little Traditions, rooted in animistic beliefs and practices could not be transplanted to the West and were dependent on India's sacred geography. The Great Tradition, however, did survive, becoming transportable to overseas Indian communities.

The cultural trajectory of embodiment and presence, which had evolved from the tap root of Hindu society, was one of the most important components of the Great Tradition, forming links between temple and text. Yet, as this text will demonstrate, among overseas Hindu communities in Western societies, it is increasingly separated by generation and often replaced by the dominant cultural trajectory in the West based on rationalism, symbolism, and meaning. Temples have become the repository of embodiment while in homes, India associations, and among the population of South Asian Hindus living and working in the West, expressions about images as symbolic representations of deity are common among the sons and daughters of the immigrant generation.

On one hand, through the sustained flow of first-generation immigrants to the West, the role of *mūrtis* has been continued in temples and in many homes as a form of divine presence. However, at the same time as the U.S. Hindu population ages and second- and third-generation families establish their own ritual patterns, sacred objects have increasingly been seen as symbolic and often without the sense of presence that has defined their historical role in India. Much more than the result of generational changes and assimilation, this transition has also been influenced by immigration and the length of time that parents spent in India, and by sectarian traditions. Perceptions have also been influenced by the movement of many second- and third-generation children into professions rooted in science where the dominant way of knowing is empirical.

Because of the number of variables that can influence Hindus abroad, multiple attitudes toward sacred objects can be found in the same family. Some second-generation students showed confusion both recognizing the role of their parents in continuing ritual practices based on embodiment and at the same time acknowledging their own acquired empirical nature that refused to examine the more intimate connections between objects and spirit.

In the age of globalization, *mūrtis* have become visitors in the West where they have acquired multiple roles in a society that is also debating the connections between the spiritual and material. Acquired through inheritance, ritual production, mass production, and export, they have entered a variety of roles. Within this process the essential characteristics of Hindu tradition have also witnessed dramatic change, forging American, European, African, and Australian forms of Hinduism that have begun to evolve differently from the long history of the parent tradition.

Two

Bringing God to Life
*The Trajectory of Presence
and Ritual Production*

This chapter describes the origins of the trajectory of embodiment and its evolution over the course of several thousand years. The trajectory has been part of the infrastructure of classical Hinduism from the inception of the Hindu temple through the evolution of the *Vaiṣṇava*, *Śaiva*, and Shakti (*Śakti*) traditions. Although this text is primarily focused on the role of sacred presence in images, rather than in aniconic forms such as the *liṅga*, embodiment has remained a central part of both iconic and anionic Hindu traditions.

The chapter is a reminder that cultural trajectories have lengthy histories and have survived because of their resilience which has been supported by centuries of diversified traditions that surround core patterns of belief and practice. They also have sustained challenges philosophically and historically. These dynamics are illustrated in the origins and development of the trajectory of embodiment which evolved with the Hindu temple tradition. The chapter is a reminder that cultural trajectories have lengthy histories and have survived because of their resilience which has been supported by centuries of diversified traditions that surround core patterns of belief and practice. They also have sustained challenges philosophically and historically. These dynamics are illustrated in the origins and development of the trajectory of embodiment which evolved with the Hindu temple tradition. This chapter presents the trajectory in three parts: a discussion of the origins of the trajectory in part 1, the processes of ritual production in part 2, and a study of a single iconographic tradition, *Balkrishna*, in part 3.

Part 1: Origins of the Trajectory

Studies of the origins of image worship frequently conclude that it became part of Hindu tradition during the Buddhist period, gradually gathering momentum within the wider fabric of ritual tradition. While the Vedas contain sparse references to image worship, these references are not central to the tradition and are not described in terms of ritual embodiment. Sthaneshwar Timalsina concludes,

> Textual references that can be roughly dated from around the time of the Buddha until the Common Era provide sufficient clues about the scope and nature of image worship in the earliest period. With the later emergence of Smārta and Tantric Hinduism, images moved to the center of religious experience.[1]

While Hindu literature provides glimpses of the gradual evolution of the trajectory, it was during the early periods of empire, in the *Mauryan* (322 BCE–185 BCE), *Gupta* (320 BCE–550 CE), and *Chola* periods (300s BCE–1279 CE) that it became visible. As monarchs established governing dynasties they also used patronage to support temples which became residences of the gods. As the purview of priests the trajectory of presence found a continuous foothold in text and practice. Later, codified in a diverse collection of scripture, the *Śilpa Śāstras*, the trajectory achieved a level of orthopraxy that has for centuries been maintained in temples and home shrines where deities in iconographic form were awakened, bathed, fed, dressed, and entertained daily.

While it is possible that the beginnings of the trajectory may lie much earlier in the Indus Valley and adjacent Neolithic civilizations, there is no firm evidence and considerable debate. Proponents of the Indus origins for worship of figurines cite contemporary civilizations including Egypt, where, they suggest, similar practices occurred,

> … civilizations in ancient Egypt and the Indus Valley were contemporary sharing a number of socio-cultural practices. Both were theocratic societies, shared patterns of trade often connected with seals and amulets connected to religion, and practiced religious traditions where the divine was focused on anthropomorphic images. While we know far more about Egyptian religious practices than those of the Indus Valley because of access to written sources, it is still possible through the careful use of analogy to suggest that in both civilizations, as in other contemporary ancient societies, images were likely understood as objects of divine presence.[2]

Evolving in two urban areas, Mohenjo Daro and Harappa, and a wider region that extended as far south as the present day Gujarat, deities were portrayed in terracotta statues and on seals in anthropomorphic forms.

Archaeologist Dilip Chakrabarti concludes that Indus figurines were ritual objects,

> There is no specific ritual place or context associated with these figures, but their ubiquity and abundance cannot be easily discarded; they are unlikely to be merely children's toys. The ritual use of such terracottas varies in modern India; a common context is to place them under a tree as offerings to a wish-fulfilling deity. The small female figurines may also be fashioned for use in various household folk rituals by women.[3]

This argument can be supported by the use of Formal Analogies in ethnoarchaeology which are "...justified by similarities in the formal attributes of archaeological and ethnographical objects and features."[4] In Egyptian and Babylonian civilizations where trade with the Indus Valley flourished, trajectories of presence in sacred objects was an important component of civilization.

Additional support for this argument comes from the evolution of symbolic thought. The notion that material objects represent, but do not contain, larger realities is a product of modernity. While the nature of Indus Valley religion is the subject of numerous theories, and the identity of the terracotta figurines that represent deities cannot yet be known, it is possible to argue by analogy that in ancient near eastern and south Asian civilizations, sacred objects were likely to be construed in terms of presence.

A number of strong arguments from archaeologists, however, would seem to cast doubt on these claims. Rejecting the early assumptions by Sir John Marshall and Mortimer Wheeler that Indus figurines were forms of the mother goddess, or that they had ritual use, Gregory L. Possehl concludes that the role of female figurines produced in Mehrgarh-Nausharo, "...tips slightly toward the concept of motherhood, fertility, reproduction. It does not seem to favor religion, ritual, and goddesses quite as much; although there can be elements of magic and wish fulfillment."[5]

Debates about the connections between the Indus Valley civilization and contemporary Hinduism are complicated by interpretations of Hinduism that want to find origins of mother goddess worship and early representations of other deities in the Indus. A case in point was the early debate about a *"proto-Shiva"* discovered in 1929 on a terracotta seal which showed a horned deity sitting in a *yogic* position and wearing horns. Orientalist scholar Sir John Marshall interpreted this image to be *Pashupati*, a form of *Shiva* presented as lord of the animals, and subsequently as a *"proto-Shiva"* image. However, revisionist approaches have subsequently rejected this idea, presenting a variety of other theories.[6]

Temples as Conduits of Presence

While knowledge of Indus religion remains incomplete, evidence of the trajectory of presence is easily found in the evolution of the Hindu temple tradition. While perceptions of embodiment were probably far older, the temple tradition provides a window through which the evolution of the trajectory can be observed. Maintained through royal favor, and administered by retinues of priests, temples became undisputed sources of authority across the Indian subcontinent, reifying sacred presence. Temples evolved as the arm of both monarch and deity—controlling vast amounts of land including entire villages, conscripting laborers, establishing parameters of purity and pollution, and doing all of that in support of the beneficence of the gods.

Beginning in the early *Gupta* period, monarchs supported the construction of temples which were established as divine residences.[7] As patronage expanded, temples became more ornate and began to expand the trajectory of presence beyond the inner sanctum. The towns that serviced larger temples not only became residences of workers but also were planned to meet the needs of the gods. In time, temples became part of a sacralized landscape, in which both urban and rural areas became integrated within the trajectory of presence, creating a sacred geography.

The evolution of these changes can be seen in the earliest construction of stone temples. Primitive temples in Sanchi and Jaipur were erected as divine residences and often included little more than the inner sanctuary or *garbha gṛha*. At temple #17 in Sanchi (circa 400 CE) the only architectural addition to the sanctuary is an outer portico.[8] At Mahabalipuram, near Chennai, the *garbha gṛha* is accessed through a portico with a distinctive hanging roof, in an analogy to a Bengali hut.[9] At the Ladkhan temple at Aihole (5th century CE), planners added a path for circumambulation of the inner sanctuary, magnifying the role of the structure as a divine residence and its central occupant as the focal point of the temple.[10] The practice of circumambulation, magnified the significance of the cosmic center within.

By the sixth-century northern and southern patterns of temple architecture had become established with increasing levels of sacred space surrounding the inner sanctuary.[11] Large gateways or *gōpurams* became part of the South Indian landscapes as temples embellished their identity as bastions of sacred space. Inside, the *garbha gṛha* also became more defined, embodying the deity's presence and maintained by stringent standards of purity. The large *gōpurams* of southern Indian temples were augmented by bulbous spires (*śikhara*), erected directly over the sanctum sanctorum. The location and architecture of temples in the North, South, and in the Deccan, where a syncretistic style of temple architecture developed, also placed primary importance on the *garbha gṛha*, purifying the space below where the deity would reside through elaborate rituals and *homa* ceremonies, and insuring the receptivity of the area to the divine through *maṇḍalas.*

In *Śaiva* temples that relied on aniconic imagery with the enshrinement of the *liṅga*, similar patterns evolved. In southern India, near Chennai, as early as first to second centuries BCE, the *Guḍimallam liṅga* combined the aniconic imagery of *Shiva*, with a three-headed sculpture of the deity incised in the image. The *liṅga* was more than symbol or metaphor, and marked the full presence of the deity,

> There are many kinds of *liṅgas*, but the most important distinction is between those that are *svayambhū*, "self-manifest" and those that are fashioned and consecrated by human hands, *sthāpita*, literally, "established." Many temples old and new have a Śiva *liṅga* with a finely shaped shaft and base, placed in the sanctum and consecrated with elaborate rites to be the permanent presence of Śiva. *Svayambhū liṅgas* are, instead, already there. The powerful presence of Śiva is *discovered,* revealed in the earth, not established by human hands. These *liṅgas* are said to be spontaneous, perhaps miraculous, appearances of Śiva....[12]

The driving force behind the social and ritual power of the temple was the life force that resided in the inner recesses of the *garbha gṛha* (sanctum sanctorum or "womb room"). Bharne and Krusche suggest, in this regard, that temples were always erected from the *garbha gṛha* outward, supporting the primacy of a divine center.[13] As pillared hallways and porches (*maṇḍapas*) were added to the structures, the inner energy of the deities was interpreted not just as a local but also as a cosmic center. Temples became microcosms of the cosmos—an idea that had been used to create the *maṇḍalas* that helped define the space before construction began. Using precise astronomical calculations, these geometric patterns looked to the center, creating "maps" that would help define the sacred presence within.

The concept of sacred presence was so significant that both resident *mūrti* and the temple itself were understood to be alive. Temples were designed in a scale that reflected human proportions to support the life force within. The final act that brought *mūrti* and temple to life was the *Prāṇ Pratiṣṭhā* which was performed when the god was established in residence, "Prāṇa means vital force or energy that surrounds life. Within the ceremony the idol's eyes are sculpted open, marking the birth of both the statue and the temple itself."[14]

As temple architecture became more refined, temple towns expanded the purview of the divine presence so that the deity could periodically leave his residence to survey the city built in his honor. At Chidambaram, the city evolved in keeping with the deity's needs, providing routes for the god's ritual circumambulation of the temple. Temple towns were organized hierarchically so that the castes (*jātis*) that served the temple would be accessible.[15] In Vijayanagar, this practice also led to the separation of the sacred zone of the temple proper from the mundane, again insuring that the purity associated with the deity would be preserved.[16]

The idea of a divine center also affected entire regions, sometimes constructing a sacred geography which, "...not only connects places to the lore of gods, heroes, and saints, but it connects places to one another through local, regional, and transregional practices of pilgrimage. Even more, these tracks of connection stretch from this world toward the horizon of the infinite, linking this world with the world beyond."[17]

Within the evolving sacred topography, urban areas became cities of the gods and more rural regions their playgrounds. Kashi became the residence of *Shiva* and, in its own right, as an important place of pilgrimage. In parts of Rajasthan and Uttar Predesh, Braj became the homeland of *Krishna*. Myth reinforced temple traditions.

A case in point was the oral and literary traditions about Braj (an area in Uttar Pradesh and Rajasthan). In a rural area not far from Mathura, Mount Govardhan became significant both as a manifestation of the deity's presence and as a locus of myth. The story of *Krishna* and Govardhan in the *Bhāgavata Purāṇa* magnified the identification of the land with the deity and at the same time separated *Krishna* from the *Vedic* god, *Indra*, distancing the earlier sacrificial tradition from the nuances of *bhakti* traditions. In the *Bhāgavata's* account, India required his subjects to submit offerings. However, the infant *Krishna* suggested that as farmers they should concentrate on their work and not make the offering. Jealous of the popularity of the child god, *Indra* unleashed a punishment of a torrent of thunder and rain. Remaining loyal to his devotees, *Krishna* lifted the mountain so that they could find shelter. The myth and the mountain created a mutually identifiable level of sacred space, magnifying the tradition of presence and justifying the removal of a *Vedic* god and his sacrificial cult.

The trajectory of presence emerged from the antiquity of Hindu civilization as the confluence of myth and art, ritual and image. The role of priests was to meet the needs of the life force within the temple, awakening, bathing, anointing, feeding and entertaining deities in both iconic and aniconic form. Temples became the most visible parts of Hindu tradition but also mirrored the reification of the trajectory of presence at home. As the gods moved into the temple, at times creating cities around them, so they were also resident in homes where the same processes of purification defined their realm and established their presence.

Hindu Temples, Embodiment and the Dynamics of Patronage

If Hindu temples were the visible manifestation of embodiment, housing a resident deity inside, the dynamics of patronage helped establish the broad power of the trajectory of presence. From the earliest evolution of the temple, connections with royalty were readily apparent. The temple became a landlord, controlling vast amounts of territory, exerting authority over multiple villages, and exacting tribute from crops that the temple lands controlled. In the early ruling dynasties of southern India monarchs constructed temples as living evidence of their political and economic power. The ritual power inside became another level of authority, perpetuating the role of embodiment.

> Tenth-century Chola monarch, Rajaraja I, ... also gave land, making over the royal share of produce from numerous villages throughout his dominion and as far afield as Sri Lanka. These endowments yielded an annual income of roughly a quarter million bushels of rice paddy. To supply ghee for cooking and for burning oil lamps, livestock was donated to the temple. One inscription details 2,832 cows, 1,644 ewes, and 30 she-buffalos that were assigned to 366 cowherds, who in turn required to supply ghee to the temple at the rate of one *ulakku* (roughly half a pint) per day for every 48 cows or 96 ewes.... Arrangements were also made for the regular supply of such cooking ingredients and condiments as fruit, pulse, pepper, tamarind, mustard, cumin, sugar, curds plantains, salt, greens, areca nut, and betel leaves. All of these were necessary for the regular offerings of worship on a suitably grand scale, and for the even grander special offerings made during the several "great festivals" held annually.[18]

The dynamics of patronage rested in economic exchange, "As a focal point for economic redistribution, the South Indian temple was the conduit through which exchange occurred: material goods were transformed into the symbols of prestige and influence known as temple honors."[19]

At the *Sucindram* Temple in Travancore the patronage of Raja Raja the Great facilitated the temple's ability to sponsor festivals, celebrations, and other manifestations of the temple as a social institution,

> Wherever he went, he seems to have aimed at ennobling the temple as the pivot of social and religious life. Bestowal of gifts on the temples, organisation (sic) of Brah-

min feeding, the establishment of the institution of Devadāsīs, the insistence on the practice of singing devotional hymns from Devaram and Tiruvacakam, and above all, the popularisation (sic) of religious festivals and ceremonies were some of the activities, which he reveled in. A master-builder of temples, Raja Raja holds also a unique place as the ruler who oranised (sic) the practices and celebrations of the temple in South India. The lofty position which the temple was ennobled as a social institution, stood the test of time during the succeeding centuries and became the dominant feature of the social history of South India.[20]

Similar dynamics were also apparent in North Indian *bhakti* temples which, even though participating in a movement of reform, also relied on patronage. The *Vallabha Sampradaya*, a sixteenth-century *bhakti* sect, was supported not only by grants from the Mughal Emperor Akbar, but also by land grants from the *Mahārāṇas* of Mewar, a staunch, independent Hindu kingdom.[21] In the seventeenth century, when Aurangzeb came to the throne and patronage of Hindu temples ended, the sect was deeded a village as a gift from the ruling *Mahārāṇa*. Moving its central deity, *Shrī Nathji*, to Mewar, the village was transformed into Nathdwara, becoming an important pilgrimage center. Patronage of ruling *Mahārāṇas* lasted through the sixteenth and seventeenth centuries until increasing influence of the East India Company made it no longer tenable.

In South India, patronage resulted in a symbiotic relationship between deity and king. Richard M. Eaton concludes,

> … not withstanding that temple priests endowed a royal temple's deity with attributes of transcendent and universal power, that same deity was also understood as having a very special relationship, indeed a sovereign relationship, with the particular geographical site in which its temple complex was located. As revealed in temple narratives, even the physical removal of an image from its original site could not break the link between deity and geography.[22]

Within the dynamics of patronage, the pattern of embodiment was so strong, that any change in mood of the deity was assumed to be a sign of trouble.

The bonding between king, god, temple, and land in early medieval India is well illustrated in a passage from the *Bṛhatsaṃhitā*, a sixth-century text: "If a Śiva *liṅga,* image, or temple breaks apart, moves, sweats, cries, speaks, or otherwise acts with no apparent cause, this warns of the destruction of the king and his territory."[23] The trajectory of embodiment was never separated from the political manifestation of the deity who jointly exercised the authority of the realm with the ruling monarch. Embodiment affected the mood of the region, predicted signs of economic or political difficulty, established ritual patterns of tribute, and affected the life cycle of devotees in such a way that no one was exempt from the trajectory.

Theologies of Embodiment

While worship of images of Vishnu or his *avatars* including *Krishna* and *Rama* assumes that the deities enshrined in temples have a fixed presence, this is not necessarily the case in other forms of Hinduism. In his study of medieval Saivism in South India, Richard Davis reveals that in the texts of the *Śaiva Siddhānta* philosophy, the presence of *Shiva* and his embodiment in an image was transient, dependent on the role of priests to bring the *mūrti* to life during each period of worship (*pūjā*).[24]

In India's medieval period, *Śaiva* temples were heavily patronized by *Cola* kings. Temples were constructed with the radiant energy of the deity inside. Each portion of the structure brought devotees closer to this center and the deity. Images were of several types. The most sacred were *lingas* which were aniconic images which did not convey the deity's presence anthropomorphically. Differentiated images or *beras* were anthropomorphic forms of *Shiva*. Finally, the *linga* with faces carved in it was mid-way between the two.[25]

Image, temple, and priest in *Śaiva* worship existed in symbiotic forms, conditioned by an "oscillating" universe in which the deity's presence in iconic form was evoked by the priest. At the same time, the priest acquired a divine body, free of defilement, and in such a state that he could communicate with the awakened deity and become absorbed in his own *Shiva* soul. This cycle of the emanation of the deity into *linga*, *bera* images and *linga* with faces, coupled with the movement of priests to a purified state in which they acquired a *Shiva* soul is part of the oscillating nature of the universe. It also forms the unique conditions in which embodiment existed during the *Chola* dynasty. As temple priests evoked the deity so they also transformed themselves so that they could enter the heart of the temple,

> As the priest moves from outside the temple toward the central linga, he must also transform his own state of being. Before entering the temple, the worshipper reaches a state of personal purity through performing his daily ablutions and bath.... He then enters into its outer precincts. Offering worship to the various deities who inhabit the door frame and protecting the temples against intruders (vighna). Next he must transform himself with a more thorough purification and the construction of a divine body.... Only then may the priest enter the central abode of the linga, again worshiping the deities of the sanctum's door frame and protecting it against intruders as he enters.[26]

When worship has concluded and the *pūjā* is done, the priest dismissed *Shiva* from the embodied form that he has taken. Unlike *Vaiṣṇava* traditions in which embodiment is permanent for temple images, *Chola* *Śaivas* required that *Shiva* be evoked and dismissed with every *pūjā*.

Since *pūjās* were conducted daily this oscillation of the deity's presence was a regular occurrence and formed the conditions within which deity, royal patron, and his subjects lived their lives. Temples became abodes of this oscillating presence which also mirrored the movement of the universe and the cyclical pattern of creation and destruction associated with *Śaiva* theology.

Daily or *nitya pūjā* in the temples of the *Saiva Siddhanta* also differed with the absence of *prasād*—the ritual sharing of food blessed by the deity.[27] Davis suggests that this was because of the central dynamic of purity and the inability of the deity's worshippers to enter into this same state. The connections between theologies of embodiment and ritual purity in all Hindu traditions are central to the experience of *pūjā* and the ability of the deity to receive food in anthropomorphic forms. However, in the practices of the *Śaiva Siddhānta* temples were seen as bastions of ritual purity so significant that the presence of the deity could only be experienced when priests entered the same state which was inaccessible to devotees.

What the example of *Śaiva Siddhānta* theology shows is that in India's medieval period, more than one theology of embodiment existed. Within each of these complex systems in both *Vaiṣṇavism* and *Śaivism*, the deity's presence was interpreted in different ways. However, in both cases, temples became bastions of divine energy and presence. Through systems of royal patronage, embodiment deeply affected economic and social systems. Food offerings, a constant supply of milk and butter, clothes for the deity, crops, and any number of staples were all affected by the presence of the deity. The authority of the ruling monarch was also enhanced by the deity's presence, wedding perceptions of embodiment with the internal and external health of the realm.

Challenges to the Trajectory

The process of establishing the centrality of embodiment was not without challenges. In the early medieval period the transition from *Vedic* sacrifices to temples which housed embodied deities produced intense debate among priests. Support of *Vedic* authority found strength in the *Upaniṣads* and the evolution of monistic thought which led to the nondual philosophy of *Advaita*. Championing non-attachment and meditation, *Advaitans* did not see image worship as central and were supported by devotional poets, advocates of the *Mīmāṃsā* School of philosophy as well as early forms of Buddhism and Jainism which also gave *mūrtis* peripheral importance.[28]

Advaitan thought speculated that in the oneness of all reality there could not be distinctions nor subject or object. The role of images was not a primary path to *mokṣa*. *Advaitan* philosophy suggested that while *mūrtis* may be helpful to some, in the end they are distractions that move devotees away from the delusion of cause and effect and from access to release from the fetters of illusion (*māyā*) generated by *karma*.

When, in the seventh and eighth centuries, *Advaitan* philosophy was codified by Shankara, a more unified system of *Vedānta* was posited. Shankara argued that in an environment controlled by *karmic* processes and the dynamics of rebirth, perceptions of duality were the result of ignorance and the onslaughts of illusion. However, the codification of *Vedānta* also produced a counter reaction among devotees who, undoubtedly influenced by the expanding temple tradition, argued that theism was a viable alternative path. The chief proponent of this position was Ramanuja, who, writing in the eleventh century, codified a system identified as *Viśiṣṭadvaita* or qualified non-dualism. Within this philosophy, images remained a central part of the search for salvation, becoming translucent forms that could lead the devotee on a path of ultimate experience toward the unknowable *Brahman*. Ritual treatises argued that form was essential,

> Vaiṣṇava and Śaiva ritual treatises often frame their discussions of image worship within the question of God's accessibility. If God is by definition unconstrained by form, these texts ask, how may humans praise him, meditate upon him, and offer him worship? In the Vaiṣṇava Pāñcarātra *Paramasaṃhitā*, the creator god Brahman is perplexed by just this problem and raises it with Viṣṇu himself. "You have told me that the Highest God Viṣṇu is the ultimate cause of creation," Brahman observes "Then how should humans worship him and meditate on him? For He is not ever limited by any conditions, and his form cannot be ascertained through direction, place, time, or shape. So how should one who hopes to be successful worship Him?" ...
>
> Viṣṇu answers him firmly: "He can be worshipped in embodied form only. There is no worship of one without manifest form."[29]

As a supporter of the Shri *Vaishṇava* tradition, Ramanuja wrote nine Sanskrit treatises, struggling with Shankara's dismissal of theism. Ramanuja posited that *Iśvara*, or personal deities could be worshipped as a way of accessing *Brahman* through a teaching which he identified as *dharmabhūtāñjana*—the view that both consciousness and perception are object oriented. Constructing a theistic form of *Vedānta*, Ramanuja's addition to the corpus of Hindu philosophy created a bridge between temple and *Vedic* tradition, securing a hermeneutical lens through which the non-dualism in the *Upaniṣads* could be interpreted in a way that conformed to the continuing trajectory of embodiment and presence.

Another system of philosophy, *Pūrva Mīmāṃsā*, also argued that image worship was not of central importance. A similar, albeit atheistic position, had been posited by the ancient *Cārvāka* school. As a system of logic, *Pūrva Mīmāṃsā* drew its authority from the *Vedas, Pūrva Mīmāṃsā* philosophers denied divine embodiment.[30] Jamini (writing in the fourth century) and Sabara (writing a century later) gave theism little credence, disavowing the idea of divine embodiment. "Sabara was arguing explicitly against a way of interpreting Vedic sacrifice, and at the same time he argued implicitly against the theistic schools that advocated the worship of divine icons."[31]

These critiques occurred at a time when temple traditions were expanding within an accelerating system of royal patronage. Allowing monarchs to control vast amounts of land, temples not only became conduits for embodiment, but were the mainstays of empire. The political strength of this union between temple and state reduced the possibility of any lasting threats to the trajectory of embodiment. The ancient atheistic *Cārvāka* School, for example, had found image worship irrelevant but achieved little support in grounding its assumptions within an expanding Hindu civilization supported by temple traditions.

Ironically, it was a series of historical events, all portents of globalization, that created the most distress for practitioners of embodiment. The penetration of Islam into the Indian subcontinent by Mahmud of Gazni (beginning in 1001 CE), the establishment of the Delhi Sultanate, and the more enduring Mughal Empire, brought the Hindu trajectory of presence into direct contact with Islam which assumed that divine embodiment was heretical.

Stereotypes about Islamic presence in India have often led to the premise that image worship was severely threatened by Muslim conquest and conversion and that images were routinely defaced during the Mughal period. However, there is scant evidence of this happening, except during the reign of Aurangzeb (1618–1707), and even then not on a scale that would have posed a threat to the entire trajectory. As part of his military campaigns Aurangzeb destroyed Hindu temples in Mathura and Varanasi, erecting mosques over the ruins. However, there is no record of the wanton or wholesale destruction of *mūrtis*. Hindu sects (*sampradāyas*) fearing the loss of freedom and, as was the case with the *Vallabha Sampradaya*, sought refuge in areas away from Aurangzeb's armies.

Far greater threats to the trajectory of presence came from colonial empires. The religious organizations created as part of the nineteenth-century Hindu Renaissance brought the Western trajectory of symbolism into contact and conflict with the Hindu perception of embodiment in an early portent of a more globalized world. The Renaissance also reflected the division in Indian society precipitated by 300 years of British colonialism in which some Hindus sought to emulate their British colonizers while others staunchly defended *Vedic* authority. In both cases, embodiment was denied by Ram Mohun Roy, who championed monotheism, and by Hindu reformer, Swami Dayananda.

Ram Mohan Roy was a Hindu monotheist who is most often identified with the *Brahmo Samaj*, a Renaissance organization that advocated Christian principles. The *Samaj* had broken away from the British Indian Unitarian Association, an organization that Roy had worked with as the Calcutta Unitarian Association. Championing Western education he had also founded the English-Language-Anglo-Hindu school in 1822.[32] A Hindu social reformer, he advocated for women's rights and disavowed *satī* (widow burning).

Roy was a staunch opponent of embodiment, attempting to convince followers to renounce image worship. American Unitarian missionary Joseph Tuckerman was convinced that Roy supported the *Brahmo Samaj* "...not because he believes in the divine authority of the Veda, but solely as an instrument for overthrowing idolatry."[33] These sentiments had precipitated Roy's insistence that members of the *Atmiya Samaj*, which he founded in 1815, abstain from image worship and not advocate it. He had taken a public stance in concert with these views debating image worship with a well-known Brahmin in Madras. The debate caused such a public outrage that Roy was forced to disband the *Atmiya Samaj*.[34]

While Ram Mohan Roy advocated Christian monotheism in a way that condemned image worship, so, from an entirely different part of the Hindu Renaissance, Swami Dayananda Saraswati sought to re-establish *Vedic* religion, also disparaging image worship. While on the surface, Dayananda appears to have been completely immersed in *Vedic* tradition, like Ram Mohan Roy, he borrowed from Western perspectives that disavowed the Hindu trajectory of presence. Blaming image worship on the Jains, Dayananda did not voice the *Advaitan* position which understood *mūrtis* as peripheral but instead lashed out at them as idolatry, claiming, "The soul is possessed of consciousness, while idol is dead and inert. Do you mean to say that the soul should also lose its consciousness and become lifeless like the idol. Idol worship is a fraud."[35]

Dayananda borrowed the missionary zeal for his reforms from Christian missionaries, whose work he also denounced. Instead, attempting to do charitable work for Hindu children before missionaries could reach them, and sanctioning mass conversions of Muslims, Dayananda sought to establish a purified version of Hinduism devoid of image worship and focused on a single God. Borrowing from the Christians he hated, Dayananda rejected caste, seeking to return to a golden age of Hindu culture and religion.

Dayananda's iconoclasm was one of a number of precursors to Hindu nationalism, as were the effects of other Renaissance reformers. The disparate sectarian traditions that formed the Hindu Renaissance found common ground in creating religious movements that would establish India as an independent secular state in 1947. By presenting a reformist movement that saw image worship as antithetical to Hinduism, Dayananda also succeeded in embedding the Western trajectory of symbolic meaning in Indian culture. While his reforms were precursors to the Hindu fundamentalist movement and the formation of the *Bharatiya Janata* Party, they also created a climate in which Hindu orthodoxy was redefined. His work became a precursor of the shift in trajectories of sacred presence and symbolic meaning that would arise more than a century later but with an important difference. Dayananda's process of conversion created a cadre of Hindus who were conscious of the shift in perspectives and interpreted them as reform. In the twenty-first century Hindu diaspora the same shift is no longer tied to reform but to the dynamics of assimilation and acculturation.

A Diversified Trajectory

The question of diversity within the iconography of the trajectory of embodiment is a subject of long standing debate in India. It is tied to discussions about Hindu national identity. On one hand, Hindu iconographic tradition presents a complex array of images, styles, and theological positions. Yet, on the other hand, there is an overall level of consistency. In his *tour de force* on Hindu iconography, *Indian Sculpture & Iconography: Forms and Measurements*, V. Ganapati Sthapati attempts to resolve this discussion by describing the work of *sthapatis* as part of a national tradition,

> During the course of our research in the *shilpa parampara,* we became aware of the similarities and resemblances of the grammar or order of sculpture in all parts of India whether Karnataka, Maharashtra, Orissa or Bengal. We realized that a national tradition existed in our midst, which had been mistakenly put into contradictory slots due to variations in styles. The underlying principles and rhythms have evolved from a common and powerful base. In fact the work methodology, measuring techniques, habits, ethics, and material handling of the *Viswakarma*

community show a remarkable similarity through the length and breadth of the whole of India. The *Viswakarma* have been one large united family and it is their genius and creativity that has contributed to the identity of our culture today.[36]

While Sthapati is correct that there is a "national tradition" of image making, differences within the craft are equally important, giving the global trajectory of presence strength, and resilience. In addition to the aesthetic differences achieved through style, pose, and adornments that are unique to each deity, the tradition allows for variation through the work of the *sthapatis* who are charged with ritual production.

The inherent diversity within the craft is also a product of the historical *bhakti* tradition in India which expanded the variety of images through the growth of sectarian movements. Originating with the teachings of the *Śaiva Nāyanmārs* (sixth to eighth centuries CE) and the *Vaiṣnava Ālvārs* (fifth to tenth centuries CE), *bhakti* emerged in poetry as a devotional attitude and the veneration of a personal god. Spreading across North India during the Delhi Sultanate, *bhakti* emerged as a populist movement, championing unrestricted access to Hinduism through a path of surrender. Among other deities, *Krishna* became increasingly popularized in a number of *bhakti* sects with differing theological perspectives. In the Gujarat, *Pushtimarg* became a powerful movement in the sixteenth through eighteenth centuries, garnering support from *Rājpūt* princes and establishing temples (*havelīs*) through a lineage stemming from the founder, Vallabhacharya. At the same time in Bengal, followers of Chaitanya established a competing tradition, elevating the worship of the divine couple, *Krishna* and *Radha*, to a new level of popular appeal. Other *sampradāyas* emerged including the *Radha Vallabha Sampradaya* as the movement gathered increasing support.

In each case, the emerging *bhakti* movement developed new forms of religious authority, distinct from the classical South Indian tradition and the ritual requirements of the *Vedas*. Each sect also developed its own scripture and methods for transmitting the authority of the tradition. In *Pushtimarg*, the lineage of the sect, beginning with Vallabhacharya and his son Vitthalnath, became the locus of authority.[37] As the sect developed, the seven sons of Vitthalnath (who is dubbed *Śrī Gusāīmjī*) spread through Rajasthan and the Gujarat, establishing centers of tradition with the heart of the faith in Nathdwara, home of the image of *Shri Nathji* which Vallabha had unearthed on Mount Govardhan. Each son was given another *swarūp* or image of the infant *Krishna*, further diversifying the iconographic traditions within the movement. *Swarūps* were judged to be more complete forms of the deity than *mūrtis*.

The *bhakti* movement emerged as a populist tradition that championed both theological and regional diversity. As this growing differentiation of tradition increasingly separated itself from classical South Indian Hinduism, the faiths also established iconographic traditions. While adhering to common poses and styles of ritual production established in the south, *sthapatis* in the north found increasing freedom to represent god in ways that appealed to the emerging sects which encouraged the veneration of personal images. As a result of these combined influences, Hindu *mūrtis* intended for home devotion show differences in regional expressions of style, in the composition of the figures, and in the way that each image reflects a mood (*bhāva*) which is transmitted to the devotee.

Part 2: Process, Technology and Ritual Requirements

Beyond its philosophical underpinnings in the work of Ramanuja, the Hindu trajectory of embodiment was given form and technique in the *Śilpa Śāstras*, a diverse collection of architectural and iconographic treatises. At the same time, it also was strengthened through regional variation. *Sthapatis* formed iconographic styles not only to meet scriptural regulations, but adapted them to regional styles and practices learned through genealogies of ritual production. Each *sthapati* is part of a lineage that reflects the insights of a branch of the total tradition. Lineages embody technique, style, and essential skills in a way that makes their work distinctive, yet well anchored in iconographic tradition.

The *Śilpa Śāstras*

The *Śilpa Śāstras* are a broad collection of Hindu literature focused on the arts, architecture, and the ritual production of images and are revered as the scriptural basis for embodiment. Representing a multiplicity of sources, they form a composite picture of the processes involved in the creation of an image that is crafted for the express purpose of hosting the divine.

The origins of the *Śilpa Śāstras* are heavily mythologized and have been attributed to four figures: Agastiya, Kasyapa, Maya, and Nagajit whose origins are quasi-historical.[38] Agastīya was first presented in the *Rāmāyana* as a sage. Becoming widely identified with the origins of Hindu sculpture, he was identified as the author of the *Agatīya Sakalādhikāra*, a *Śāstra* on iconometry. Kasyapa was also identified as a *ṛṣi* (sage) and presumed to be the author of the Kasyapa, another *Śāstra* that assumed importance in the tradition. Maya was credited with four texts, the *Mayamata*, *Maya Śilpa*, the *Maya Śilpa Satika*, and the *Śilpa Śāstra Bilhanam*. Nāgajit left no surviving texts but is often quoted as the creator of the system of *angulas*—divisions of the basic unit of measurement, the *tāla*, employed by *sthapatis*.

While these origins are attributions, scholars assume that the *Śāstras* were collected by priests and copyists and transcribed in the tenth and eleventh centuries.[39] While the total corpus of *Śāstric* literature about the ritual production of *mūrtis* carries authority, the texts are not linear and should not be interpreted as if they were a form of canon law. Instead, in keeping with the transmission of devotion and skill in a Hindu context, they have been employed by master craftsmen, who, analogous to *gurus* and spiritual teachers (*ācāryas*), memorize sections and descriptions of particular techniques and instill the same values and skills in their students. The origins of the *Śilpa Śāstras* undoubtedly also reflects this same process, beginning with oral tradition and moving toward codification as the processes associated with ritual production matured.

Some *Śāstras*, such as the *Vastu*, are sources related to the construction of Hindu temples and architecture. Others, such as the *Mānasāra Śāstra*, contain detailed information about lost wax casting and the preparation of *mūrtis*. However, in conjunction with the *Āgamas*, collections of sectarian literature, they present a body of work that is understood as the principle source of technical information about the ritual production of *mūrtis*.

The *Śilpa Śāstras* are concerned with relative measurements and the proportions of the human body that are used as a basis for the production of *mūrtis*. In order to accomplish this they articulate a unit of measurement called the *tāla*,

> The basic unit of measurement is called the "tāla," (sic) which literally means the palm of the hand which is equal to the measure of the length equal to that between the tip of the middle finger and the end of the palm near the wrist. The length is in all cases taken to be equal to the length of the face from the scalp to the chin.[40]

While parts of the *Śilpa Śāstras* suggest that *tāla* is derived from the size of the hand, other sources within the tradition connect the *tāla* to the face. This derivation is used to construct the relative proportions for the rest of the human body in a system of nine units call *navatāla*,[41]

Head	¼ *tāla*
Face	1 *tāla*
Neck	¼ *tāla*
Chest	1 *tāla*

Navel	1 *tāla*
Genital belt	1 *tāla*
Thigh	2 *tālas*
Knee	¼ *tāla*
Leg	2 *tālas*
Foot	¼ *tāla*
Total	9 *tālas* or *navatāla*

Keeping the assumption that each *tāla* has 12 divisions or *virals*, and that each *viral* contains a lesser measure of 8 *yavai*, different *tāla* systems based on this measurement are available. These include *sapta tāla* (7 *tālas*), *saṭṭāla* (6 *tālas*), *pāñcatāla* (5 *tālas*), *catuṣtāla* (4 *tālas*), *tritāla* (3 *tālas*), *dvitāla* (2 *tālas*), and *ekatāla* (1 *tāla*).[42] While the designation of *tāla* may refer to the palm, or the face, Mayan (mythological author of a number of treatises on iconometry within the *Śilpa Śāstras*), claims that it is a measure of the foot.

These differences not only reveal variation within the *Śāstras*, but also suggest connections between sculpture, dance, music, and sculpture,

> It is very significant that the word *tāla* is used in the field of dance as well, where it denotes the rhythm of footwork. It may be noted here that, in the artistic traditions, *tāla* or time-measure and distance or space-measure are viewed on the same plane. In the field of music, the rhythmic time-measure called *tāla* ensures the order and sweetness of a melody. Similarly, *tāla* in the sculptural field ensures the order and beauty of an image. In architecture and poetry, *tāla* is replaced by the word *pada*, which also means foot. One will recognise (sic), thus, the supreme role of rhythm in the world of fine arts.[43]

This theory of the inter-relationships between *tāla* in the arts is called— *Ayādi Lakṣaṇa Vidhi* which perceives images as representations of a vital, inner rhythm of life.[44]

This juxtaposition of *tāla* is a critical part of the tenets of iconometry in the *Śilpa Śāstra* system. While the *Śāstras* incorporate exacting ratios and present specific techniques for the process of lost wax casting, their real value is in the system of harmonious relationships that they seek to provide for *darśan* to take place. Unlike secular systems of art, which build aesthetics from the vantage point of an observer, the *Śāstras* are much more concerned with establishing an environment where the divine can be seen, experienced, and understood. Moreover, because *darśan* is a reciprocal process, temples become settings where not only can god be seen, but also where he or she can cast loving glances at those who worship them. *Pūjās* and *sevā* ("service" to a deity in *Pushtimarg*) incorporate a number of sensory qualities that vary from the sound of bells, to the voices and instruments presenting a *kīrtan* or *bhajan*, to a blend of colors—all in an attempt to foster this kind of environment. Through the theory of

Ayādi Lakṣaṇa Vidhi devotees are presented with a total environment which is radically different from galleries or exhibitions in the art world.

Temples also share in this same rhythm and both image and temple are crafted in proportions and measurements that facilitate the direct experience of this internal cosmic rhythm. The use of this theory also suggests that there are direct benefits that are accrued from image worship.[45] Calculations for images are based on this theory and are done so that devotees can experience the maximum level of embodiment possible.

The *Śāstras* categorize *mūrtis* through a number of variables including mobility. Images intended for installation in a temple are considered immovable and once installed, must remain in the *garbha gṛha*, often directly above the pit that was dug for initial consecration of the space. Temple *mūrtis* are cast in metal or carved from stone. *Mūrtis* designed for home worship are considerably smaller, designed to be movable, and often crafted from metal. Still other forms of images are made from clay and are designed for festival (*utsava*) use. In India, clay *mūrtis* are found in great numbers in rivers which are understood as an acceptable way of disposing of these temporary forms of God.

Mūrtis may be sculpted or painted, and are further defined by temperament and posture. Gods may be depicted in meditative positions (*yoga mūrtis*), in positions of enjoyment and happiness (*bhoga mūrti*), in heroic stances (*vīra mūrti*), in protective modes (*ugra mūrti*) or as defeating enemies (*abhicārika mūrti*).[46]

Deities in iconographic form are also depicted with symbolic hand gestures known as *mudrās*. Common *mudrās* include the *Abhaya*, in which the palm is presented in an upward sign of fearlessness. In the *varada mudrā*, depicting generosity, the palm points downward. When first finger and thumb are touching, the deity presents the chin *mudrā*, signifying teaching. When hands are folded one over the other, the *mudrā* is *dhyāna*, signifying meditation. Finally, the *tarjanī mudrā*, with one finger pointing upward signifies vigilance.

In addition to gestures, *mūrtis* frequently hold objects. Images of *Krishna* often present him with a flute, and, in the case of *Balkrishna*, show him with a mound of butter in his right hand. Standing images of *Shiva* depict him with the *damarou*, a drum whose beat marks the cycles of existence. *Ganesh* often holds a variety of objects including the *pāsha* or noose (binding us to rebirth), the elephant goad (as an incentive for spiritual practice), and an axe, demonstrating severing of attachments.[47] In each case the symbolic identification of objects is often multiple, allowing the *mūrti* to contain a variety of meanings.

The *Śāstras* also contain specific injunctions for casting that draw on ritual and assumptions about the nature of deity. Maya concludes, "If the face of the image is cast downwards, the *shilpin* would be ruined, he would no longer be respected and the wealth of the master would also be lost. If the nose (of the image) measures more than three *yavas*, it would kill the king soon for certain."[48]

In classical, South Indian construction, a blend of five metals (*pañchaloha*) is used including gold, silver, iron, copper, and lead (or tin). Writing in the early twentieth century as Orientalist interest in Hindu sculpture declined, O.C. Gangoly concluded,

> Bronze is technically known by these artists as Panchalouha (sic), literally the "five irons"—the amalgam being composed of the five metals—copper, silver, gold, brass and white lead. The copper forms the chief ingredient and according to the present practice the gold and silver are generally dispensed with. In most of the modern images the amalgam is made of the following proportions: 10 parts of copper, ½ part of brass and ¼ part of white lead.[49]

However, in practice the combination of metals varies. A modern manufacturer who advertises on the internet suggests that for display purposes gold is not used while the traditional combination of five metals is employed when images are intended for worship.[50] However, as the following pages will show, traditional *sthapatis* in South India whose craft is more secluded use a different combination of metals. Moreover, forensic analysis of images also demonstrates a wide variety of alloys and combinations of metals.

A Traditional *Sthapati* in Swamilalai, South India

The application of text to process and the techniques associated with the ritual production of images are best understood through the work of individual *sthapatis*. Each artisan interprets and applies the scriptural injunctions of the *Śilpa Śāstras* through their role in a lineage of *sthapatis*, their own experience, and the demands of industrialization and the market that they serve. This is the case with Ratnam Krishnamurti Ashok Kumar, a *sthapati* in the village of Swamimalai, a traditional locus of ritual production in Tamil Nadu.

SWAMIMALAI

Swamimalai is a village of 7,289 (2011 census),[51] in the Thanjavur district of Tamil Nadu.[52] Like the much larger city of Kumbakonam, Swamimalai is a regional center of ritual production, known throughout the subcontinent for the high quality of its artistry. Other areas in Tamil Nadu also have long histories of *sthapatis* including Tiruchirapalli, Madurai, Chengleput, and Salem.[53]

Not only does Swamimalai have a lengthy history of traditional patterns of ritual production, but it also reflects changes in image manufacture since Indian independence in 1947. Utilizing Gandhian principles of autonomy and self-sufficiency, cottage industry systems of image manufacture were organized in the 1950s. In Swamimalai, the *Swamimalai Icon Manufacturers Cooperative Cottage Industry Society Limited* was organized in December 1958.[54] As part of a burgeoning cottage industry system, this organization provided Swamimalai with a national market. The Icon Manufacturers Cooperative also helped facilitate a training site in the village:

> The establishment of the co-operative provided an organization not only to help market icons, but also insure standards for artistic quality by having a sthapathi master craftsman on the board. In the 1950's, the department of industries and commerce at Swamimalai established a training institute called Poompuhar, to train both Sthapathi and non-sthapathi boys in the traditional of icon production described in the Silpa Śastras. Thus, following India's independence to help and develop the village economy of Swamimalai, the traditional social organization of icon craft specialization changed radically by making icon manufactures mostly with the aim of reaching the handicrafts market.[55]

As India achieved greater industrial self-sufficiency in the late twentieth century, ritual production also facilitated a growing variety of business primarily targeted both at temples in India and in the evolving Hindu diaspora. Ritual production of images is now done by hereditary family owned manufactories, hereditary family workshops, individual hereditary skilled craftsmen, entrepreneur owned manufactories, family/entrepreneur workshops, and individual skilled craftsmen.[56]

However, beyond the evolution of varieties of business, traditional patterns of *sthapati* organization also continue,

> The Sthapathi community in Swamimalai is a patrilineal society organized along clan lines who trace their descent back to an ancestor named Agora Veerapathira Sthapathy from the time of the temple construction. They are endogamous in the sense that marriages are arranged between the different clans of the Vishwakarma community. For example, the males of the icon producing Sthapathis will often marry women from the goldsmith/jeweler's group.[57]

Not only does Swamimalai reflect the voice of modern India with an ability to market its products throughout the subcontinent, but at the same time its role in the Hindu *jāti* system also enables it to affect patterns of marriage and patrilineal organization.

Ratnam Krishnamurti Ashok Kumar

Ratnam Krishnamurti Ashok Kumar (Figure 4) is a middle-aged *sthapati* who runs an entrepreneur owned manufactory in Swamimalai.[58] He is part of a declining community of artisans in India that continue to practice ritual production. Elsewhere, in Indian factories and abroad in China, mass production techniques have eclipsed the traditional craft and the practices of evoking embodiment that have been part of it. Kumar's evolution as a *sthapati* reflects both the traditional craft and at the same time also demonstrates the opportunities afforded by industrialization. He is the product of both worlds. Following a path common for entrepreneurial *sthapatis*, Kumar is a graduate of Poompuhar College and holds a certificate in Architecture and Sculpture.

In establishing itself as an educational center for twenty first century *sthapatis*, Poompuhar College also reflects the fusion of religion and craft. Founded in 1964 through a grant from the Hindu Religious and Charitable Endowment Administration, the College emphasizes classical South Indian Tamil culture as well as traditional skills. However, the presence of a regional college does not take the place of apprenticeships which remain an important part of the *sthapati* tradition.

Following graduation, Kumar was apprenticed to a

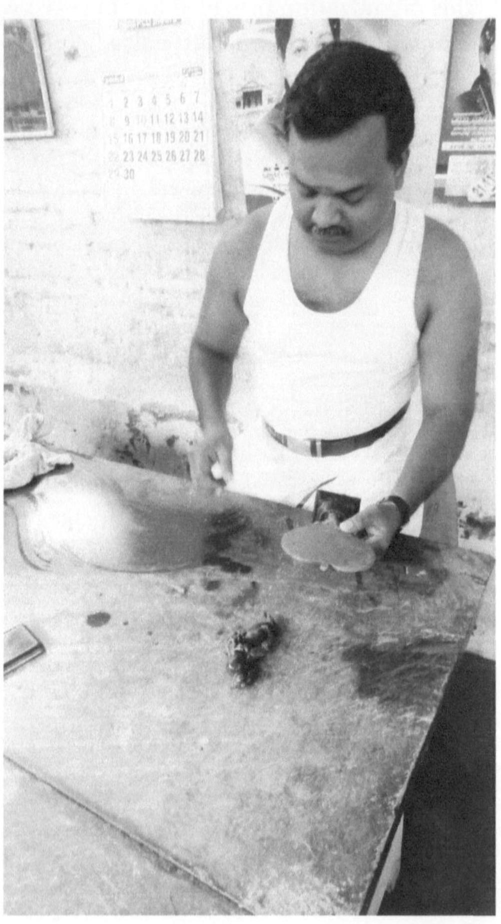

Figure 4: Ratnam Krishnamurti Ashok Kumar (courtesy Rajendran Srinivasan).

well-respected master, Guru Sambashivam Samiyar, for three years.[59] The apprenticeship not only provided Kumar with the skills that he needed to begin a business, but also established him with a lineage of *sthapatis*. In Swamimalai, *sthapatis* are linked to their craft through genealogy of master and student, caste, and clan. Clans are patrilineal and are linked to a distant ancestor, Agora Veerapathira Sthapathy.[60] Linkages to *jātis* (endogamous groups who share a common occupation) are perpetuated in the same manner so that the *sthapati* tradition is preserved. Marriage alliances are forged with a goldsmith/jeweler *jāti* insuring that both the skills of the *sthapati* and the goldsmith continue in familial lines.[61] As a result of these alliances, the genealogies of *sthapatis* extend over ten generations. In Swamimalai, this is directly linked with the Swaminatha temple, appropriately constructed in the center of the village.

Kumar's shop employs twenty-five people, each skilled in different parts of ritual production. The process reflects a synthesis of material, craft, and spiritual concerns. The creation of an image begins when a customer (usually a temple) commissions a *mūrti* to be produced in an interesting blend of the traditional craft with ancient methods of ritual production. While the requirements of the temple dictate the choice of deities and their size, Kumar uses *tāla* measurements to define the proportions of the image, consulting a book of line drawings produced in accordance with text.

Text and tradition also govern purity requirements for the entire shop. Employees are required to take daily baths. When the image is initially carved in wax, traditional dress is required in the form of a *dhotī* which is fastened at the waist covering the legs, leaving the chest bare. In addition, before the wax figure can be created, a *pūjā* is done to *Ganesh*, which is considered auspicious and is often done before a new venture. In addition to these requirements, astrology plays an important role in dictating the time that an image can be created. Charts are available for this purpose identifying five times each day that are auspicious and five times that are not.[62]

Once an image has been identified, the wax is carefully carved (Figure 5) using a variety of tools including hot iron rods which can smooth the surface of larger areas. Every mark in the wax must be exact and will be reproduced in the finished casting. The most difficult part of the procedure is creating the face which is critically important in reflecting the mood (*bhāva*) of the image and also meeting the requirements of the temple that will house it.

In yet another medium, *sthapatis* who work in stone often comment

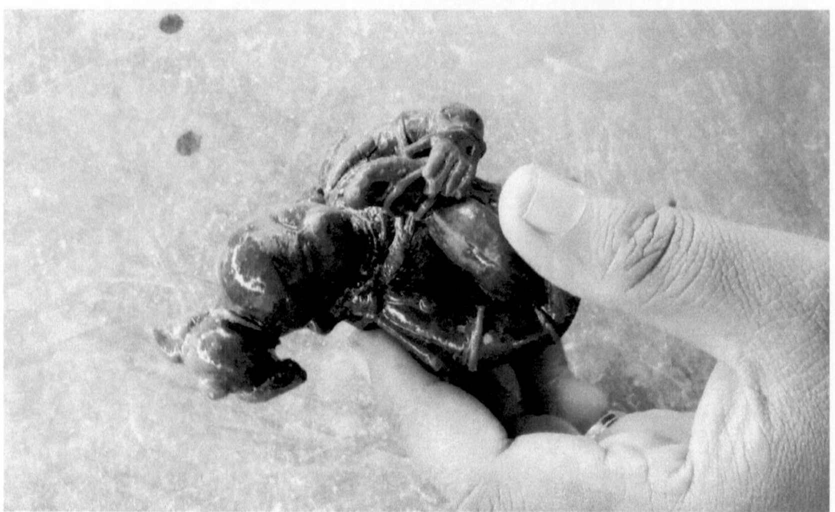

Figure 5: A completed wax image (courtesy Rajendran Srinivasan).

that the presence of the deity is also in the raw stone before it is ever shaped into iconographic form. Priests from temples that commission a stone *mūrti* frequently visit the *sthapathi's* shop, examining the stone to be sure that it is free from flaws and a suitable residence for the deity. In the same way, the metals that are used in Kumar's shop must be pure and capable of producing the finest quality image.

After the figure is carved in wax (Figure 5), it is carefully laid on a cloth over a bed of sand. Clay drawn from the adjacent Kaveri River produces an especially fine medium which is carefully applied over the wax. Small amounts of clay are carefully pressed into each part of the wax figure in a time-consuming process to be sure that each detail in the wax is also formed into the clay. Once this has been completed the river clay is allowed to dry so that on the next day it can be turned, applying clay to the reverse side. Each surface of the wax figure is covered in clay so that the completed form, once fired, becomes a detailed cavity for the metal.

When the casting has been completed, Kumar's artisans begin a labor intensive process of filing (Figure 6). Sprues, conduits that have received the molten metal, are removed. All rough edges of the casting are taken off in preparation for a final polishing. This too is not easy since *mūrtis* routinely include a variety of decoration built into the casting including details of clothing and jewelry. Large polishing wheels would blur the edges of these details, creating the need for fine polishing in small areas throughout each figure.

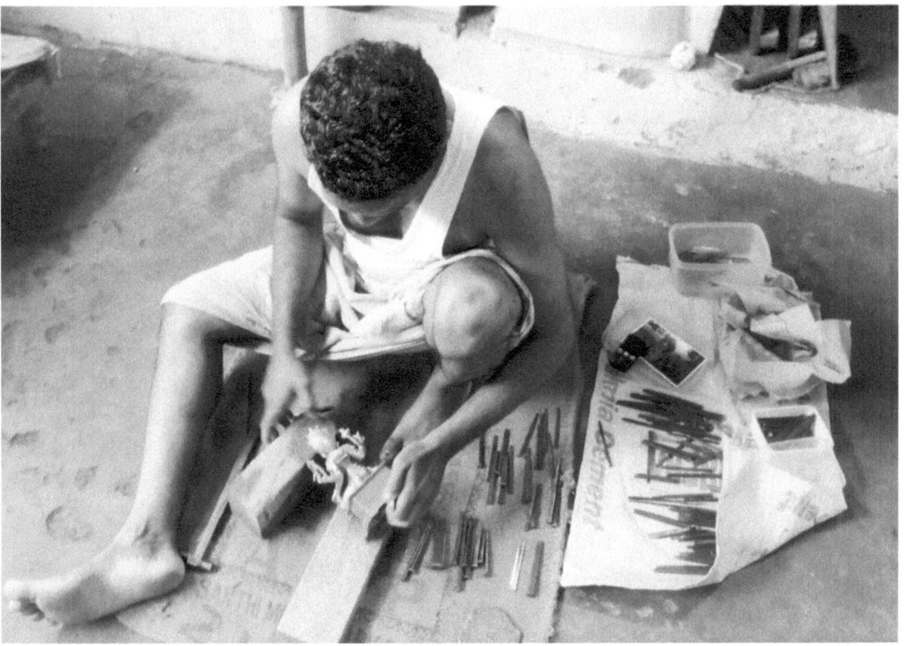

Figure 6: A worker finishes a casting (courtesy Rajendran Srinivasan).

Once the casting and polishing have been completed (Figure 7), the figure is ready for its first ritual requirements. Nine orifices in the figure must be opened including eyes, nose, ears, mouth, naval, and urinary tract. A *Brahmin* priest is called in to perform this task. This is especially significant for the ears and eyes, which allow the deity to hear and to see. Once this has been accomplished the deity can no longer be left on its back or side and must remain standing up. A mirror is placed in front of the *mūrti* so that the god can see his image. Readings are done to further instill life into the figure.

When these requirements have been met and the image is alive, it is delivered to priests who will conduct the *Prāṇ Pratiṣṭhā* ceremony at its installation in a temple. This ceremony frequently includes rituals that only the priests can be allowed to see as the deity is placed on an altar designed for their presence.

Kumar's staff works through each of these processes in recognition of their symbiotic nature. Skilled metal work is essential so that the resulting image will provide the best possible residence for the deity. At the same time, workers who help sustain this process must meet a variety of their own ritual requirements. The shop is kept pure, and free of any source of ritual pollution.

These elements of traditional ritual production are all dependent on the trajectory of embodiment. The role of artisans blends seamlessly with the function of priests. Acting together in a symbiotic relationship, *śilpi* and priest work together to evoke the presence of the deity in the image. Small shops like this are an important connection for temples in the United States which rely on ritual production and traditional methods to supply them with their central images.

Style and Regional Differences in Iconography

Because Hindu iconography is a traditionally based sculptural tradition designed to evoke the presence of deities in images, change happens slowly. However, because of

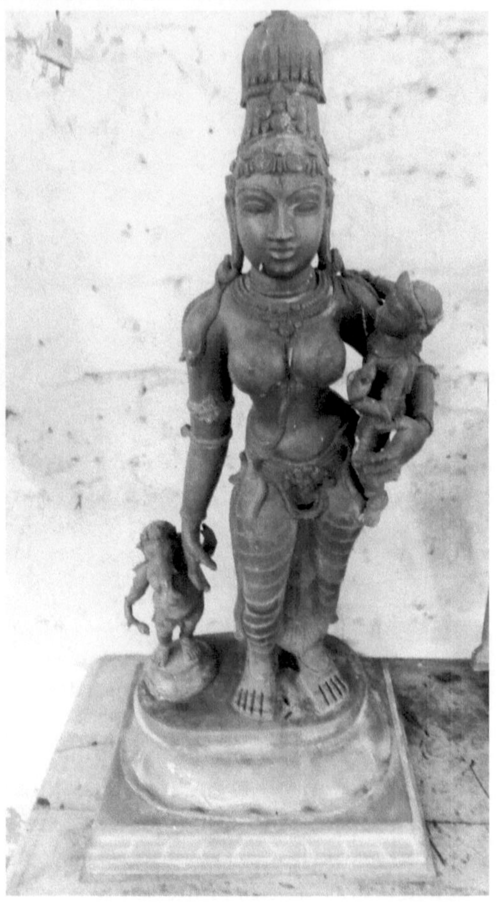

Figure 7: A finished *Mūrti* ready to be brought to life.

its innate conservatism sometimes the extraordinary diversity within it is difficult to see. While stylistic variation is readily apparent in periods of Hindu Empire and can readily be identified by distinct patterns of artistic composition that were unique within the *Maurya, Gupta, Chola, Vijayanagar* and other kingdoms in the last 500 years, regional differences are more difficult to discern. Particularly in North India, where *bhakti* traditions have produced significant theological and cultural variation, it is difficult to distinguish regional differences from the variation between the work of individual *sthapatis.*

However, broader levels of difference can be distinguished between northern and southern Indian images. Anatomical proportion and iconographic differences provide important clues that separate the work of *sthapatis* in the North and the South. Southern Indian images emphasize a level of stylistic conformity and proportion in the measurement of *Vaiṣṇava* and *Śaiva* images that is readily apparent, often strictly adhering to the *tāla* system in the *Śilpa Śāstras*. Characteristics such as hair style or crowns (if any), show distinct differences from figures produced in the North.

Beyond these broad differences between North and South more specific patterns of regional identity are often a matter of conjecture. However, in some instances where regional patterns of image making reflected distinct theological and cultural differences, the origins of images can be more precisely identified. This is the case where groups of deities appear together, reflecting regional patterns of belief. For example, the association of male deities with female consorts varies in different parts of India,

> In Behar and Bengal Vishnu invariably is accompanied by Sri-Lakshmi and Sarasvati. Sri-Lakshmi has been associated with Vishnu from ancient times, but Sarasvati became his second spouse only in eastern India not much earlier than the tenth century. Elsewhere in India Sarawvati generally is regarded as the wife of Brahma. In the South, however, Vishnu's spouses are Sri-Devi or Sri-Lakshmi, and Bhudevi, the earth goddess who stands between Vishnu's feet in Kashmiri images. In the South Vishnu's Garuda seems not to have been necessary as Siva's bull and Durga's lion.[63]

Variation in iconographic tradition is also supported by changes in patterns of composition which, while reflecting differences among regions, is much more the result of the work of lineages of *sthapatis*. As individual craftsmen create images that reflect their heritage as artisans, so in a similar fashion individual variation is also reflected in the devotional life of the metal workers. Unlike factory manufacture, ritual production assumes that the image maker acts on his internal insights in producing an image. While often employing priests to help bring the image to life, the *sthapati* incorporates moods and emotional responses that he brings to the process. While the persona of *mūrtis* also reflects theological and cultural traditions, it is this subjective level of emotion, which the tradition identifies as *bhāva*, which contributes to essential variation within the tradition.

Bhāva and Emotive Differentiation

Bhāva is an emotive state with a wide range of meanings in Hinduism and Buddhism with deep connections to the role of embodiment. Connoting mood, *bhāva* is an important aspect of the iconographic form of deities and is understood to be part of the visual experience of *darśan* in which seeing god produces an ecstatic state. *Mūrtis* are created to evoke these states of awareness.

Among devotees of *Krishna*, *bhāva* is seen as essential, particularly with the sects associated with the historical *bhakti* tradition. *Bhakti* sects including ISKCON, *Pushtimarg*, the *Radha Vallabha Sampradaya*, and others, stressed *bhāva* as an essential ingredient for facilitating the devotee's inner experience of devotion and identification with the deity. These emotional states are not universal and reflect the cultural connotation of emotion in South Asia.

Yet, emotions are culturally relative. This subjective nature of emotion is enhanced even further by complex formulations of meaning which are difficult for Western societies to understand,

> It is difficult to convey through simple and misleading English terms the complex meanings assigned to both the identities of mother, female lover, slave, and so on in this culture and the manner in which each form of personhood is construed, constructed, and experienced emotionally. Moreover, a systematic play of differences (or difference to borrow Derrida's phrase) works in the various interpretation folk and sectarian traditions give to the same set of emotions.[64]

Moreover, as cultural constructions, emotions are not the same as feelings,

> In the English language the verb "to feel" is so intimately linked to understanding of emotion that one can scarcely imagine the Other without it. Yet in Hindi and Dravidian languages there is no such specific equivalent verb, and Indians get along quite well without it.... Emotions are not and cannot be accurately identified by specific feelings.[65]

These linkages between emotion and language are also reflected in art which seeks to give visual expression to rarified states of emotion that are expressed in written format. For emotions that are uniquely tied to religion, the subtlety of expression in the visual arts can be even more difficult, as the concept of *bhāva* suggests. Moreover, the role of *bhāva* is an essential part of embodiment, creating a rarified level of experience in which connections with the divine can be readily accessed.

Bhāva is linked to the aesthetic experience of emotion or *rāsa*. Within this framework, religious art has a unique quality in which it is executed as a means of inducing *bhāva* and creating *rāsa*. This function is easily seen in painting but is also visible in sculpture and the creation of *mūrtis*.

Nine expressions of *bhāva* are associated with *Krishna* and are commonly collapsed into five,

> *Janatā Bhāva*—expressions which show *Krishna* as a supreme being
> *Dāsya Bhāva*—showing *Krishna* as Lord and Master
> *Sakhya Bhāva*—*Krishna* is presented as a cowherd, friend, and equal
> *Vātsalya Bhāva*—the deity is shown as a child who is adored and
>   cared for by his mother
> *Mādhurya Bhāva* (or *Sṛŋgāra Bhāva*)—showing sweet emotion

The experience of *bhāva* is subjective and is dependent not only on the countenance that is presented in a work of sacred art, but also on the receptivity within the devotee.

Yet, the identification of one *bhāva* does not necessarily negate the presence of others. Some *Balkrishnas* exhibit *Mādhurya Bhāva*, presenting a state of infinite bliss which transcends worldly emotion (Figure 8). However, others also show aspects of *Sakhya Bhāva* and at the same time also reflect *Vātsalya Bhāva*.

As David Haberman suggests, in order to be understood, *bhāva*, must be disassociated from perceptions of reality grounded in historical authenticity,

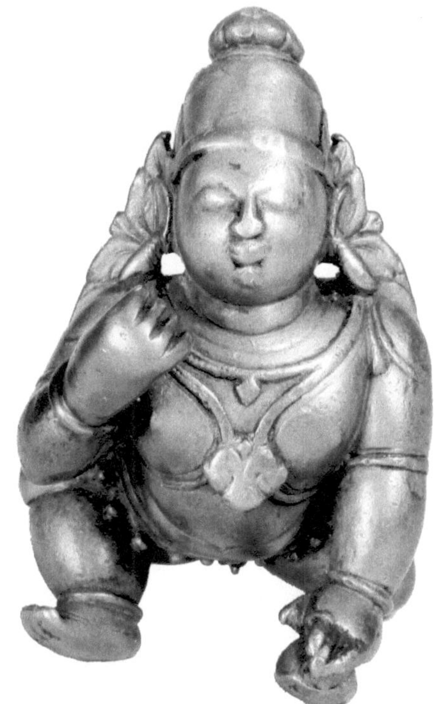

Figure 8: *Balkrishna* (15th–16th century, *Vijayanagar* Period, South India) (courtesy Tom Ardizzone).

> Reality is not set for human beings; multiple realities or worlds of meaning are available to us. Judgments of realties are difficult, because there is nowhere to stand that is not situated within a particular reality, which by its very nature regards other realities with suspicion ... such questions as "Did this really happen here?" are really concerned with the issue of historical authenticity, but this way of thinking is somewhat alien to the religious thought of Braj. For most of the people with whom I discussed this problem, it had more to do with the issue of *bhava,* that is, with the investment of a certain kind of emotional and imaginative energy.[66]

Haberman's comments were prompted by the *ban yātrā*, a pilgrimage in the forests of Braj associated with the life of *Krishna*. However, they also have important ramifications for *mūrti* worship and for the shift in cultural trajectories that has accompanied globalization.

If Hindu images are approached as material culture, with emphasis on the bronze or stone, they immediately become associated with an object that exists in space and time—defining reality. Material culture tends to look at other perceptions of reality with suspicion in a similar way to a focus on history and place. When *mūrtis* are viewed through a cultural lens that understands them as images that can be recognized through considerations of style, age, patina, and a host of other variables, they are defined by authenticity. To perceive some *thing* that is authentic is to ground it in a level of reality that dismisses copies and emphasizes the uniqueness of an object. But *bhāva* cannot exist when tied to a single level of reality. It has nothing to say in the face of claims about authenticity. Rather, its "life force" rests with the power of imagination and emotional energy in which images are translucent, opening windows to wider, more pervasive realities.

Finally, *bhāva* is subjective, emanating from the devotee but always nurtured by the image which is crafted to evoke it. This suggests that the emotional experience of one devotee may not be the same as for another when both are confronted with the same image. These differences were apparent to a *Pushtimarg* devotee who visited Nathdwara,

> When I was younger, I used to feel envious of temple servants (sevaks) at Nathdwara, thinking how lucky they are to serve Sri Nathji in person every day! When I stayed there for an extended period in 1989, I asked some of them how they felt being in the presence of God all the time.
>
> I was surprised that many sevaks were afraid of Sri Nathji! To them Sri Nathji was a stern task master who they had to serve and obey with great diligence.
>
> Sevaks often refer to Sri Nathji as "anna-data" (food giver—i.e., pay master). I was surprised that they did not see Sri Nathji as I did—a child or a friend or a lover or God who liberates the soul. To them, Sri Nathji was their employer and a tough one at that![67]

The visitor discovered that the *bhāva* he had always associated with Shri Nathji was very different from the emotions that he had experienced in his childhood with the images (*swarūps*) that became his closest friends. At the same time, after living in Nathdwara, he came to realize that the *bhāva* that temple servants felt was altogether different from any emotion that he had associated with deity. Yet, in their context, the *bhāva* that they experienced made perfect sense.

The subjective nature of *bhāva* is also an important component in *Vaiṣṇava* scripture. The *Bhāgavata Purāṇa* presents an image of *Krishna* in which the deity is seen in different ways in a number of encounters:

The various groups of people in the arena regarded Kṛṣṇa in different ways when He entered it with His elder brother. The wrestlers saw Kṛṣṇa as a lightning bolt, the men of Mathurā as the best of males, the women as Cupid in person, the cowherd men as their relative, the impious rulers as a chastiser, His parents as their child, the King of the Bhojas as death, the unintelligent as the Supreme Lord's universal form, the yogīs as the Absolute Truth and the Vṛṣṇis as their supreme worshipable Deity.[68]

Reading this passage in the context of *bhāva* suggests that the emotional response of devotees is also subjective. The emotions and insights that one person feels may not be the same as those of another.

Sthapatis have incorporated this level of subjectivity into their work but at the same time have also identified particular *bhāvas*, or combinations of *bhāvas*, in the images that they have created. For example, Figure 9 is a South Indian *Balkrishna* presented in a moment of ecstasy. *Krishna* dances with his left foot barely touching the ground and his right foot held in hand in an axis directly below his chin. The position is both that of a young child in a moment of play and at the same time a meditative state in which the distractions of the world are gone. The figure presents a facial expression of complete calm, reflecting a state of absolute transcendence far removed from the push and pull of everyday life. Evocative states of *Dasya Bhāva* (*Krishna* as Lord and Master) and especially *Janatā Bhāva* (*Krishna* as a supreme being) are both possible within this image.

Figure 8 is a sixteenth-century image from the *Vijayanagar* period whose countenance reflects traditional elements of *Karnataka* style. The deity wears a crown and is presented wearing jewelry. His expression is serene. However, presented in a more traditional *Balkrishna* format, the image is moving, carrying butter in his left hand. A number of different *bhāvas* can easily be seen in the figure. *Krishnu* is clearly Lord and Mas-

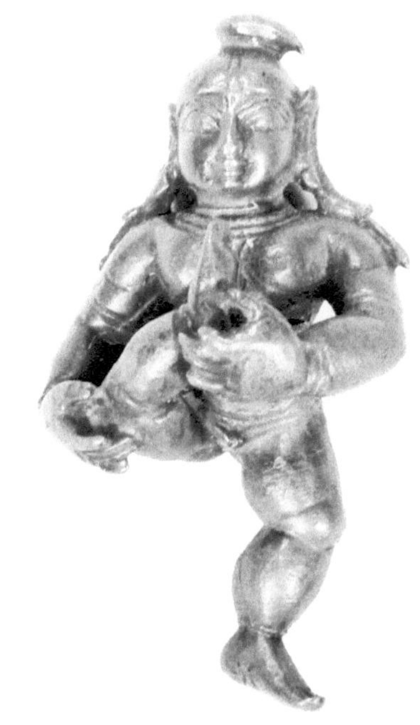

Figure 9: Dancing *Balkrishna* (19th century) (courtesy Tom Ardizzone).

ter, but could also be understood as friend (*Dasya Bhāva*), or child (*Vātsalya Bhāva*). While his countenance is more formal he may also be seen as emoting sweetness (*Mādhurya Bhāva*). Since facial expressions are central in realizing *bhāva*, it is possible to understand how each devotee's own experiences, moods, and feelings could be realized in this figure resulting in combinations of emotional states.

Figure 10 presents two *Balkrishnas* in dancing form, again from a South Indian perspective. The figures have expressions that countenances royalty or the qualities of a supreme Lord and Master. Yet, while these emotional qualities are easy to identify, the *bhāva* that this image of *Krishna* produces in devotees depends on the life experiences of the devotee.

Finally, figure 11 shows a North Indian form of *Balkrishna* with visibly different anatomical proportions than the South Indian examples. The expression of this figure is that of a child (*Vātsalya Bhāva*) but could also be interpreted as a friend and equal (*Sakhya Bhāva*), or that of sweet emotion (*Mādhurya Bhāva*). The choice is not a selection of a single *bhāva* but often a combination of evocative states that form a mood

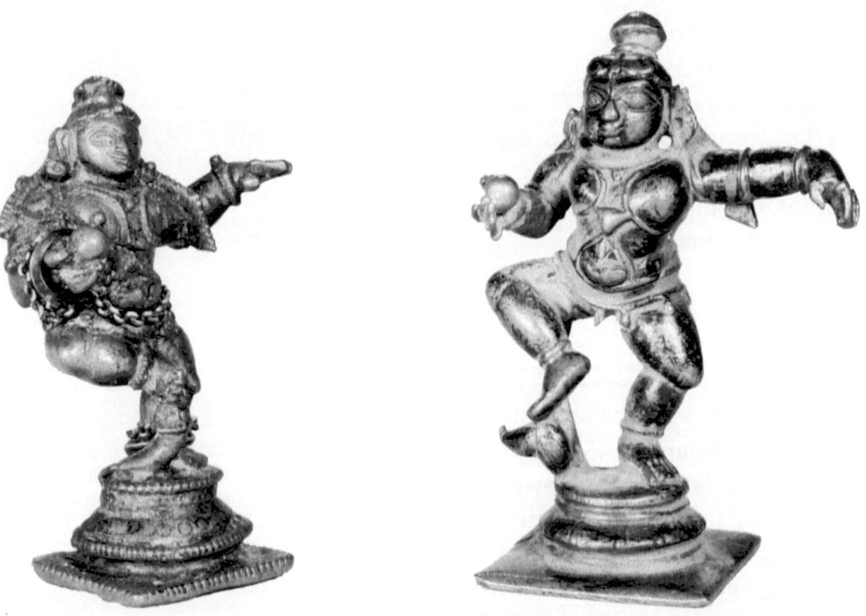

Figure 10: Two dancing *Balkrishnas* (18th–19th centuries, South India) (courtesy Tom Ardizzone).

entirely unique to the individual and beyond the capability of language to represent.

Differentiation Through Composition

Diversity within images can also be demonstrated through their composition. The traditional mixture of metals suggested in the *Śilpa Śāstras* is *pañcaloha*, an alloy of five metals including copper, zinc, tin, silver, and gold. While this expensive combination of metals is used for the finest of images, in practice more affordable amalgams of metal characterize images intended for home devotion. Thomas and Levy suggests that "... today the metal used in most icons is prepared by weighing out the desired proportions of three metals—copper (82 percent), brass (15 percent), and lead (3 percent)."[69] While the authors are correct, suggesting that alloys of copper, zinc, and lead, are frequently employed, the composition of images is far more diverse than these percentages suggest and rarely conforms to either the dictates of scripture or to a precise formula. Instead, this diversity allows each *sthapathi*, within each lineage of tradition, the latitude necessary to create their own visions of God. For *sthapathis* in the South, the dictates of tradition that are rigidly adhered to include anatomical proportion while in the North regional and individual differences emerge. In both cases the composition of the *mūrtis* may employ the amalgam of copper, zinc, and lead that Thomas and Levy observed but vary the percentages or even add small amounts of other metals. Since images are never signed in the same way that a work of art would be in the West, the only evidence of the *sthapathi's* hand are stylistic nuances in the interpretation of iconographic tradition and the combination of metals that was used to create the figure.

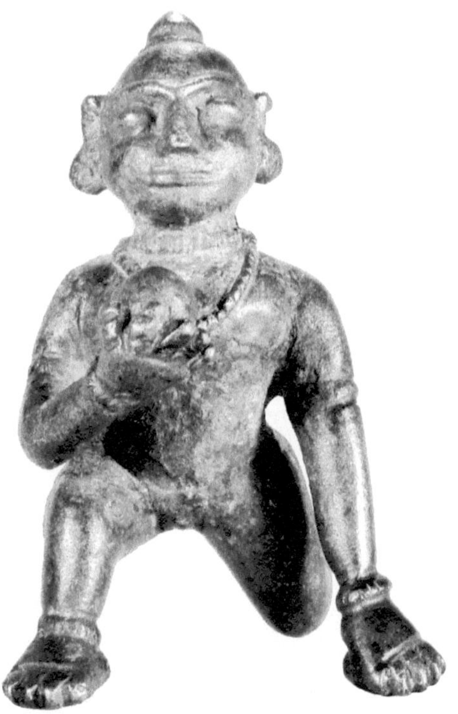

Figure 11: *Balkrishna* (North India, 19th century) (courtesy Tom Ardizzone).

Part 3: Krishna as a Butter Stealer: A Study of Balkrishna *Iconography as an Example of Variation*

The Butter Thief in Texts

While images of the Butter Stealer exhibit variation in style and composition, they exhibit an overall unity in keeping with textual tradition. Each figure is connected to stories that are as widely known in India as "mother goose" is to us which appear in scripture, poetry, and even in Hindi movies.[70] The stories of the butter stealer magnify the image of *Krishna*, who as he crawls carries a ball of butter in his right hand and a butter pot in his left, protesting when his mother, Yasoda, confronts him,

> O mother mine, I did not eat the butter
> come dawn, with the herds,
> you send me to the jungle,
> o, mother mine, I did not eat the butter.
> all day long with my flute in the jungles
> at dusk do I return home.
> but a child, younger than my friends
> how could I reach up to the butter?
> all the gopas are against me
> on my face they wipe the butter,
> you mother, are much too innocent,
> you believe all their chatter.
> there is a flaw in your behavior [sic],
> you consider me not yours,
> take you herd-stick and the blanket
> I'll dance to your tune no longer.
> Surdas, Yasoda then laughed,
> and took the boy in her arms,
> mother mine I did not eat the butter.[71]

The poem by the fifteenth-century poet Surdas, reflects the value of play (*līlā*) in the context of the butter thief. *Līlā* has a variety of meanings including deception, thievery, and dance but also connotes the spontaneity and freedom that is associated with play.[72] *Krishna* steals butter, grabs a churning stick from a cowherdess (*gopī*), and pulls calves' tails.[73] In performing these pranks he exemplifies the Jungian archetype of the divine trickster. Scolded for his mischievous acts, but beloved by all who encounter him, he represents the unpredictable nature of the divine which does not do as we expect but nevertheless is present in the most ordinary of human affairs. The image of the butter stealer is supported by scripture, with a number of treatises providing a context that is recounted in literature and dance. Chief among these is the *Bhāgavata Purāṇa* which, developed in the eighth through tenth centuries inspired numerous other texts including the *Sūr Sāgar* by Sur Das.[74]

While the textual tradition of the butter stealer developed from a variety of sources, it also created a more unified corpus of mythology that is well known. Representations of *Krishna* as a butter thief can be found in art and in dramatic "miracle plays" such as the *Rās Līlā*. The stories about the butter thief tie the infant to a cross-cultural tradition of the divine trickster—in this case, the god who steals. But as he steals butter, one of the most valuable substances in a rural agrarian economy, so those nearby who see him breaking butter pots and sticking his hand in butter jars, can only smile. He has become the face of the transcendent in the realm of ordinary experience. There is nothing as ordinary as butter and *Krishna* uses that to create an image of divine play (*līlā*) that encapsulates the mystery that lies at the ground of all experience.

Iconographic Variation
of Butter Stealer Images

While retaining the essential qualities of the butter stealer which are supported by text in the *Bhāgavata Purāṇa* and the wider *Vaiṣṇava* literary tradition, *Balkrishna* images exhibit significant iconographic differences. Influenced by region, period of manufacture, *sthapati* and the lineage within which he worked, this variation, within a single *Vaiṣṇava* iconographic tradition, shows how the trajectory of embodiment maintained an essential level of diversity.

Compare, for example, images produced during the *Vijayanagar* kingdom in southern India in the fourteenth through seventeenth centuries with the same figure from other *Karnataka* traditions. Figure 8 shows a South Indian *Balkrishna* from the *Vijayanagar* Empire in the traditional pose, clutching a lump of butter in his right hand, clutching it near his chest. His other hand rests on the butter pot as he pauses, while in motion. The face of this *Balkrishna* appears distant and yet at the same time radiates authority with a countenance that is regal yet inviting.

Figure 12 shows the same figure although this time created from a tribal pattern of iconography. This *Balkrishna* is flowing, presenting a glimpse of a figure who pauses just long enough to display the butter in his right hand. The deity's hair is worn in tightly formed curls on either side of his face. However, the figure incorporates a number of additional differences which are startling. The butter pot, which is normally under the left hand, is barely discernable. The butter ball, normally clutched in the right hand with fingers wrapped tightly around the butter to hold it, has changed. The hand is flat with the butter barely clinging to it.

A small percentage of *Balkrishna* images also show significant differences in the position of the right arm and hand and almost appear as if the deity is giving the butter to someone else as depicted in Figure 13. This pose creates a number of contextual and theological questions which also relate to the diversity of the figures. Is the butter thief actually presenting his find to someone else? And, if so, what is the context for that action? Or, instead, is the position of the butter in the right hand a product of iconographic tradition in which individual *sthapatis* incorporate artistic license when creating images?

While there is no easy answer to these questions, the issue of context is the easiest to approach since the butter thief is a product of specific tex-

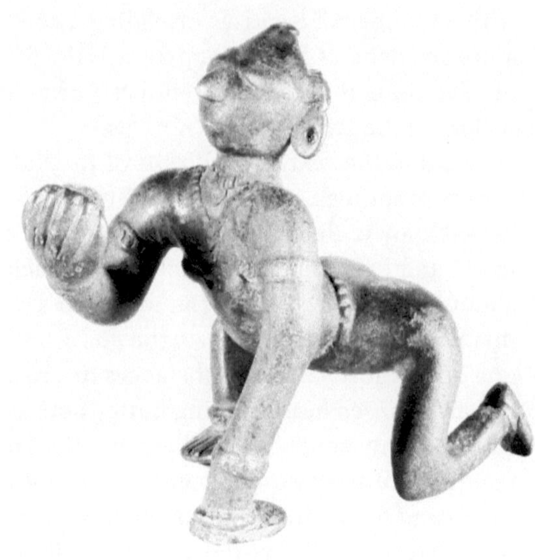

Figure 12: Tribal *Balkrishna* (North India, 18th–19th century) (courtesy Tom Ardizzone).

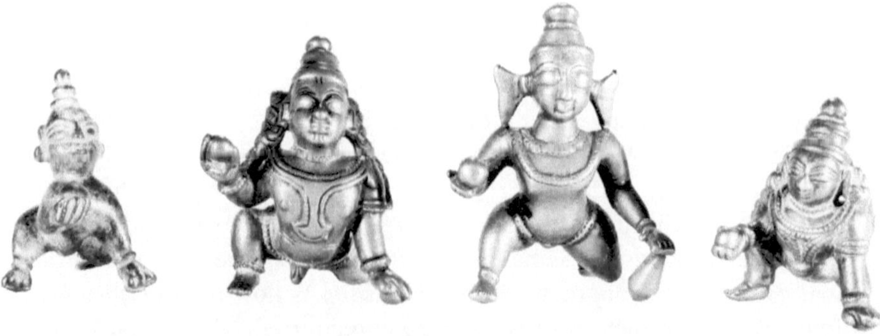

Figure 13: Four *Balkrishnas* with right hands outstretched (South India, 18th–19th centuries) (courtesy Tom Ardizzone).

tual traditions. Much of the imagery about the young *Krishna*'s love for butter comes from the 10th canto of the *Bhāgavata Purāṇa.* In one instance, seeing the suspended butter pot hanging above him the child stands on a mortar and turns it over, offering its contents to monkeys nearby.

In another instance called the *Maṇikhambh Līlā, Krishna* views his reflection in one of the polished pillars in the house where he seeks butter. When, writing in the fifteenth and sixteenth centuries, the blind poet Surdas read this account he described the way that *Krishna* sought to feed the butter to his reflection, asking his reflection, "Here, have some butter. Don't let it drop!"[75]

Both examples have problematic connections with this variation in iconography. In the first, the butter put is hanging from the ceiling and *Krishna* breaks it. Yet, despite this, the *Balkrishnas* that show *Krishna*'s right hand "appearing" to offer butter also show his left hand holding the pot with no indication that the pot had been suspended. In the second example the pillar, or any suggestion of a reflection, is absent in the iconography. If *Krishna* is offering butter to his image, there is no indication from the form that this is the case.

The absence of a convincing correlation with text suggests that this element of stylistic variation is the result of artistic license by *sthapatis* who chose to present *Krishna*'s act of defiance as more open than closed.[76] The butter is held away from the body at arm's length as the mischievous child drags the butter pot along. Excited with his most recent find, his arm holds the butter, outstretched, for all to see.

Iconographic variation can also be found from north to south and are evident both in anatomical proportion and in hair style. Proportion is more likely to be uniform in images created in the South (Figure 14) than in those produced in the North (Figure 15) which demonstrate significant

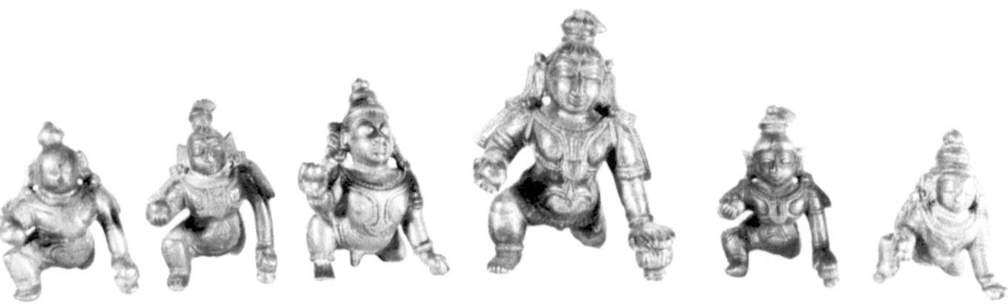

Figure 14: South Indian *Balkrishnas* (18th–19th centuries) (courtesy Tom Ardizzone).

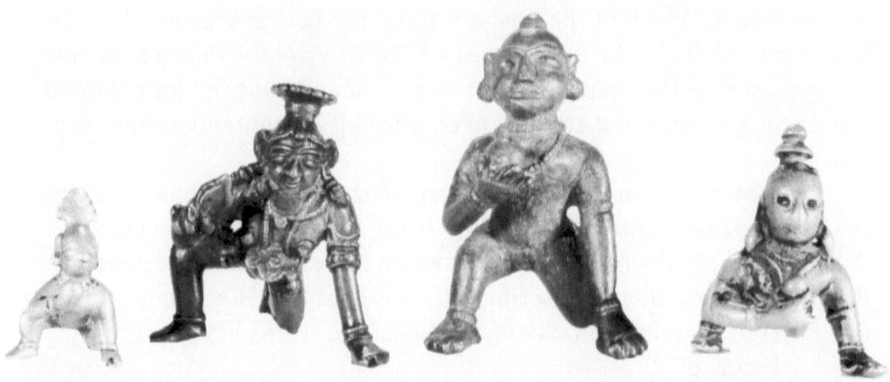

Figure 15: North Indian *Balkrishnas* (18th–19th centuries) (courtesy Tom Ardizzone).

variation in proportion. In Figure 15, the third image from the left has a more spindly figure that makes him appear gangly and long limbed. He carries a butter ball with a flame above it. Atop his head is a crown unlike those that appear in the South.

Iconographic differences are also visible in the hair and crowns. South Indian *Balkrishnas* can easily be recognized by the head adornments that have become typical of the classical Indian *sthapati* tradition. Stapathi lists 13 styles of decorated hair, several of which (the *Kiriīṭa Mukuṭam, Keśa Bandham, Jaṭā Bandham,* and *Jaṭā Makutam*) incorporate conical, highly decorated and stylized hair patterns.

Images from other regions in India demonstrate other anatomical differences. For example, the small *Balkrishna* in Figure 16 appears mischievous and presents a *bhāva* associated with a small child—typical of many forms of the same image. This *Balkrishna* does not display the detailed anatomical features or proportional scale

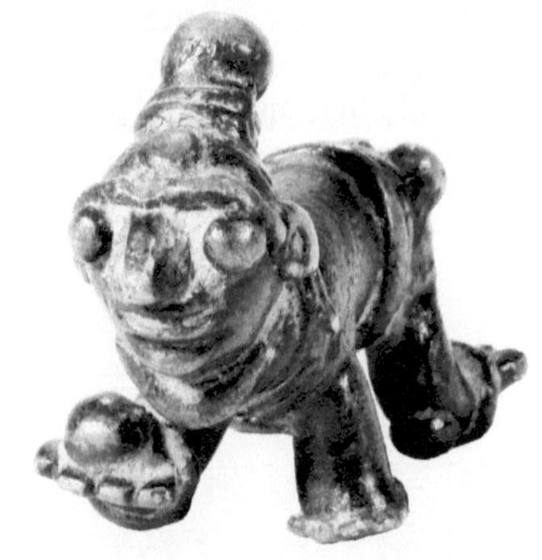

Figure 16: Small 19th-century *Balkrishna*— Odisha (courtesy Tom Ardizzone).

that would be found in Karnataka. However, the large eyes of the figure may provide a clue as to its origins.[77] Devotional art in Odisha depicting *Jagannath* (a form of either *Vishnu* or *Krishna* as lord of the universe) is often rendered with large eyes which can also be seen in this figure. Odisha is also known for its tribal art which may also explain the cruder characteristics of the figure and for differences in composition which include an especially high percentage of lead. The crude characteristics of the image, coupled with these differences, may link it to the tribal regions in Odisha.

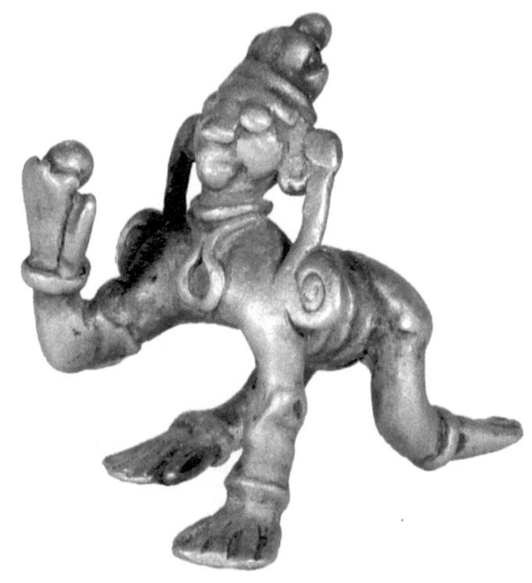

Figure 17: Tribal *Balkrishna* (19th century) (courtesy Tom Ardizzone).

Figure 12 is also a tribal image and, unlike other images, has a more curved and flowing form than seen in northern or southern forms of the same figure. Eliciting a *bhāva* of innocence and playfulness, the rounded lines of the figure contribute to its childlike aura. Yet another tribal figure (Figure 17) also exhibits more of a curved body than would be seen among conventional *Balkrishna* images but exhibits large hands and feet and an almost quizzical expression. Unlike other *Balkrishnas* he is not in motion, but has stopped, admiring the butter ball in his right hand. The butter pot is absent. Images of the child *Krishna* may show additional patterns of variation such as Figure 18, which presents a more fluid, curved rendering.

In sum, although *Balkrishna* images represent only a fraction of the ritually produced images of *Krishna*, and within that a small proportion of the totality of Hindu iconography, they exhibit significant

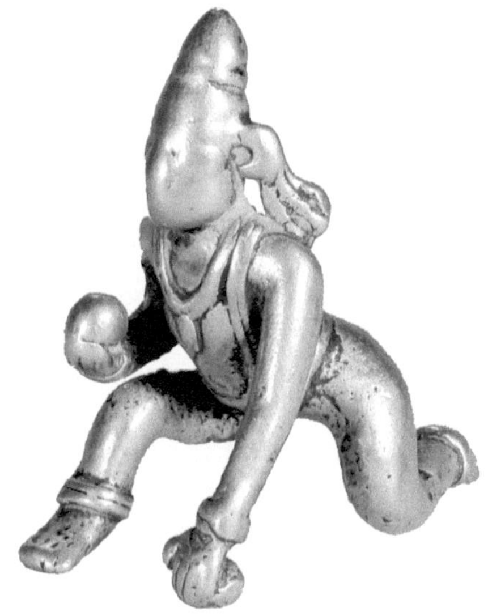

Figure 18: North Indian *Balkrishna* (courtesy Tom Ardizzone).

differences in style, regional identification, composition and in the *bhāva* that they elicit. *Bālakṛṣṇa* images also exist in multiple forms including *Navanit Priya*—which is common in *Pushtimarg*.[78] Facial expressions, which are finely crafted by each *sthapati*, also vary and are an important part of each figure.

Variations in Composition of *Balkrishna* Images

A comparative study of ten ritually produced images of small *Balkrishnas* showed diversity not only in style but also in composition.[79] While this sample is too small to be interpreted statistically, it shows remarkable variation that undoubtedly is replicated in hundreds of other figures, demonstrating that *sthapatis* in both North and South India regularly departed from the formulaic approach to ritual production detailed in the *Śilpa Śāstras*. The images were all between 100 and 200 years old and included figures from both North and Southern India.

Table 1—Approximate Age of the Images

Image	Origin	Approximate Age Before Present
1	North India	100 years
2	North India	100–150 years
3	South India	100 years
4	South India	100 years
5	Tribal	100–150 years
6	South India	100–200 years
7	Eastern India	100–150 years
8	North India	100–150 years
9	South India	100 years
10	North India	100 years

Significantly, none of the ten figures was composed of the traditional alloy of metals, *pañchaloha,* nor was there any uniform composition across the samples, reflecting the latitude that individual *stapathis* have in creating images.

There was also no evidence that diversity of composition was tied to either region or age of the figure. While sometimes it may be possible to make a specific regional identification, this is often subjective and was omitted from the study. However, based on age and style of each figure, distinguishing between images that were made in the North and those that were crafted in the South was possible.

METHOD

The images were tested on a scanning electron microscope (SEM) using a Philips XL-20 with IXRF. This instrument allows for determining elemental composition of metals. Tests were conducted on samples taken from each image and magnified between 200 and 500 times. Atomic ratios of other metals were compared with copper as the standard (1.000).

FINDINGS

Images 1, 2, and 10 (all from different regions in North India) are composed of copper, zinc, lead, and tin. However, while the SEM tests were normalized for copper which was found in each image, the relative amounts of lead, tin, and zinc varied.

Image 3 (from South India) is composed of copper, lead, and zinc but unlike any of the others also has a surface coating of silver.

Image 4 (From South India) is entirely formed from copper.

Image 5 (from South India) is composed of copper and lead in a ratio of 1 to .32.

Image 6 (from South India) has body composed of copper and a crown that, while mostly copper, also contains zinc in a ratio of 1 to .32. As a result, the crown (6b) appears as brass.

Image 7 (from Eastern India) exhibits more lead than any of the others in a ratio of lead to copper in almost a 1 to 1 ratio.

Image 8 (from North India) contains both copper and zinc in a ratio of 1 to 1.5.

Image 9 (from South India) is composed of copper and zinc in a ratio of 1 to .5.

Table 2—Composition of the Images Relative to Copper Content

Image	Magnification	Copper	Zinc	Lead	Tin	Silver
1	500x	1.0000	0.0614	0.4016	0.0845	0
2	500x	1.0000	0.0484	0.2960	0.0326	0
3a	200x	1.0000	0.0121	0.4339	0	0
3b	200x	0.0153	0.0535	0.3179	0	1.0000
4	500x	1.0000	0	0.3746	0	0
5	200x	1.0000	0	0.3200	0	0
6a	200x	1.0000	0	0	0	0
6b	200x	1.0000	0.3200	0	0	0
7	500x	1.0000	0	0.9291	0.4244	0
8	200x	1.0000	1.5350	0	0	0
9	500x	1.0000	0.5134	0	0	0
10	200x	1.0000	0.2927	0.5255	0.0046	0

Image 3a refers to tests done on the figure itself while 3b refers to tests completed on the surface coating on the figure.

Image 6a refers to tests done of the body of the image while 6b refers to tests done on the crown.

Comparisons to Modern Factory Produced Images of *Balkrishna*

For purposes of comparison, two recently factory produced images (Figure 19) were secured and tested in the same manner as the previous ten images. Both images were created in Baroda and brought to the United States for sale in *Pushtimarg* temples. These images were found to be far more uniform than the images which were ritually produced with no stylistic or iconographic variation and a uniform composition of copper, zinc, and lead. The ratios of copper and zinc were almost the same with some variation in the amount of lead which may have resulted from the sampling process.

Table 3

Image	Magnification	Copper	Zinc	Lead	Tin	Silver
1	500x	1.0000	0.8536	0.4374	0	0
2	200x	1.0000	0.6158	0.2979	0	0

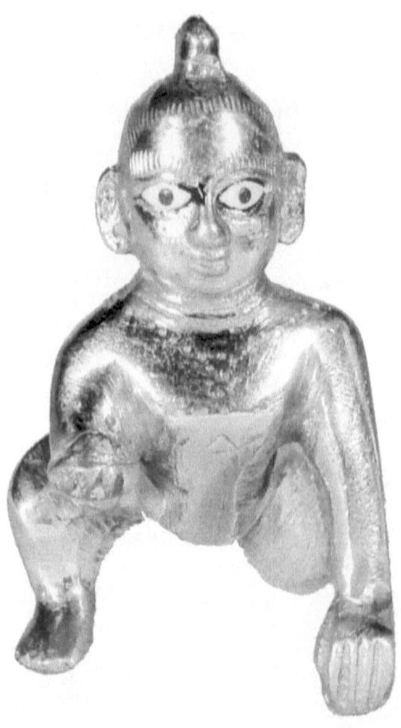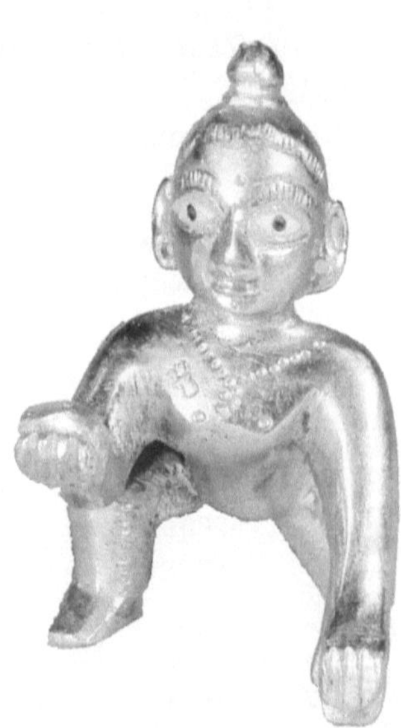

Figure 19: Factory Images (North India, 21st century) (courtesy Tom Ardizzone).

Conclusion

This chapter has demonstrated the origins and antiquity of the Hindu trajectory of embodiment and presence. Perhaps originating much earlier, texts referred to image worship from the time of the Buddha. With the construction of Hindu temples the embodiment of the gods became part of the Indian religious landscape, expanding in the *Chola* dynasty. The chapter has also shown its resilience, surviving the expansion of Hindu tradition into Southeast Asia, encountering numerous challenges to its centrality in Hindu ritual through variant systems of philosophy and colonial condemnation of idol worship.

In all of this the trajectory achieved strength and continuity through its ability to foster the work of ritual specialists who oversaw complex traditions that when enacted brought images to life. In time, techniques for the construction of images were recorded in the *Śilpa Śāstras* and referred to in a variety of the non-canonical *smṛti* literature, giving it both voice and physical expression. *Prāṇ Pratiṣṭhā* became a culminating act, completing the work that *sthapatis* and priests had done together to create images that would become receptacles for divine energy.

The development of the craft of image-making also added resilience to the trajectory by giving *sthapatis* license for individual variation. The ritual production of images did not coalesce around techniques of mass production but instead relied on the devotion and artistic expression of each artisan, trained in accordance with the techniques of his teacher and his teacher's teacher before him. Trained through apprenticeship and learning the craft through lineages descended from master craftsmen, *sthapatis* became independent artisans in a system of production guarded by a sense of mystery and grandeur. It was only through the finely tuned techniques that had been passed down through skilled artisans for centuries that embodiment could take place. Ritual production meant that the intricacies of lost wax casting and the secretive *mantras* of priests worked together in a symbiotic relationship. Only in this fashion could the divine energy of the gods be funneled into images which expressed ultimate reality symbolically but also housed a presence that transcended meaning.

Diversity of expression in the *sthapati* tradition was achieved in a number of ways. While conforming to iconographic patterns each artisan gave the images that he created unique expression that within established styles, showed remarkable variation. Through a study of *Balkrishna* images within a two hundred year period of manufacture, the chapter showed how this was accomplished. Regional variation between northern and southern styles of iconography established stylistic parameters that each *sthapati* worked within. Other regional styles expressed a variety of differences, recognizable throughout the subcontinent. In the case of *Balkrishna* images, distinctive styles emerged among tribal populations, more freely interpreting the figures.

As but one example of the variation that *sthapatis* were permitted to incorporate in their images, *Balkrishnas* showed remarkable differences in the position of the hand carrying the butter ball. Some figures seemed as though they were offering it while others clutched the butter to their chest. Differences in facial expressions also became important indicators of the *sthapatis* own devotion, creating *bhāva* that would in turn be different for each devotee that worshipped an image.

A study of the composition of a sample of *Balkrishnas* revealed the diversity in composition that also accompanied ritual production. While the *Śilpa Śāstras* advocated an amalgam of five metals, none of the images that were studied and which were intended for use in home shrines, showed such a formulaic mode of production. Instead, copper, tin, lead, and silver were used in varying percentages with no single formula being typical of a region. While some of the finest copper images are crafted in southern India, images made of pure copper are also found in the north. By contrast, in an analysis of two images manufactured in Baroda through small scale factories, the percentages of metals were almost identical as were the expressions and countenance of each piece.

The variation in style, execution and composition of *mūrtis* created through the process of ritual production thus created a level of diversity that could not easily be dismissed. By contrast, current modes of factory production depend on the viability of a single product. Theologies of embodiment and techniques of ritual production are absent from the process which depends entirely on a global market economy. The trajectory of embodiment could not be so easily contained and the system of ritual production insured that image production was supported by a wide range of sources of cultural authority, separated from commercial economic systems and tied to a craft that retained a level of authority through its connections with the transcendent.

However, with the advent of globalization, and modes of factory production spread across continents, ritual production has become a rarity. While temples in India and in transnational forms of Hinduism require it, images produced for home use widely vary and are often the product of sources of manufacture outside India. For second-generation Hindu

Americans, who grow up in homes where parents and grandparents perform *pūjās*, direct experience with *mūrtis* is often occasional rather than an integrated part of their daily experience. Because the international market of images has been so heavily supplied with mass produced images, the children of first-generation Hindus in the United States may not be prepared to understand the differences in modes of production, nor have they been exposed to the intricacies of theologies of embodiment. The decline in demand for ritually produced images in India has shifted the role of traditional *sthapatis* away from individual markets to supplying temples. For American temples, these contacts are retained with the utmost discretion and are not widely revealed, insulating the processes of ritual production from a globalized world that is ill equipped to understand them.

Moreover, as the next chapter will show, the dominant mode of interpretation of sacred objects in the West is symbolic, separating the material from any form of embodiment. The trajectory of symbolism and meaning, akin to the trajectory of embodiment, has a long history of evolution, stemming from the Enlightenment when the use of reason created a hermeneutic that shaped Western civilization. However, while the trajectory of symbolism relied on Aristotelian logic its impact is only a matter of three centuries. Yet, it continues to shape attitudes in the modern world toward material culture and the role of images, creating a global terrain of divergent attitudes toward image worship.

THREE

Imagining God
The Trajectory of
Sacred Objects as Symbols

In India, the trajectory of embodiment was supported by a single, dominant institution—the Hindu temple. In turn, the temple was empowered through patronage and the support of dynastical traditions. Patronage reached deeply into cities and villages as Hindu temples became land owners, controlling entire villages and achieving economic benefit from the lands that they controlled. In this, the trajectory of embodiment became embedded in both grass roots culture and in a state-driven religion. While there were challenges to its dominance, philosophical alternatives to image worship never achieved economic or political support, which could compete with the expanding temple tradition in India's medieval period.

By contrast, the trajectory of symbolism and meaning, although informed by Greek philosophy and ancient traditions, was a product of a much shorter period of time gathering momentum in the eighteenth-century Enlightenment which was also a revolt against religion. Through the Enlightenment and its reaction against religious dominance, the Scientific Revolution and the rise of rationalism in the West, religion achieved a common level of meaning, tied to "...inner mental and emotional states, to cognition and the production of meaning."[1]

This chapter explores the foundations that have shaped this primary level of association. Sacred objects were defined by an ambiguity about images in the biblical and early Christian traditions, a struggle in the Middle Ages about the role of presence that had begun with relics, Roman Catholic debates about transubstantiation and embodiment, and, finally, by a pervasive revisionist paradigm in the Enlightenment that replaced images of presence with perceptions of symbolism and meaning. Further defined by economic theory, and the industrial revolution, sacred objects were treated as material culture, creating a trajectory that has influenced religion, the arts, and the self-image of Western civilization. However, akin to the Hindu trajectory of embodiment, the Western trajectory of symbolism and meaning garnered strength through diversity of thought and repeated challenges to its assumptions.

The Trajectory of Sacred Objects in the West

Greek Philosophy

Plato uses an allegory to describe the importance of the intelligible world, which he perceived as reality, over and above the perception of the physical world which he saw as illusion. While the allegory did not distinguish between matter and spirit, it did posit a duality between the intelligible world and shadows. This duality, in concert with the Aristotelian emphasis on pre-scientific investigation of the material world, created an early conceptual framework for the trajectory of symbolism and meaning,

> Attitudes toward material culture were shaped by Aristotelian logic and by discussions about the nature of matter in pre–Socratic philosophy. Writing in the sixth century BCE, Thales, searching for a single substance that could explain the material world, initiated a conversation about the nature of the cosmos focusing on the role of water. A century later, Democritus posed an atomic theory as a way of explaining the nature of material substance, foreshadowing scientific assumptions in the modern world about the nature of physical reality. Plato continued this interest in the nature of things proposing a theory of forms. In his allegory of the cave he imagined prisoners, chained in a cave where they could only see their own shadows and the shadows of objects.... Behold! human beings living in a underground cave, which has a mouth open towards the light and reaching all along the cave; here they have been from their childhood, and have their legs and necks chained so that they cannot move, and can only see before them, being prevented by the chains from turning round their heads. Above and behind them a fire is blazing at a distance, and between the fire and the prisoners there is a raised way; and you will see, if you look, a low wall built along the way, like the screen which marionette players have in front of them, over which they show the puppets.[2]

Biblical Attitudes

The West has been deeply affected by biblical attitudes about images which have commonly been described negatively as idols. However, the Hebrew Bible also presents a level of ambiguity, denying the role of embodiment but in alternative passages condemning idols as forms of "lesser gods," and not denying their existence. Examples of the first type of iconoclasm occur in a variety of books which suggest that idols cannot speak (Psalm 115:1–18), hear or know (Daniel 5:23), breathe (Jeremiah 51:18) or answer (Jeremiah 10:3–16). Jeremiah likens them to "a scarecrow in a cucumber field" claiming that they cannot answer.[3]

Other passages in the *Tanakh* that condemn image worship, while using extraordinarily negative language, do not rebuke an ontological claim. Jonah (2:8) suggests that idols are vain and despicable but implies that they may have life. Jeremiah (7:18) declares that they provoke anger. Isaiah (57:13) suggests that the wind will carry them away implying that they are weak and fragile. Isaiah (42:17) calls them shameful while Hosea (4:12–14) describes them as whores.

The New Testament continues the same themes. Idolatry is freely condemned but an ontological ambiguity remains. Galatians 4:8 declares that they are not gods, denying their divinity but leaving the question of existence open. Act 17:29 declares "Therefore since we are God's offspring, we should not think that the divine being is like gold or silver or stone—an image made by human design and skill."[4] 1 Corinthians (12:2) continues the theme of nonexistence describing them as "mute."[5] A number of other passages such as Revelation 2:20–22 link them with sexual immorality but remain silent about their existence. Some apocalyptic passages imply the existence of other gods such as 1 Timothy 4:1 which declares, "The Spirit clearly says that in later times some will abandon the faith and follow deceiving spirits and things taught by demons."[6]

The biblical injunctions against idolatry are complicated by the fact that archaeologists have uncovered considerable evidence that the textual imagery of Hebrew monotheism in the *Tanakh* were increasingly compromised by folk religion, which continued Canaanite practices of image veneration. Biblical archaeologists have uncovered images of female fertility figurines that attest to the continuation of image worship even after the formation of the Hebrew monarchy. In addition, passages such as 2nd Kings 23:4–14, which makes a reference to the cult of Asherah, provide further evidence that image worship was prevalent, since this was the dominant form of veneration of the goddess.[7] William Dever concludes that cultic practices, image worship, and a variety of other characteristics of folk religion were practiced in Israel and that, "...the *majority* of the people, not just an easily ignored minority, were doing them—and, I would argue principally doing them in a family context, where women played a highly significant role."[8]

The biblical ambivalence about image worship carried over into the early history of Christianity where in the Roman world religious images were common. Images of dying and rising gods such as *Mithras* and mother goddesses such as *Demeter* and *Isis* dominated popular religion. Despite the Christian iconoclasm that followed after the conversion of Constantine, the influence of theologies of presence in Romanized gods continued to be felt.

There is significant evidence that Roman gods were not only associated with agency but with affirmations of full embodiment. Roman gods were fed, bathed, and dressed, in a series of practices that are also found in Hindu *pūjās*.[9] However, as Troels Myrup Kristensen points out, Roman iconic tradition differed from Buddhist (or Hindu) practices in that priests were not required to consecrate the images which were often produced through entirely secular means.[10] However, while the cultural context, nature of the rituals, and personality of the gods were entirely different from images in the Eastern traditions, the markers of embodiment were nevertheless part of Roman tradition.[11]

The most obvious iconographic connection between Hellenized gods and early Christology was Isis and her affinity with the Virgin Mary. While earlier approaches posited that the cult of *Isis* was transformed into that of Mary, later analyses suggest that this view may be too extreme. Tran Tan Tinh has effectively shown the iconographic parallels between *Isis* and the Virgin Mary but avoids the suggestion that the two deities merged into the same figure.[12] Yet, while such direct historical connections cannot be confirmed, there is little doubt that the role of the mother goddess in the ancient near east impacted the theological formulation that saw venerated Mary.

However, while attempts to avoid reductionism are important, the parallels between earlier Egyptian images of the goddess and later images of the Virgin Mary are nevertheless quite striking,

> From 700 BCE ... the goddess is sitting on a throne with no backrest or a very low one; sometimes she has a throne on her head or she wears a horned sun-disk; her legs are parallel and her feet are flat on the floor; her proper right hand is placed on her left breast and her left hand holds up Horus's head; the legs of her son hang over the left side of her lap; and she holds his hands toward his body, while avoiding the gaze of his mother....[13]

Parallel examples of iconography in the *Isis* cult and early Christian traditions are not difficult to find. Painted images of the virgin holding the infant Jesus were found as early as the second century in the catacomb of Priscilla. Others followed with paintings of the "Protectress of the Roman People" in the fifth century and the "Madonna and Child Enthroned among the Angels and Saints" in the sixth century. Perhaps most striking, the *Codex Aureus of Loresh* composed in the late eighth and early ninth century shows numerous parallels to images of Isis from late antiquity. In the *Codex*, the virgin is seated on a low throne with little back, with her right hand placed on her left breast, and her left supporting the infant Jesus. While early medieval images of the mother and child are not exact

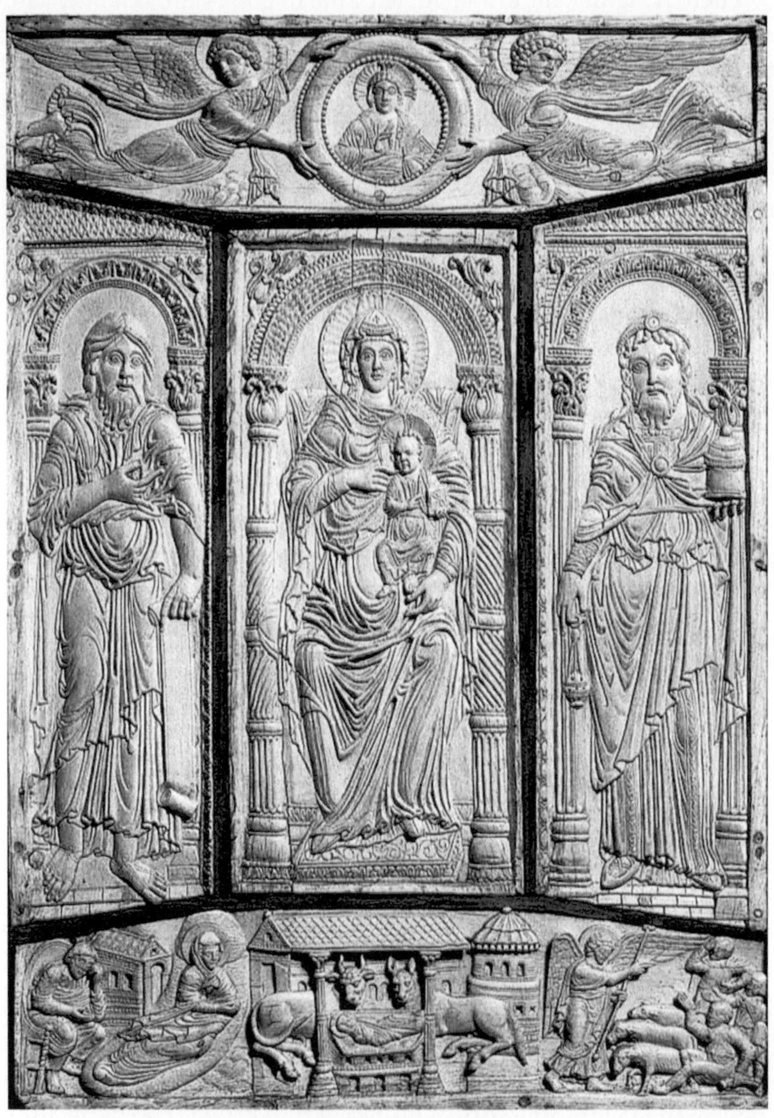

The *Codex Aureus of Lorsch* showing the Virgin and Child.

parallels with Egyptian portraits of *Isis* the influence is unmistakable. While the cover of a codex is not an image, a subtle transformation has already taken place with the creation of religious art rather than a goddess who needs to be bathed, dressed, and fed.

These examples of syncretism and the influence of earlier theologies of embodiment in the Hellenistic world alternated with the iconoclasm that followed the creation of a Christian Roman Empire after the conversion of Constantine in the fourth century. Iconoclasm prevailed not only destroying statues of embodied gods but also damaging secular statues, which were understood to have a more limited presence. Kristensen describes instances of mass "executions" of images through fire, which had been used in Egyptian society as a form of capital punishment for rebels.[14] As a form of punishment which insured the complete destruction of the body, burning was both cruel and humiliating. However, the use of this form of punishment to destroy images also implies embodiment. Kristensen notes an ancient source, the *Life of Severus*, in which the author implies that pagan gods before Christ had power, concluding that "...the rationale of burning is made explicit in the *Life of Severus*, in which the author notes that 'we wanted to show them that all the power of the pagan gods and demons has actually been dissolved and lost after Christ, the word of God, had come and become human.'"[15] While Kristensen concludes that this form of destruction would have also been a powerful way of showing that the images were "...nothing more than pieces of wood,"[16] the ancient text once again implies that pagan images before Christ had life. However, while these examples clearly suggest an ontology, the question about whether Roman statues had life is also complex and was never fixed as, the determination of life in an image was a question of magic or theurgy.[17]

As the Christian church grew, eventually splitting in to eastern orthodox and the Western Catholic traditions, image worship became a highly disputed topic as the church sought to distance itself from pagan religions. In the Byzantine Empire, images were rejected although religious iconography appeared on coins from the period. However, as Eastern Orthodoxy developed into a variety of forms, images developed special significance, not only representing the liturgy of the church but also connoting power and presence.[18]

As the Western Roman Catholic tradition expanded in the Middle Ages in Europe, sacred objects took a number of forms. Relics associated with Jesus, the cross, and the bones of saints developed special significance and were perceived as divine. "Bleeding sites" that were associated with the blood of Jesus were claimed to exist in over 100 places in Germany.[19] Many of these sites involved desecrated hosts, often in places where pogroms had taken place and where large numbers of Jews had been executed, and were perceived as part of the corpus of bleeding sites where Christ could be experienced directly.[20] Any destruction of the Host was also understood as a place of special power and significance.

Relics were also associated with the death of Jesus and have been dubbed, "passion relics." During the Crusades in places where "saints relics" were not found,

> ... passion relics—bits of the true cross or the crown of thorns, etc.—were eagerly collected and imported by the powerful to endow churches and monasteries. Relics of Christ's blood—supposedly gathered on Calvary by Longinus, Mary Magdalene, or Joseph of Arimathea—were often perceived as being literally Christ and therefore as trumping other relics, even passion relics.[21]

As typologies of relics evolved, images also accrued power as they became the center of cult veneration. In Sori, near Genoa,

> ... in 1509, a returning sailor brought home a panel painting of the Virgin Mary and Christ Child, which he had picked up on his travels. The sailor's house lay in what was effectively a suburb of the little port, separated by a river from the urban center and from the principal parish of the town. Very soon word spread that the picture had occasioned a miracle: upon its arrival in the house, the sailor's daughter, who had been dumb from birth, had begun to speak. The sailor promptly declared his wish to found a chapel adjacent to his home, in which the image might be venerated by all, and in which services might be held in particular for the inhabitants of the immediate neighborhood. That neighborhood was defined as Sori in the parish of San Michele, distinguished from the main town that lay in the parish of Santa Margherita.[22]

The authors conclude that following the painting's establishment in Sori, it not only became a source of veneration but also was an important part in defining a neighborhood.

In each of these cases, albeit in the form of relics, paintings, and the Host, medieval Catholic culture assumed that the sacred could be embedded in material objects. In each case, sacred objects accrued power not through their symbolic association with the holy as symbols, but rather from the perception that they were receptacles for divine energy and presence. The association of object and power was so strong, that remnants of the Host became pilgrimage sites while visual representations of the Virgin Mary and Jesus influenced the formation and sanctification of entire urban neighborhoods.

In 1640, in the midst of the English Civil War, similar perceptions were recorded when Puritan encountered a crucifix,

The soldiers were headed for Scotland, pressed into service, and probably angry: "The Soldiers went into the church and pulled up the rails and pulled down the images (which as I hear cost the parson to set up thirty pounds) they tied the images to a tree and whipped them then they carried them 5 miles to Saffron Walden and burnt them and roasted the roast and heated the oven with it, and said if you be god, deliver yourselves."[23]

What is fascinating about this account is that in this post-medieval period, Protestant forces who treated Catholic veneration of images with disdain, were not convinced that the images that they encountered were only symbolic. The soldiers challenged the images to reveal their power but were only willing to take this "risk" after they had whipped, burnt and roasted the images. The incident reveals perceptions in popular Christian culture of the period that was well aware of the power of images and assumed that the divine had the ability to reside within them. However, in less than a century, with the rise of the Enlightenment, empirical science and rationalism, that view would begin to falter.

Transubstantiation and Reformation Debates About Embodiment

A theology of embodiment had been adopted by the Roman Catholic Church in the fifteenth century at the Council of Trent. However, this belief never achieved the level of dominance of embodiment in the Hindu temple tradition. It was contested in the Reformation, in the English Civil War and in the conflict between Catholic and Protestant traditions that consumed European political life in the sixteenth and seventeenth centuries. Moreover, the Catholic theology of presence was a limited form of embodiment. Bread and wine were understood to become the body and blood of Christ during the mass, evoked by ritual formula, and lasting until the host was completely consumed. Once the mass was over, the elements could be distributed to the infirmed who had been unable to receive them in church. However, because of their fragility they could no longer be retained or enshrined. Their presence dissolved with the consumption of the food, to be recreated in subsequent masses.

John Wycliffe was the first to deny the Catholic doctrine of transubstantiation arguing that since time could not be divided into segments, it was impossible for the bread and wine to be changed. Wycliffe insisted that since divine knowledge was also eternal that it was equally impossible for any substance such as bread and wine to be destroyed and changed into something else.[24]

Later, Zwingli, accepted an argument of Corneilius Hoen, who had, "...suggested that the word *est* in hoc *est* corpus *meum* should not be interpreted literally as "is" or "is identical with," but rather as *significat*, "signifies." For example, when Christ says "I am the bread of life," (John 6:48), he is clearly not identifying himself with a loaf of bread or bread in general."[25]

However, Luther disagreed with Zwingli. While Zwingli was only willing to see the Eucharist as symbolic, Luther was willing to concede that the host retained the presence of Christ. Luther would accept consubstantiation, affirming that the presence of Christ coexisted with the bread and the wine but the elements were not changed into the body and blood of Jesus.

Calvin, like Wycliffe, was only willing to understand the Eucharist as a sign, also rejecting transubstantiation,

> It was the goal of Calvin's theological and pastoral endeavor to restore divinity to God. In eucharistic terms this meant that the immediate imperative was not sacramentality but union with Christ. To attain this objective he partially developed and partially inherited a eucharistic personalism and a greatly modified objectivism which stood in contrast to the eucharistic mechanism, empiricism, and to the raging objectivism of Rome's sacramental doctrine and liturgical practice as Calvin conceived them. In both ecclesiology and sacramental theology he sought inwardness and interiority.[26]

As Reformation thought developed, transubstantiation was increasingly identified as a form of idolatry, affirming the continuing difficulty that Protestant reformers had with even the limited idea of embodiment that had become such an important part of Catholic theology. As a form of "idol worship" Protestant thought could not deny the presence of Christ in the elements any more than it could reject Jesus' presence in the world. However, the Catholic notion that physical elements could be changed into the body and blood of Jesus was different, affirming that the Eucharistic host became Christ, albeit with a form of embodiment limited by time and space.

The Enlightenment and the Affirmation of Rationalism

Emergence of the Trajectory

Seventeenth-century mathematician, scientist, and philosopher Blaise Pascal was known for his work in physics, geometry, and probability theory. He was also a Jansenist, an *avant-garde* Roman Catholic theological tradition that both challenged existing doctrine and advocated a rigorous devotional life. In the mid–seventeenth century, Pascal was caught between these two world views, one the forerunner of Enlightenment rationalism and scientific inquiry and the other a theological tradition that emphasized the primacy of faith. Suffering from both tuberculosis and depression, the differences between the two world views that had consumed his life came to culmination on November 23, 1654, when, filled with ire and desperation, he wrote a pronouncement on parchment, sewing it into his coat where it would be found after his death,

> In the year of grace, 1654
> On Monday, 23rd of November, Feast of St. Clement, Pope and Martyr,
> and of others in the Martyrology,
> Vigil of St. Chrysogonis, martyr, and others,
> From around half past ten in the evening, until about half past twelve.
> FIRE
> God of Abraham, God of Isaac, God of Jacob,
> not of the philosophers and scholars.[27]

Pascal's dilemma was created by a radical shift in cultural trajectories as the Age of Enlightenment began to eclipse the role of religion as the dominant paradigm. The Enlightenment and the Scientific Revolution placed rationalism and empiricism on a pedestal. The beginnings of social science and the role of economics also challenged earlier perceptions including those about material culture.

In a shift of emphasis, objects were not looked at as part of a divine creation but instead through the lens of wealth. When John Locke described the nature of material objects, he cast them as property, suggesting that ownership was an intrinsic human right. Locke's narrative about a hundred bushels of acorns or apples is well known, and illustrates the ways in which the accumulation of material goods was equated with the origins of money,

> He that gathered a hundred bushels of acorns or apples, had thereby a property in them; they were his goods as soon as gathered. He was only to look that he used them before they spoiled; else he took more than his share, and robbed others.... If he gave away a part to any body else, so that it perished not uselessly in his possession, these he also made use of. And if he also bartered away plumbs that would have rotted in a week, for nuts that would last good for his eating a whole year, he did no injury, he wasted not the common stock; destroyed no part of the portion of goods that belonged to others, so long as nothing perished uselessly in his hands. Again, if he would give his nuts for a piece of metal, pleased with its color; or exchange his sheep for shells, or wool for a sparkling pebble or a diamond, and keep those by him all his life, he invaded not the right of others, he might heap up as much of those durable things as he pleased; the exceeding of the bounds of his just property not lying in the largeness of his possession, but the perishing of any thing (sic) uselessly in it.... And thus came in the use of money, some lasting thing that men might keep without spoiling, and that by mutual consent men would take in exchange for the truly useful, but perishable supports of life.[28]

Articulating principles of individualism, and the ownership of property, Locke connected the land and material goods to natural law, equating the acquisition of things as an inherent right.

Drawing on Locke's argument, in *The Wealth of Nations*,[29] Adam Smith cast objects as forms of wealth but added the dimensions of a free market, creating the basis of *laissez-faire* capitalism. In capitalist societies objects were understood as transient. While their accumulation was a measure of wealth, so by the same token the need to share, trade, and move objects through an economic system became the hallmarks of Enlightenment thinking, ideas that would later influence John Stuart Mills' philosophy of utility.

At the same time, the Scientific Revolution re-cast material objects as subject to laws and conforming to emerging theories about the nature of matter. There was no room in this increasingly dominant world view for discussions of medieval alchemy or of sacred objects. Instead, science relied on rational discourse, the creation of hypotheses, and experimentation under controlled conditions, as ways of gaining knowledge.

These components of the evolving Western trajectory for material culture were also shaped by the industrial revolution which, through the creation of interchangeable parts, saw objects as transient and replaceable. While some goods, such as art, were more durable, they too were governed by principles of wealth, free trade, and the commodification of material goods which were seen as assets. Within capitalist ideology the sacred was irrelevant. Instead, all forms of material culture were connected with the acquisition of capital and the ability of societies to utilize the ebb and flow of the free market to their advantage.

While Western ideology changed direction, moving ideologies of material culture into the domain of capitalism, in India the Hindu trajectory of Embodiment remained unchanged. While sectarian *Vaiṣṇava* and *Śaiva* theology each developed their own perspectives and variant philosophical approaches about material culture, the rhetoric of presence remained stable in Hindu society. This was supported by the symbiotic role of Hindu temples which were bastions of presence and embodiment. Temples had significant economic functions that allowed them to control vast amounts of land and, in addition, the economic well-being of the villages that supported them. In addition, systems of royal patronage conjoined religion with affairs of state creating a socio-economic fabric of society that saw embodiment as its foundation. Conversely, in the West, during the same period, capitalism eroded the dynamic of presence that the medieval church had depended on, moving material culture into systems of production and consumption and transforming the dynamic of presence into symbolism.

Emile Durkheim and Material Culture as Symbolic–Sacred Objects as Conduits of Cultural Identity

Writing more than a century after Locke, Emile Durkheim, began to define sacred objects through the same lens that he applied to religion using scientific inquiry to shape analysis. Applying rationalism to religion he delved into what he understood as primitive religion, hoping to find the seeds of religious identity that could also be applied to contemporary practices. Durkheim saw objects as a necessary vehicle for creating awareness of collective feelings and at the same time differentiated sacred things from those that were profane.[30]

Perhaps the most applicable part of Durkheim's work to the discussion of sacred objects was his work on totems. For Durkheim, the totem was a visible sign with enormous symbolic power that encapsulated the energies of the clan that produced it,

> These totemic decorations enable us to see that the totem is not merely a name and an emblem. It is in the course of the religious ceremonies that they are employed; they are a part of the liturgy; so while the totem is a collective label, it also has a religious character. In fact, It is in connection with it, that things are classified as sacred or profane. It is the very type of sacred thing.[31]

Durkheim's assumption that totems were more than symbolic and greater than an emblem led him to explore the way in which sacred objects were ritually empowered. While they functioned as symbols pointing to greater levels of meaning, at the same time they garnered power that went beyond traditional assumptions about how symbols functioned. Extrapolating from Durkheim's perception of ritual empowerment, through taboos and rituals, objects were approached with fear, awe, and wonder.[32]

Semiotics, Cultural Anthropology and the Meaning of Things

Originally developed by Ferdinand de Saussure, semiotics evolved as a system of linguistic analysis that could be applied to material objects in order to understand meaning. Saussure evolved a system based on the symbiotic relationship between an object (signifier) and the ideation that was brought to bear on it (signified). Together, in dynamic juxtaposition, these two components produced a sign. Objects evolved multiple signs as the interpretations of what was signified changed. In the same way that words evolve, Saussure suggested that the relationship between signifier and signified was entirely arbitrary but also produced structure. However, while semiotics created a fresh approach to understanding material culture, it concentrated on meaning rather than a perception of embodiment.

If Saussure's semiotic analysis were to be applied to an image (*mūrti*), form and perception would produce a sign with multiple ways of understanding the meaning of the figure. In this way an image of the deity *Ganesh* would be viewed in its physical form in concert with the abundance of stories about the god. The signs that were produced as a result of this dynamic process would incorporate both conventional perceptions (through accustomed meaning or *parole*) and would also reflect the larger corpus of mythology (more systemic meaning or *langue*) embedded in Hindu scripture about *Ganesh*. Signs would also multiply in association with different poses of *Ganesh* (dancing, sitting, trunk facing left or right) which in each case would produce a different signifier. *Ganesh* with a trunk facing right is seen as a male signifier. When the trunk faces the left the orientation is female.[33]

As semiotics rose and waned in popularity as a form of analysis, anthropologists, also influenced by Durkheim, explored other facets connecting objects and meaning. Following the work of Saussure, Pierce, and others the structuralism that had influenced linguistics and anthropology, and the post-structuralism that followed, archaeologists and anthropologists began to look at material culture in new ways. Among these interpretations were theoretical discussions of objects as metaphors. Christopher Tilley concludes that objects function as metaphors when they

> ... move from a whole to one of its parts to another whole which contains that part, or from a member to a general class and then back again to a member of that class. (4) Metaphors involved metonymy in their ability to represent a greater level of reality and synecdoche in which metaphors are relational, moving "...from a part to a whole or a whole to a part."[34]

Tilley took the association of metaphors as a part of language and developed the concept of objects as solid metaphors. Assuming that the human mind was largely non-literal he examined the way that objects, architecture, and landscape were also metaphorical.[35] Drawing on myth and the image of collective consciousness from analytical psychology, he speculated how houses reflected prevailing images of the cosmos while artifacts also acquired metaphorical meaning that transcended their denotative characteristics.

Symbolic Consumption

Insights from semiotics and anthropology emerged in the literature of symbolic consumption which looked at, "…the tendency for consumers to focus on meanings beyond the tangible, physical characteristics of material objects."[36] This interdisciplinary body of literature that developed in the late twentieth century drew heavily from semiotics and the trajectory of symbolism and meaning, placing all objects in a framework of capitalism and consumption,

> Consumers now occupied a world filled with goods that carried messages. Increasingly they were surrounded by meaning-laden objects that could only be read by those who possessed a knowledge of the object-code. Of necessity they were becoming semioticians in a new medium, the masters of a new code. In sum, more and more social behavior was becoming consumption, and more and more of the individual was subsumed in the role of the consumer.[37]

Using this approach sacred objects were taken out of their ritual context and construed as commodities in which they were subjected to the same criteria of authenticity as antiquities and art, supporting the evolving cultural trajectory of symbolism. In this emerging context, as antiquities, the value of images as a generic form of material culture was connected to their age which could be judged, in part, through the chemical coating or patina that resulted from years of exposure to the environment. In *Culture and Consumption*, Grant McCracken identified patina as a way of ascertaining the provenience, relative value, and antiquity of sculpture in a way that was readily transferable to Hindu images.[38] Although McCracken's discussion is limited to Western art, his discussions of the history and nature of patina reflect the cultural lens through which *mūrtis* continue to be evaluated my museums and collectors.

McCracken discussed the role of patina as a symbol of status, authenticity, provenance, and value.[39]

> In Western societies, (patina) is treated as a symbolic property. In these societies, the surface that accumulates on objects has been given a symbolic significance and exploited to social purpose. It has been seized upon to encode a vital and unusual status message. What makes this message unusual is that it is not, strictly speaking,

concerned with claiming status. This relatively simple, even banal, message is left to other, more mundane, aspects of status symbolism. Patina has a much more important symbolic burden, that of suggesting that existing status claims are legitimate. Its function is not to claim status but to authenticate it. Patina serves as a kind of visual proof of status.[40]

McCracken went on to suggest that patina exists on objects in direct proportion to their age and that it can be used to determine the duration and enjoyment of social status.[41] Patina emerged as a market tool that defined patterns of acquisition within an evolving class structure.

In formulating this argument, McCracken traced observations of patina to the eighteenth century. Subsequent studies about the role of patina became an important factor in distinguishing the durable objects that *nouvelle riche* could purchase. Patina was a measure of authenticating status rather than claiming it.[42] In the case of a sixteenth-century silver plate, "The presence of this patina reassured an observer that the plate had been a possession of the family for several generations and that the family was, therefore, no newcomer to its present social standing."[43]

Patinas were, therefore, part of the symbolic nature of property. In the international art market, where Hindu images are regularly bought and sold, the presence of patina can be a determining factor in reifying the symbolic nature of the image and further disconnecting it from the trajectory of embodiment within which it was produced. Curators and collectors develop skills in discerning chemically induced patinas from those caused by age. For example, a scientific analysis of a Chinese bronze from the Shang dynasty used patina as a way of separating an authentic piece from a fake, "This microscopic cross section of the ritual object (*zun*), approx. 1600–1050 BCE … reveals the many layers of various colors, with the corrosion penetrating deep into the bronze. Modern fakes may look corroded on the surface, but when studied in cross section under the microscope the deep, irregular corrosion of an authentically old bronze such as this is lacking."[44] Among users of *Ebay* and large auction houses, similar descriptions of authentic patinas and chemically induced corrosion can easily be found.

Challenges to the Trajectory of Sacred Objects as Symbolic

As the Western world evolved from the Middle Ages through the Enlightenment and the Scientific and Industrial Revolutions, the trajectory of sacred objects became subjected to increasing secularism in the nineteenth and twentieth centuries. This process was also tied to the early history of globalization when colonialism created emerging patterns of consumption in Europe for Asian goods. European adventurers and explorers found sacred objects in Egypt and other parts of the Middle East, as museums became repositories of religious art removed from their cultural contexts. Sacred objects emerged as a sub-category in what came to be known as material culture and could be identified as physical metaphors of the larger society. However, that view had also been challenged during the Enlightenment by Immanuel Kant.

Immanuel Kant's "The Thing in Itself"

Prior to Kant, things were assumed to be knowable through the senses and any assumption that they existed *a priori* was assumed to be false. Kant challenged these ideas through a dualistic approach to phenomena, suggesting that there was another level behind the sensual reality of experience which he called *noumenon*. *Noumenon* could not be known and, since objects and events also exhibited this other level, they exhibited a level of transcendence. The-thing-in-themselves became a metaphor for the supposition that objects were more than appearance and that they incorporated a higher level of reality and presence.

Noumenon was also a Platonic construct which Kant revised, equating it with the world of ideas. As part of the Copernican revolution, Kant rejected the idea of a theocentric universe in which humanity had little active role and instead shifted his lens to human perception.[45] However, when this new paradigm was applied to the distinction between phenomena and *noumenon*, it produced a way of knowing that was forced to conclude that the nature of things could be experienced through the senses and that the realm of ideas, the *noumenon*, was also the realm of God.

Kant's perception of material culture as a vehicle for *noumenon* thus shifted the emphasis of objects away from the supposition that they were entirely separate from spirit. However, this assumption was rejected by other Enlightenment thinkers including Hegel. In his *Phenomenology of Spirit*, Hegel both challenged Kant's perspective on the thing-in-itself and at the same time added a new dimension to assumptions about material culture in Western philosophy.[46] Hegel was convinced in conjunction with scientific reasoning that objects could be known, rejecting Kant's idea of the *noumenon*. However, in so doing he created an

Enlightenment philosophy with parallels to Hindu non-dualism. Hegel concluded,

> ... but the thing is a One, and we are conscious that this diversity by which it would cease to be a One falls in us. So in point of fact, the Thing is white only to *our eyes,* *also* tart to *our* tongue, *also* cubical to *our* touch, and so on. We get the entire diversity of these aspects, not from the Thing, but from ourselves....[47]

While rejecting Kant's argument, Hegel also established an explanation for the reasons that we do not experience the level of oneness in material culture. He speculated that this happens because of the ways in which objects define themselves from each other, and at the same time the inability of our senses to experience oneness in the same way that we see a color as either white or black.

Following the work of Kant, and continuation of his challenge to the expanding trajectory that characterized material culture, other philosophers also began to question the consensus of scientific rationalism that matter and spirit were entirely separate domains. An Anglican bishop, George Berkeley, added to the Enlightenment dialogue about material objects by positing that they did not exist outside of the mind,

> ... It is indeed an opinion strangely prevailing amongst men, that houses, mountains, rivers, and in a word all sensible objects, have an existence, natural or real, distinct from their being perceived by the understanding. But, with how great an assurance and acquiescence soever (sic) this principle may be entertained in the world, yet whoever shall find in his heart to call it in question may, if I mistake not, perceive it to involve a manifest contradiction. For, what are the fore-mentioned objects but the things we perceive by sense? and (sic) what do we perceive besides our own ideas or sensations? and (sic) is it not plainly repugnant that any one of these, or any combination of them, should exist unperceived?[48]

For Berkeley, the essence of things was spirits. Spirits could perceive "sensible objects," and were aware of their own self nature.[49] In Berkeley's thought there could not be a universal spirit, because each spirit existed unto itself. Objects existed when they were perceived but it was the ability of each spirit to see them that gave them form.

Since Berkeley denied the existence of matter, his philosophy has been called immaterialism. Yet, by positing that the perception of matter rested within the individual spirit, he was really suggesting that the spiritual and material were one in the same. Departing from the Enlightenment separation of matter and spirit, Berkeley's world was one of complete spirit, albeit separated into a pluralistic universe where each spirit was independent of the other.

The Challenge from Phenomenology and the Search for the Essence of Things

Kant's "the-thing-in-itself" continued to create reactions in western philosophy well into the twenty-first century. The debate was profoundly affected by the development of phenomenology which was articulated most notably by Edmund Husserl. Husserl asserted that phenomena must be encountered directly and experienced for what they are. Affecting the study of psychology, and what later became religious studies, phenomena were to be approached through unbiased analysis, free from the associations that thinking about them produced. William James added to this conversation through assumptions about the fringe—the thoughts that we attach to an object when we perceive it and the differences between these perceptions and the experiences of the object itself.

The early development of phenomenology was influenced both by Husserl and by theologian Martin Heidegger.[50] The debate centered on the reality of objects and the content that the mind produced in association with them. For Husserl, the discussion championed the kind of idealism contributed by Hegel and placed the object and content squarely within the realm of consciousness. Rejecting Kantian assumptions about the presence of objects, and, instead, constructing his argument on Hegel's idealism, Husserl concluded that the role of phenomenology was to disentangle objects from the experience of them.

In contrast, Heidegger asserted that the nature of an object was beyond its function. In an often recounted metaphor of a hammer he concluded that while the tool was defined by "handiness," as an object it only became useful because things have a "being-in-themselves." Moreover, theoretical approaches to objects lack an understanding of handiness which can only happen through an association with them. In this sense, he asked whether handiness had a linkage to ontological presence concluding that "...if handiness proves to be the kind of being of beings first discovered within the world, if its primordially can ever be demonstrated over and against pure objective presence, does ... (it) contribute in the least to an ontological understanding of the phenomenon of the world?"[51]

Challenges from Theology–Teilhard de Chardin and the Spiritual Power of Matter

Pierre Teilhard de Chardin was a French Jesuit priest who also became a paleontologist, incorporating both religion and science as valid ways of knowing. With an abiding interest in the processes of evolution, de Chardin studied ancient human remains in China and Mongolia. Appointed to participate in a French paleontological expedition he also participated in the American Central Asian Expedition in 1930 and collaborated in the excavation of Sinanthropus. Also venturing to India, he saw the origins of humankind in profoundly theological terms. For de Chardin, there was no argument between science and religion. Instead, the empirical nature of science was a vehicle for demonstrating much larger insights.

As a child, de Chardin had been obsessed with matter. Writing in *The Heart of Matter*, he concluded, "I was certainly not more than six or seven years old when I began to feel myself drawn by Matter, or, more correctly, something that 'shone' at the heart of Matter."[52] Later, this obsession led him to envision an "iron God" which included "the hexagonal head of a metal bolt which protruded above the level of the nursery floor" and "shell-splinters lovingly collected on a neighbourhood (sic) firing range...."[53] Iron was important for de Chardin since it was a symbol of the Absolute, leading him to develop a worshipful attitude toward the objects that he treasured.

In the "Cosmic Life," written in 1916, he realized not only the divine nature of matter but also the need to surrender to it,

> One day, I was looking out over the dreary expanse of the desert. As far as the eye could see, the purple steps of the uplands rose up in a series, toward horizons of exotic wildness; again, as I watched the empty bottomless ocean whose waves were ceaselessly moving in their "unnumbered laughter"; (sic) or, buried in a forest whose life-laden shadows seemed to seek to absorb me in their deep, warm folds__ on such occasions, maybe, I have been possessed by a great yearning to go and find, far from men and far from toil the place where dwell the vast forces that cradle us and possess us, where my over-tense anxiety might indefinitely become ever more relaxed.... And then all my sensibility became alert, as though at the approach of a god of easy-won happiness and intoxication; for there lay matter, and matter was calling me. To me in my turn, as to all the sons of man, it was speaking as every generation hears it speak; it was begging me to surrender myself unreservedly to it, and to worship it.[54]

De Chardin's unitary perception of matter led to the conviction that ultimately, one must surrender to it, a concept that already had ancient roots in the Hindu trajectory of embodiment where the natural world was deified.

In 1919, de Chardin put these convictions in a poem, "The Spiritual Power of Matter,"

> Blessed be you, harsh matter barren soil, stubborn rock:
> you who would

Yield only to violence, you who forces us to work if we would eat.
Blessed be you, perilous matter, violent sea, untamable passion:
you Who unless we fetter you will devour us.
Blessed be you, mighty matter, irresistible march of evolution,
reality ever new-born...
Blessed be you, universal matter, immeasurable time ...
you who by over-flowing and dissolving our narrow standard
of measurement reveal to us the dimensions of God....[55]

The poem was based on a number of influences that were part of de Chardin's spiritual development. As a child, in addition to looking for an ultimate expression in iron and in rocks, de Chardin thought of collections of rare things because they too expressed a level of uniqueness and drawing him closer to what he perceived as the final essence of things. Later, as a Paleontologist, de Chardin began to see matter and spirit not as dual, but as dimensions of the same cosmic essence. He wrote, "Matter is the matrix of spirit. Spirit is the higher state of Matter."[56] This realization dissolved the duality of the separation between the spiritual and material that had driven Western philosophy since the Enlightenment. He no longer saw separate domains but an overall sense of unity.

As a scientist, de Chardin was increasingly convinced that yet another, deeper and more penetrating level of reality could be found in addition to the Biosphere. This was a higher realm of spirit which he dubbed the Noosphere. He thought, "Deep down, there is in the substance of the cosmos a primordial disposition, *sui generis,* for self-arrangement and self-involution."[57] In this, the Noosphere was analogous to a halo that enveloped the Biosphere.[58] As he wrote about evolution he posited that the world was moving toward this realm of spirit in which individual cosmogenesis reaching out to a Christo centric point of unity.

By the time that he composed *The Heart of Matter* in 1950, de Chardin's spiritual evolution had drawn him completely away from the trajectory of symbolism.[59] Material culture became a window to a level of oneness in much the same way that a Hindu image draws the devotee deep inside to the wider reality of *Brahman*. Both were ultimately transparent, yielding to the astute observer a deeper perception of ultimate reality. The journey inward was not a voyage of reason nor was it about Enlightenment rationalism. Rather, at its core was a level of experience and a different way of knowing.

In *Teilhard de Chardin and Eastern Religions*,[60] Ursula King suggests that de Chardin had some contact with Hindu thought. He had also been influenced by William James' *The Varieties of Religious Experience*.[61] James' presentation of religious experience was individual, non-judgmental, and framed by the realization that ultimate reality was more than a question of meaning. In Hinduism, de Chardin came into contact with an experiential model of religion in which the divine is manifest in dreams and visions. However, King reports that de Chardin also read the nineteenth-century Hindu reformer, Vivekananda, and was aware of his monistic emphasis on the Hindu school of *Vedānta* philosophy.

While *Vedānta* presented a vision of unitary religious experience that made images almost unnecessary, Vivekananda also was aware of the West's condemnation of image worship and railed against it. In his public addresses at the World's Parliament of Religions, he defended the use of images, casting aspersions at the West for limiting their understanding of God. While de Chardin did not capitalize on Vivekananda's defense of image worship, he was compelled by his Christian theology to reject *Vedānta* monism, suggesting that its emphasis on *Brahman* as ultimate reality was devoid of personhood. Instead, de Chardin's theology was centered on the transcendental nature of personhood and, in his view, the elevated position of Christianity in affirming it.

There is some evidence that de Chardin was aware of other forms of Hinduism including the *tantric* and *bhakti* traditions. Affirming the role of sexuality as an expression of the divine, he was willing to accept the underlying premise of the *tantric* traditions. However, he concluded that the *bhakti* faiths also lacked connections with personhood in the same way that he had identified shortcomings in *Vedānta*.[62]

King reports that de Chardin had made contact with a *guru*, Swami Siddheswarananda who worked with him on the French branch of the World Congress of Faiths.[63] The Congress, which was an attempt to build understanding between different religious traditions, was a continuation of the effort begun in 1893 at the World's Parliament of Religions in Chicago. Meeting in Chicago in 1933, the Congress of Faiths affirmed a belief in "...a sense of Oneness that transcends particular religions...."[64] However, de Chardin could not bring himself to accept Siddheswarananda's premise that the mysticism inherent in *Vedānta* was the same as for seminal Christian figures such as Saint John of the Cross. Rejecting any attempt to equate the two views, de Chardin reaffirmed the need for a more personalized view of ultimate reality than *Vedānta* had to offer.[65]

However, de Chardiin's understanding of mystical experience was strikingly similar to Shri Aurobindo, a Hindu mystic who was an important part of the Hindu Renaissance and the Indian nationalist movement.[66] While both figures came from entirely different cultural and religious backgrounds, each with profound influences from their own cultural trajectories, each sought a synthesis of East and West,

> In one respect, however, Teilhard and Aurobindo are curiously alike: despite their efforts to find a synthesis of thought between East and West, both remain locked in their own religious and cultural perspectives. Aurobindo emphatically claims that the future development of religion is linked to his reinterpretation of Indian mysticism in the form of "integral yoga," whereas Teilhard conceives of it mainly in terms of a new "road of the West" or a western-based "mysticism of evolution." These positions are opposed to, and exclusive of each other.[67]

While de Chardin's approach to mysticism shared some commonality with Shri Aurobindo there is also evidence that, like others in the West he was influenced by Vivekananda's interpretation of *Vedānta* philosophy, which he misconstrued as a form of *Vedic* religion and denigrating popular Hinduism. On one occasion, observing a festival in honor of Shiva in a village de Chardin wrote,

> With its groups of palms and venerable mango trees, the whole place seemed to have been transformed into a setting for some Oriental "Midsummer Night's Dream." ... Apparently, the god had visited their fields a few days ago in the guise of a flood, leaving behind numerous symbols of his procreative power in the shape of some longish pebbles, which were regarded as an especial mark of divine favour. From the temple, where the festivities were in full swing, came the sound of flutes and drums and the nasal incantations of the priest.... The whole village seemed to be involved in the festival. In several houses we glimpsed old men seated by candlelight, holding their hands before their foreheads in prayer ... and chanting continuously from books with such devotion that for a moment we felt ourselves carried back in time to the far-off days when the Vedic hymns still formed part of daily worship.[68]

For de Chardin, the mystery and magic of that experience came from its ability to evoke *Vedic* religion. Echoing Vivekananda's praise for *Vedānta* as the purist form of Hinduism, de Chardin looked to *Upaniṣadic* religion as the essence of Hindu tradition.

However, arriving in Bombay in 1935, when de Chardin encountered forms of popular Hinduism he expressed disappointment, "So far as I have been able to form an opinion of them, the Hindus have been a disappointment to me. In them, too, the creative power seems in a pretty poor way, and you have to go to India to realize the numbing and deadening effect of a religion obsessed by material forms and ritualism."[69] While de Chardin found enormous congruity between his unitary views of mystical experience and *Vedānta*, he could not carry these perceptions over to popular Hinduism. In some senses he was akin to the Transcendentalists who were so captivated by the monism in Hindu scripture, that they never applied these insights to Hindu worship. Like many Americans, de Chardin also found Vivekananda's interpretation of Hinduism enthralling, undoubtedly assuming that Hindu culture in India would reflect the same high ideals. Unprepared for what he saw in his short visit to India, he perceived ritualism as something entirely different even though the focus of Hindu *pūjā* was a sacred image.

Despite his inability to connect *Vedānta* with Hindu ritual culture, de Chardin attempted to find a synthesis between the two trajectories of symbolism and presence. His mystical journey focusing on matter had begun as a child and remarkably continued in his scientific career. The scientific method and the processes of observation, crafting hypotheses, testing and experimentation, did not stand in the way of his conviction that spirit and matter were essentially the same. Yet, he was also trapped within a cultural trajectory that did not have the conceptual tools to understand the Hindu perspective of presence in material objects.

De Chardin's transition to a trajectory of embodiment did not alter or change the momentum in the West that had since the Enlightenment separated the material from the spiritual. But it did provide a window through which proponents of symbolism and rational thought can understand embodiment. The genius of de Chardin was that he was able to use scientific thought as a means to refine these insights. In this he demonstrated that perhaps more affinity exists between the two cultural trajectories and that both can coexist not in a realm of absolute separation, but in a symbiotic process where outer and inner journeys eventually become one.

Paul Tillich

Paul Tillich was one of the most articulate voices about the symbolic nature of religious objects in the twentieth century. However, connecting the role of objects in religion to ultimate concerns, Tillich advanced a position that went beyond the representational nature of symbols. Tillich identified six characteristics of symbols. First, "...they point beyond themselves to something else."[70] Both signs and symbols shared this common task. But, Tillich proposed a second difference positing that unlike signs, symbols participated in the reality to which they pointed. Therefore, a flag "...participates in the power and dignity of the nation for which it stands."[71] Third, a symbol, "...opens up levels of reality which otherwise are closed for us."[72] In this sense both art and poetry make access available to a level of reality that cannot be known in any other fashion. Writing from a Christian perspective, Tillich affirmed a fourth characteristic in which while opening access to a hidden level of reality, symbols also make the same reality in our soul available to us revealing "…hidden depths of our own being."[73] Citing a fifth characteristic Tillich affirmed that symbols cannot be produced intentionally and are related to the unconscious, "They grow out of the individual or collective unconscious and cannot function without being accepted by the unconscious dimension of our being. Symbols which have an especially social function, as political and religious symbols, are created or at least accepted by the collective unconscious of the group in which they appear."[74] Finally, Tillich suggested that symbols cannot be invented and that they have both a life and a death. Influenced by both culture and history, "They die because they can no longer produce response in the group where they originally found expression."[75]

While all symbols exhibited these characteristics, Tillich posited that religious symbols required an added dimension of ultimacy. Since the absolute can only be expressed through symbols they also become vehicles through which ultimate concerns are accessed. This also suggests that the finite cannot incorporate the infinite. Hence, the word "God" is a finite expression of a higher level of reality. The word finite, cannot contain the absolute and instead points to an ultimate level of reality that language, as a symbol system, can access.

When applied to sacred objects, Tillich's assumptions about the nature of symbols moved them into a different terrain than classification systems based on pose, style, or hand gestures (*mudrās*) could suggest. The *mūrti* becomes a symbol that participates in the reality to which it points. This suggests that an image also contains an aspect of the deity it represents. While images are created intentionally, and conform to a variety of iconographic expectations, their true symbolic character moves beyond the finite. For both Tillich and for Jung, they connect with the collective unconscious, which automatically distinguishes them from consideration only through finite realms of aesthetics or beauty.

However, despite Tillich's ability to broaden earlier perceptions of symbols as representations, he still casts his argument within the Western trajectory of symbolic meaning. Symbols are gateways to ultimate concerns—but the gateway is different than the reality that lies beyond them. The symbol participates in this wider reality otherwise it could not point toward it. But, like the word "God" it is finite and cannot, by Tillich's own admission, contain the absolute. By contrast, the trajectory of embodiment affirms that the finite *can* become the absolute. A Hindu image or *mūrti* is a symbol before it is installed and can be touched, displayed or recognized as an art form. However, it is also a vessel. Once filled, the symbolic meaning is replaced with the full presence of the deity and the image is no longer defined by what it represents—but rather by what it has become.[76]

The Challenge from Analytical Psychology— Sacred Objects and the Spirit Within

Although Carl Jung did not write much about Hindu images, his work on the nature of matter, and the role of *maṇḍalas* and *yantras*, reflects a perception far beyond the trajectory of symbolism and meaning. Although Jung discovered eastern spirituality later in his career, he was intensely interested in Hindu deities. Pictures of the Hindu *trimūrti* (*Brahma, Shiva* and *Vishnu*) attracted him as a child. Later, this led to a fascination with images of the gods and an interest in meditation. While he did not develop a systematic approach to *mūrtis* or a method for approaching Hindu material culture, Jung's insights suggest an alternative to the rationalism that became the primary means in the West of understanding sacred objects.

Jung and Matter

As a boy, Jung had been fascinated with material objects. He described a rock on which he used to sit,

> There was a large rock in my garden. It was my stone. I often went there to sit when I was alone. It was the beginning of a game of fantasy which went more or less like this: am I the one sitting on the stone or am I the stone on which he is sitting. (sic) I had no doubt that the stone had some obscure relationship to me and I would sit there for hours, fascinated by the enigma it presented. The stone has no uncertainties. It does not need to express itself. It is eternal and lives for millennia, I thought. While I am but a passing phenomenon that consumes itself through all kinds of emotions like a flame that burns and then dies out. I was merely the sum of my emotions and some other element in me was the timeless stone.[77]

Jung's interest in matter was similar to de Chardin's perceptions of the spirituality that he saw in the natural world. Each reacted against the evolving secular world view that saw objects as commodities and as transient.

Jung's encounter with the stone led to another experience in which he crafted an image,

> I had in those days a yellow, varnished pencil case of the kind commonly used by primary-school pupils, with a little lock and the customary ruler. At the end of this

ruler I now carved a little manikin, about two inches long, with frock coat, top hat, and shiny black boots. I colored him black with ink, sawed him off the ruler, and put him in the pencil case, where I made him a little bed. I even made a coat for him out of a bit of wool. In the case I also placed a smooth, oblong black stone from the Rhine, which I had painted with water colors to look as though it were divided into an upper and lower half, and had long carried around in my trouser pocket. This was *his* stone.[78]

The narrative is remarkable since Jung had few connections with Hindu image worship which is not described in his writings. Despite this, his procedure of dressing the wood image in a coat, hat, and boots had remarkably close affinity with the importance of dressing a *mūrti* in which use of clothing confirms embodiment. The stone placed alongside the image also paralleled more complex rituals in temples in which images are brought to life by connecting them to sanctified ground. Even more striking, Jung would have had no way of knowing about traditions like *Pushtimarg* in which embodied images are given a bed in a wood box so that they can be transported. Yet, while Jung created his image spontaneously with no reference to these remarkable parallels in the Hindu tradition, he was fully aware of the nature of *maṇḍalas* or sacred designs in the tradition.

Maṇḍalas as Repositories of Sacred Energy

In both his personal life, and in his writing, Jung used the *maṇḍala* as a gateway to a spiritual center, dissociating it from the Hindu and Buddhist traditions, but incorporating it as a way of healing. Jung concluded,

> The fact that images of this kind have under certain circumstances a considerable therapeutic effect on their authors is empirically proved and also readily understandable, in that they often represent very bold attempts to see and put together apparently irreconcilable opposites and bridge over apparently hopeless splits. Even the mere attempt in this direction usually has a healing effect, but only when it is done spontaneously....[79]

Jung's adoption of *maṇḍalas* as a symbol for the Self was also influenced by the assumption in both Hinduism and Buddhism that they define reality by establishing boundaries around a sacred center. Because Jung saw spirituality as tied to hidden aspects of the Self whose domain was the unconscious, the use of a *maṇḍala* as a device to access the inner psyche was subjective. Jung was acutely aware of this, creating his "Red Book" in which he drew elaborately detailed *maṇḍalas,* using them to discern patterns of unconscious thought.

While Jung was aware that he was removing *maṇḍalas* from their cultural origins, he was also adapting a tradition that had developed over centuries in diverse forms. *Maṇḍalas* have been used as meditative devices, often appearing on the floors of temples. They have also had a significant role in the Hindu *tantric* tradition where sacred and profane are dissolved in a complex tradition that includes sexual imagery as a way of accessing the holy. *Maṇḍalas* have been employed within the ritual life of a number of Hindu sects including the *Siddhanta* school of *Śaivism* and the *Smarta Vaishnava* tradition. In some *Śaiva* traditions, *maṇḍalas* are also employed as a form of initiation. Candidates undergo a ritual process of blindfolding in which the *maṇḍala* becomes their first sight.[80] In related traditions such as Tibetan Buddhism, *maṇḍalas* are significant parts of meditation and are incorporated within *thangkas*, sacred designs used by *lāmās* as meditative devices. *Maṇḍalas* have even had practical functions including an architectural role and have been used in town planning.[81]

However, Jung's most significant adaptation of *maṇḍalas* came about as a way of redefining the nature of symbols. Like Tillich, Jung saw symbols as participating in the reality they pointed to. However, extending his argument well beyond where Tillich had gone, Jung linked symbols with the unconscious,

> ... a word or an image is symbolic when it implies something more than its obvious and immediate meaning. It has a wider "unconscious" aspect that is never precisely defined or fully explained. Nor can one hope to define or explain it. As the mind explores the symbol, it is led to ideas that lie beyond the grasp of reason.... Because there are innumerable things beyond the range of human understanding, we constantly use symbolic terms to represent concepts that we cannot define or fully comprehend. This is one reason why all religions employ symbolic language or images. But this conscious use of symbols is only one aspect of a psychological fact of great importance: Man also produces symbols unconsciously and spontaneously, in the form of dreams.[82]

For Jung, symbols were more than conscious constructions of meaning but instead arose from within, both "unconsciously and spontaneously" in dreams and through archetypes. This perception empowered symbols, making them not just points of reference to hidden meaning, but aspects of an inner world that was connected to the collective unconscious.

As a symbol, the *maṇḍala* became a gateway,

> Their pictures work not because they spring from the patients' *own* fantasy but because they are impressed by the fact that their subjective imagination produces motifs and symbols of the most unexpected kind that conform to law and express an idea or situation which their conscious mind can grasp only with difficulty. Confronted with these pictures, many patients suddenly realize for the first time the reality of the collective unconscious as an autonomous entity.[83]

Jung's insights about the collective unconscious placed him at odds with the tenor of his times and his work was not widely accepted until after his death in 1961. His insights challenged the trajectory of symbolism which had little place in his work, replacing it with his own conclusions about embodiment. Jung had freely borrowed from both Hindu and Buddhist traditions, at times misinterpreting some of the essential parts of both traditions. He also drew from the earlier efforts of Orientalists and Hindu reformers who created syncretized versions of Hindu tradition.

YANTRAS–CREATING A CIRCUMFERENCE FOR SACRED SPACE THROUGH RITUAL

Jung not only used *mandalas* as devices for his personal reflection but he also adapted the related Hindu tradition of *yantra* with his patients. *Yantras* are geometric designs that are part of the wider tradition of *mandala*. However, while *mandalas* are used to define and embody sacred space, *yantras* are conceptualized as "instruments" that have important ritual functions. Jung saw this as an opportunity for his patients whose creative designs were,

> ... yantras in the Indian sense, instruments of meditation, concentration, and self-immersion, for the purpose of realizing inner experience, as I have explained in the *Golden Flower*. At the same time they serve to produce inner order— which is why, when they appear in a series, they often follow chaotic, disordered states marked by conflict and anxiety. They express the idea of a safe refuge, of inner reconciliation and wholeness.[84]

While Jung was aware of the Hindu aspects of *yantra*, he probably did not know that in some *bhakti* traditions these geometric drawings are an ancient method used to evoke and embody a deity into sacred art. In the *Pushtimarg* tradition, a sixteenth-century North Indian *bhakti* sect, temple hangings (*pichhavai*) are constructed on cloth by skilled artisans who view the practice as a form of devotion.

The *yantra* is created by first marking the borders of the painting and then locating the center which is analogous to the *bindu* or the center of creation. Next, a "...circle is inscribed, which touches this inner boundary line."[85] Following this, the four cardinal points are marked with lines connecting these points to each corner of the painting. When the lines are connected in this manner, the circle is squared. The process is continued by squaring the circle two more times to produce an octagon which,

> ... is found in all architecture of the Sacred, as a temple primarily represents the transition from the square (earth) to a circle (heaven) through the intermediary of the octagon (man or existence). The octagon symbolizes the eight states of matter represented as two interactive squares in their static and dynamic form. The dynamic (active) square corresponds to the cardinal directions: N, S, E and W or the four elements: fire, water, air and earth.[86]

Once the *yantra* has been completed, *pichhavai* artists paint over the geometrical designs, creating a design that is defined by the season of the year in which *Krishna* is depicted, the actions that he is performing, and the priests who accompany him.

In an analogous form of art in Tibet and Nepal, in the *Vajrayana* form of Buddhism, *yantras* are incorporated within *thāngkās* or cloth hangings used by *lāmās* as part of the ritual process of visualization. Creating a mystical state of awareness the *thāngkā* acts as a *yantra*, creating a point of entry for the *lāmā's* inward journey. Like Jung's "Red Book," the geometric design in each *thāngkā* is specific to the *lāmā* who created it and only meaningful to him. Analogous to a spiritual map, the *thāngkā* provides a path to the inner most reaches of the devotee. Although *Vajrayana* Buddhism, recognizes the existence of the self as a fiction, *thāngkās* make the leap to salvation possible by embodying future Buddhas (*bōdhisattvās*) into the painting.

Yantras employ boundaries that define the journey to the center and each is a receptacle for divine energy. As the outer lines of a *yantra* frame the space, so the form of the divine figure focuses awareness on the deity within. This is part of the rituals that prepare temples for the deities that will inhabit them. The inner space of each temple is entirely focused on the deity. Before temples are erected and the deity installed within, the earth is purified and worshipped through (*Bhūmi*) *pūjās* to the earth. Fire pits are dug and offerings of *ghī* (clarified butter) and other ritual substances sacralize the land. *Maṇḍalas* are drawn often on the temple floor, preparing the inner sanctuary for the resident deity who will inhabit the space, framing the reality inside creating the sanctified and purified conditions necessary for the deity's presence.

Mūrtis, maṇḍalas, and *yantras* act as mirrors, reflecting the self and are defined by ritual and praxis. In this context, where the sacred is everywhere, but whose focal point is specific, the *mūrti* is an instrument for finding center. The *mūrti* can deepen awareness, collapsing the distance between supplicant and deity. In much the same way Jung found that both *maṇḍalas* and *yantras* reflected the inner psyche of the person creating them, creating access to the Self in a way that otherwise could not be known.

Jung's work, as clearly identified in his "Red Book" also showed the relational nature of *maṇḍalas*. Intricate geometric designs became maps of his inner psyche, varying in appearance and significance with the changes that he was able to identify in his unconscious. Like a *mūrti*, each *maṇḍala* was a mirror, reflecting the inner Self and providing a tangible means of access to it.

While Jungian thought had little effect on the Hindu diaspora in the late twentieth century or on the ways that Hindu Americans have understood embodiment, it did challenge the prevailing trajectory of symbolism. For Jung's expansive following after his death, his rhetoric of embodiment has special significance. Yet, demonstrating the remarkable resilience of cultural trajectories, the societal perception of symbolism as the dominant quality in sacred objects continued unabated.

Challenges from Popular Culture— The Search for the Spirit Within Material Objects

The industrial revolution produced a variety of reactions to material culture, as objects became increasingly mundane. With the rise of a growing commercial world in the nineteenth and twentieth centuries, symbols were no longer the product of a craftsman, but of corporations who saw them as a way of establishing levels of meaning that connected with patterns of consumption. With the acceleration of globalization in the late twentieth century, transient goods were increasingly outsourced making it virtually impossible to assign an object to a single culture. Reactions to this loss of symbolic power in a single object have been far and wide. Peter Korn, a furniture maker, writes about the attempt to return symbolic power and meaning to handcrafted objects,

> A single piece of furniture articulates a point of view about life on many levels. I'll identify three. First, as an aesthetic whole, it positions itself within a thick cultural narrative of style and meaning. Thus this particular desk—with its streamlined traditional form, absence of hardware, natural wood, overt functionality, and exposed, hand-cut dovetails, speaks of both Shaker and modernist design precepts.... Second, as an aggregation of physical details, this desk conveys a hundred different impressions, all of which evoke meaning.... Third, as a manifestation of craftsmanship, this desk is at odds with our society's rampant consumerism.[87]

Korn speaks of meaning and the ability of things to convey not just one level of meaning but many. However, Korn is not only reacting to the loss of symbolic power of objects, but is also expressing dissatisfaction with the trajectory of symbolism and meaning itself. He writes about the ability of things to embody a level of presence that extends beyond rational assent. Using the example of a finely crafted desk he concludes:

> But the physical details of the desk speak to a more ancient materialism, deep in the human psyche. This is the belief that objects have mana: that the miraculous

power to provide spiritual sustenance resides in the object itself, not in the achievement of ownership. We enshrine the original manuscript of the Declaration of Independence because it has mana; we revere hallowed paintings in museums because they have mana; we make pilgrimages to the Shroud of Turin because it has mana.[88]

The assumptions that Korn is making are echoes of much older conversations about the material and the spiritual in Western civilization. They are echoes of Kant's the-thing in-itself. Stripped of the rigid ontology of the Enlightenment, they evoke the concept of *mana*, first voiced by anthropologists in the twentieth century to characterize the presence that natural objects were perceived to contain in animistic cultures. They reflect Hegel's perceptions that the spiritual and the material are symbiotic parts of a large whole. They also contain whispers of Teilhard de Chardin's emphasis on the spiritual nature of matter.

Korn's arguments are also part of the dialectic in Western societies, both reflecting the search for happiness in acquisition and yet at the same time, in a much quieter voice, acknowledging the inherent dissatisfaction that this emphasis has produced. His plea for finding *mana* in things is related to the assumptions in Hindu society which, without the constraints of the Enlightenment that consciousness and rationalism are the only avenues to find spirit, has developed theologies of presence.

Musical Instruments as Living Presence

One of the world's foremost cellists, Bernard Greenhouse died five months after his 95th birthday, still recounting the cello crafted by Antonio Stradivari that had been with him for 54 years. Identified after the Countess of Stainlein, a nineteenth-century aristocrat who had acquired the cello in 1854 and who kept it until her death in 1908, the cello was a living presence.[89] Greenhouse insisted during the latter stages of his life that the Countess of Stainlein be placed next to him in bed.

Other musicians who have owned great violins have expressed similar sentiments,

> The violin is not only a friend," said Aaron Rosand, 84, once a prominent soloist in the tradition of the great Romantics like Oistrakh, Milstein and Heifetz. "It's something that you live with. Every day it becomes more dear to you. It's almost like a living thing. You treat it carefully; you treat it gently. It talks to you," he said. "You're caressing your instrument all the time. Parting with an instrument that has become such a wonderful friend is just like losing a member of your family."[90]
>
> In another instance:
> Raphael Hillyer, the founding violist of the Juilliard String Quartet, was in his 90s

and repeatedly spoke of his plans to sell his viola, a late-16th-century Gasparo da Salò. Twice. Hillyer summoned Christopher Reuning to his home in order to hand over the instrument. The last time was in November 2010. Reuning went to Hillyer's apartment in downtown Boston. The violist was seated at the dining-room table. He held his instrument up and offered it to the dealer to hold. Documents were spread out on the dining table. Hillyer asked Reuning a series of questions: What would it sell for? What is the commission? How long would it take? They talked for more than an hour, with Hillyer returning again and again to the same questions.

"He sat there clutching it in his hands," Reuning recalled. "I realized he was not ready to give it up. I told him, "Why don't you keep your viola and we'll talk again sometime?" They made another appointment for just after Christmas, but Hillyer died on Dec. 27, at age 96.

"It's inconceivable that my father ever would have let it go," Jonathan Hillyer told me. "I think his life would have ended immediately if he did such a thing. It's part of what kept him alive. He played it every day, even when it got to be so painful to pick it up. It was his life force. If he had sold it, it would have been like he was giving up."[91]

Examples of other stringed instruments that were treated as living beings are not difficult to find. The sentiments that musicians have expressed for the instruments in their possession are not just due to anthropomorphizing objects. Rather, they are part of a body of commentary that has looked at them as living beings. Violinists know, in keeping with this perception, that when fine instruments are put on public display in museums they are likely to lose their magnificent sound which only emerges after repeated playing.

These examples further amplify Heidegger's perception of function verses being.[92] When in use the violin or the cello is an "instrument," a tool or device that is so finely perfected that it can evoke a level of sound that the trained ear instantly recognizes. But the perceptions of the violinists and cellists who have cared for these fine instruments for a lifetime recognize something else—a level of being and presence that not only defines the instruments identity but often their own.

In keeping with these perceptions the recorded list of the approximately 500 Stradivari instruments that remain is entitled the "Iconography."[93] Using a term usually reserved for religious figures, the association with fine violins with religious presence is not accidental. In the same way, scholars have repeatedly attempted to determine the characteristics of fine violins that have given them their exquisite sound. Some theorists have concluded that it was the varnish in contrast to others who have concluded that it is the shape of the F holes or the trees that were harvested for the wood. What is of interest here is not as much the conclusions of this academic debate, but the motivations that propel them to ask questions. Modern technology has produced many fine violins that, arguably produce even finer levels of tone than those made by the masters. Tests have been run in which musicians have been unable to identify the sound of a Stradivarius violin when played next to a finely produced more modern instrument. However, instead of quelling the debate, these studies have only heightened the discussion.

Any great stringed instrument has a provenance in which every owner of the violin, base, or cello is identified. Owners of Stradivari violins and cellos have a written record of each person who had their instrument, often accompanied by knowledge of who the person was and how long they cared for the instrument. This provenance is part of the life story of each instrument and is deeply connected to perceptions about the life within it. Together, they are part of the *mana* that Peter Korn evokes when he describes his furniture or the sense of spirit that many pocket watch collectors evoke when they first hear a 300-year-old watch begin to beat.

Conclusion—The Role of Colonialism in Solidifying the Trajectory

This chapter has shown how, through the rise of reason coupled with scientific materialism, the trajectory of symbolism became the dominant way of interpreting material culture in the West. Surpassing ambiguity in the biblical, early church, and medieval periods about the role of embodiment, the trajectory garnered strength from Enlightenment rationalism. While repeatedly challenged by philosophers, theologians, and by the rise of academic discourse in a variety of fields including phenomenology and analytic psychology, the trajectory was ultimately solidified in the West by the grip of capitalism. While the philosophy of reason and empirical inquiry defined it, the simultaneous rise of capitalism made it a form of cultural orthodoxy.

The trajectory of symbolism and meaning also drew its support from colonial Christian governments and from the increasing profit that European powers found in trade. Beginning in the seventeenth century, British, Dutch, French, and Portuguese trading companies looked for resources that could not be found in Europe. Colonial trading companies met the challenge by empowering merchants to gain access to spices, precious metals, timber and other resources desired at home. At the same time, missionaries linked the spiritual with the search for material gain.

The exploiting of nations on the periphery by core countries followed a pattern in which both Catholic and Protestant religious figures sought to construct alliances and at the same time to convince indigenous populations that their religious traditions were inferior. In the case of India this produced a European elite which remained completely segregated, structuring a hierarchical society in which Indians were prohibited from socializing with Europeans or enjoying the privileges that came with status in the army and civil service. All the while missionaries reminded the population that their religion was not only a staircase to heaven but also was a mechanism for accruing wealth and power in this life.

Evidence for implanting capitalist ideology among religious groups is not difficult to find. In 1907 the Report of the *American Marathi Mission* described the work of D.C. Churchill in Ahmednagar.[94] A graduate of the Massachusetts Institute of Technology, Churchill had developed a loom which he was convinced would be more efficient. Competitions were established with the Salvation Army loom in Madras in 1908. Weaving assistants were hired and the government opened a number of schools to help capitalize on the new invention. However, the effort ran into a number of difficulties including the reluctance of merchants to finance the new looms without assurance that they would reap the benefits.

As British colonialism took increasing hold in India, Hindu temples also became caught up in governmental regulations,

> Over the course of the nineteenth and early twentieth centuries, temples became encompassed in Anglo-Indian law under the general category of religious and charitable institutions. The social meaning of endowment took on British values, focused around ideals about secular philanthropy and Christian religion. Religious gifting came to be considered, by extension from British norms, as transcendental or other-worldly in orientation—a development with particularly dramatic implications for the evolving colonial conception of a deity and its chief devotee, the *dharma karta*. On the one hand, the deity itself came to be viewed as a kind of public property; access to it, as a public right; endowments to it, as public trusts. On the other hand, the *dharma karta* came to be defined, in the first instance, as the *trustee* of a public fund, with fiduciary responsibility for the deity. From this new perspective, if religious gifting had (by definition) the "nonreligious" side effect of creating an investable fund of capital, such a fund was considered a public resource, not the *karmic* property of private shareholders in a venture undertaken by deity and devotees.[95]

Through these mechanisms, the British *Rāj* increasingly came to redirect the enormous profits that Hindu temples had accrued through patronage systems. The result was that offerings became public property and religion was forced into a capitalistic mode in which "the public" could participate.

Both examples show the increasing ability of a colonial government to spread the trajectory of symbolism and meaning well beyond the borders of Europe, engendering international markets that were the forerunner of the globalized economic system in the twentieth and twenty-first centuries. Through its involvement with Hindu temples and the later development of Religious Endowments laws that further restricted the wealth that temples could acquire, the *Rāj* softened the trajectory of embodiment by forcing it to be part of a system defined by symbolism and meaning. A century and a half later, when Indian immigration to the West substantially increased, the ingredients for adoption of the trajectory of symbolism were already well in place. Indian entrepreneurs constructed temples and hired priests to perpetuate embodiment but at the same time as vigilant entrepreneurs taught their children the benefits of participating in a capitalist system in which symbolism trumped embodiment conforming to the growing hunger of global markets for increased profitability.

FOUR

Putting God on Display

Interpreting Hindu Images Through the Lens of Art, Symbolism and Meaning

Conversations with first-, second-, and third-generation Hindu Americans about museum displays of images often yield quite different reactions. At a conference in 2017 of first-generation teachers in a *Pushtimarg* educational program that had established religious centers in ten states, devotees agreed that museum displays of images were unsettling since they were removed from their ritual context.[1] Devoid of dress, adornment, and no longer able to receive ritual baths or food, images were on display as works of art in a way never intended in the temples that were their homes. A similar conversation among second-generation *Pushtimarg* students produced a very different conversation.[2] There was no discomfort with the prospect of museum displays of images. One student added that at least the displays presented a way of seeing images which they otherwise might not have. While this is but a single example of the different perspectives among generations that can take place, it marks the ambiguity and even confusion that museum displays often create in a Hindu transnational context. First-generation immigrants may continue the trajectory of presence, drawing on the role of temples as divine residences and continuing this perception to home shrines. Their children may be influenced by the sciences and prevailing views in the West of material culture, perceiving images as symbolic when *mūrtis* are incorporated in museum displays, acquired by private collectors, and bought and sold by large auction houses as admired art. In these instances *mūrtis* are accessed through the lens of aesthetic considerations emphasizing provenance, authenticity, skills of the artisan, and symbolism.

This shift in trajectories began in the nineteenth century when Orientalists saw Hindu *mūrtis* as objects of great beauty but also understood that the trajectory of embodiment was incompatible with biblical injunctions against idolatry and evolving Western symbolic consumption. As a result, they were displayed, collected, and admired as art.

This chapter addresses these concerns in three parts. Part 1 explores the history of museums and the display of Hindu images. Part 2 looks at ambiguity in the biblical and Renaissance discussions about the nature of idolatry and later perceptions in the art world about agency—the ability of material objects to affect emotion. Finally, Part 3 explores the role of imagination in the Hindu tradition showing its relationship to images both in the process of daily devotion and in ritual.

Part 1: Institutionalizing the Trajectory of Material Symbolism in Museums

For Hindus who perceive *mūrtis* as living presence, their display in museums is incongruous and has little to do with their role in ritual,

> Worshippers have a close relationship with their deities. They bathe, anoint, decorate them, and perform rituals that celebrate the survival of the soul over the inevitable cycle of life and death. Hence, the deity's shift from the multi-sensory temple environment into the ocular-centric museum is a reflection of its role as a living embodiment of divinity in the temple and as a visual signifier of culture and history in the museum.[3]

While temples communicate the experience of divinity through all of the senses in "multi-sensory" ways, museums, charged with the responsibility of preserving cultural artifacts, are limited in the ways that they can present *mūrtis*, often selecting "ocular-sensory" modes of display. By removing visitors from the experience of touching a *mūrti*, it is separated from the ritual world in which images are produced and experienced in home settings. At the same time, through the creation of tactile approaches to *mūrtis* in display settings especially designed for this purpose, it may be possible for museums to replicate additional parts of the temple experience.

At the same time as museums remove visitors from a multi-sensory experience of *mūrtis*, they often also depict them in ways that conflict with their appearance in devotional settings. Perhaps the most severe aspect of this transformation is the display of *mūrtis* without clothes or adornment. As Richard Davis concludes, when museums display *mūrtis* in hushed settings, deprived of the sounds of devotional atmospheres in temples, and unadorned, they are in a very different kind of space than their ritual environment.[4] In museum collections, Hindu *mūrtis* are another category of material culture,

> ... in the western world it is particularly ironic that the institutionalized activities of museums and art markets end up utilizing South Asian objects in ways that presume free customer choice as a model of and for aesthetic preference and interpretation, thereby fulfilling market-models of reality (as expressed for instance, in possessive individualism, private property, aesthetic fetishism, and the spatiotemporal practices of conservation, protection, and exhibition normalized in museum policy). Thus, what may start as unintended self-congratulation, or at best, irony, risks sinking into profound ignorance to the exact extent that the *other* dimensions of reality—the ones presumed by the ritual contexts of production, use and disposal, in which these South Asian objects were brought into being, and from which they have been removed—are, in one stroke, unintentionally, automatically, simultaneously, and reflexively, made exotic.[5]

Capitalizing on their clientele, in which visitors expect to enjoy aesthetic experiences, museum displays fulfill a number of expectations. They protect, preserve, and conserve the objects in their collections. They also appeal to "market-models of reality" in which valuable, highly prized, artifacts fall into a realm where highly prized objects are housed in secular temples of prestige and opulence. Museums, auction houses, and collectors all provide similar contexts in which material culture conforms to Michael Thompson's perception of durable goods which increase in value over time. Museum displays cater to the process, unwittingly, creating secularized environments within which *mūrtis* manufactured through processes of ritual production, cannot be adequately represented or understood.

Europeans had known of *mūrtis* since the thirteenth century when Marco Polo visited India. With no frame of reference to understand what he saw, the Venetian observer commented on their ritual use, noting the way that young girls were consecrated before an image.[6] However, as more contact with India was realized, other, profoundly negative impressions of *mūrtis* were generated when they were associated with demonic and malevolent forces,

> In short, classical monsters and gods, biblical demons and Indian gods were all indiscriminately lumped together with congenital malformations under the all-embracing class of monsters.... The indiscriminate and eclectic interest in monsters from diverse sources goes a long way to explain the consistent use of the stereotypes of demons and monsters to represent Indian gods. They were taken by travelers to be simply another variant of the multi-limbed pagan monsters and prodigies known to exist in the East.[7]

The perception of Hindu images as monsters, coupled with missionary reports describing the Hindu trajectory of presence, created a problem for Europeans who encountered them. Enthralled with the beauty of Hindu art, few English Christians would think of them as living gods. As a result, images and devotional paintings began to be collected as art. Sometimes, art was even commissioned by members of the East India Company,

> Paintings of deities in the Company style were commissioned and/or collated by European soldiers, administrators and missionaries, often as souvenirs or mementos of their time in India.... These images, as originally intended by their creators, actively engaged the Hindu viewer in a spiritual event. It was not how they looked but what they could do that was important. However, Europeans commissioning deity paintings did not participate in this visual performance between image and viewer; on the contrary, many collected them as illustrations of a spiritual belief they misunderstood and rejected and, in the case of missionary collectors, a belief from which they sought to convert the Hindu faithful.[8]

As the East India Company grew, admirers of Hindu images increased. At the same time, the work of archaeologists in India increased, creating the need for a way of understanding *mūrtis* that would not offend either Christian sensibilities about idolatry or Victorian perceptions of material culture.

The Development of Hindu Iconography—
The Nexus of Art and Archaeology

The development of museum displays of Hindu images had evolved simultaneously with Hindu iconography. The first studies of Hindu iconography followed the formation of the Archaeological Survey of India in 1861. Armed with the mandate to study India and to classify its unparalleled antiquity, leaders of the survey constructed a system of knowledge focused on the translation of scripture. Max Müller's work on the *Sacred Books of the East*, William Jones' contributions to the study of Sanskrit, and the efforts of other Orientalist scholars, attempted to systematize the wide variety of Hindu texts that they encountered.[9] Exploring and translating the Vedas, Orientalists assumed that, like monotheistic religions, Hinduism must have had a central text.[10] Emphasizing the importance of the *Bhagavad Gītā*, the total corpus of Western academic work on the Hindu tradition began to create categories of meaning. Immersed in this scholarly trend, and drawing on iconographic studies that attempted to classify Hindu images, T.A. Gopinath Rao, who had worked for the Archaeological Survey of India, began to explore Hindu images.

Rao was named superintendent of the Travancore Archaeology Department in 1908 and was trained as an epigraphist and archaeologist. In 1914 he completed his seminal work, *Elements of Hindu Iconography,* which for the first time gave Western audiences a sense of the scope of Hindu image.[11] Rao suggested that while many scholars believed that the origins of Hindu icon worship resulted from the Buddha, he believed that it was more ancient.[12] Writing well before the discovery of Mohenjo Daro in 1922 by R.D. Banerji, another employee of the Archaeological Survey of India, Rao suspected that the argument about the Buddhist origins of icons and iconography was misguided.

Rao devoted his study to the two large systems of Hindu iconography—the school associated with *Vishnu* (and his *avatārs*) or *Vaiṣṇava* and those related to *Shiva* or *Śaiva*.[13] Also acknowledging the importance of the mother goddess or *devī,* he acknowledged that his system of classification needed to be broader. He described both iconic and aniconic forms of sacred objects such as *Bāṇa Liṅgas* and *Śaligrāmas* which are naturally formed stone sacred objects that corresponded both to elements of mythology and the *yantras* that empowered them. The *Śaligrāma* stone was seen as a representation of the conch of *Vishnu* while the *Bāṇa Liṅga* was a representation of the creative power of *Shiva.*[14]

Rao also used the term "image," avoiding the more pejorative word "idol" and distinguishing it from "icons." The latter, Rao suggested, "...signifies an object of worship, or something which is associated with the rituals relating to the cults of different divinities."[15] On the other hand he concluded that the word "image" ... "has got the basic connotation of 'likeness.'"[16] He further argued that the term image also meant reflection, "...placing a mirror on a brass or copper bowl in front of the deity in such a manner that the image is reflected in the mirror. The water for bathing the deity (*snāna-jala*) is poured on the reflection there, and thus the bathing of the image is done."[17]

Rao's work was soon succeeded by other attempts to continue the process of classification as a means of understanding the nature of Hindu sacred objects. The perspective was Art History and it focused on iconography. Benjamin Rowland, writing about the art and architecture of India produced further insights into the complex nature of Hindu sacred images.[18] Rowland had received an S.B. degree from Harvard in 1928, followed by a Ph.D. in 1930. Both a noted art historian and collector he contributed to the field by taking the insights produced through archaeology and developing them in art history.[19]

Other art historians continued the process of classification. Jitendra

Nath Banerjea's *Development of Hindu Iconography* appeared in 1941. It expanded on what Rao had accomplished, describing different iconographic forms of the same deity and adding insights about the antiquity of image worship.[20] A succession of studies followed as scholars began to develop broader views of Hindu art, that moved away from the focus on authenticity.[21]

Museums and the Redefinition of Hindu Sacred Objects as Art

Museum collections of South Asian images evolved in a context of displays as "cabinets of curiosities." Within this context, sacred objects were seen as exotic.[22] The perspective of a repository for curiosities had origins in the Renaissance where galleries of paintings filled museum collections in a single, authoritative space. Later, in the early nineteenth century, museum displays of statuary underwent a transition spawned by Enlightenment rationalism. Prior to 1800, observers who saw lifelike qualities in statues were prone to attribute life to the art. However, "In the decades around 1800, with the rise of aesthetics, which were all predicated on some form of aesthetic distance, looking at and engaging with a work of art as if it was a living being became increasingly unacceptable."[23] The failure of art history and aesthetics to understand sacred objects as expressions of embodiment was even more devastating. Hindu images became appropriated in museums and private collections in the West often ignoring the long history of devotion and the presence that had been seen in them was ignored.

As museums evolved in the expanding nineteenth-century British Empire, they began not only to house the exotic but also focused on the industrial, reflecting the self-image of empire. Within these joint emphases, museums in India mirrored their Western counterparts—categorizing and cataloging artifacts, and incorporating sacred objects in the same institution that housed exhibits of Western material culture. The net effect was to separate images that had been created through long-established patterns of Hindu ritual production from their devotional context, incorporating them into the evolving cultural trajectory of the Western world in which objects were divorced from spiritual presence. In order to achieve this juxtaposition, sacred objects, as representations of material culture, were redefined as art.[24]

The British Museum was foremost among European museums displaying collections of South Asian sculpture in the context of art. Interest in the broader corpus of Asian art had been part of the museum's founding collection, gathered by Sir Hans Sloane in the eighteenth century. Later, the museum received gifts from Sir Alexander Cunningham, first Director of the Archaeological Survey on India, opening the prospect of displaying religious images. In 1880, when the East India Company was dissolved, its collections were dispersed to a number of institutions including the Victoria and Albert Museum, and the Royal Botanic Gardens in Kew. Sculptures were given to the British Museum.[25]

At the same time, with the rise of art history and anthropology as levels of rational inquiry, "...the agency and life of images disappeared from art historical research agendas to be replaced by formalism, stylistic inquiry and iconography."[26] This transition had an immediate effect on Hindu art which was increasingly consumed by iconographic studies which replaced any nuance of presence with concerns for style, antiquity, and quality of the casting.

As Hindu sculpture became increasingly displayed, art history and museology also became increasingly interdependent. This was facilitated through personal collections of Hindu art, gathered by historians such as Ananda Coomaraswamy,

> As early as 1917 Ananda Coomaraswamy had assembled a vast collection of art in India and Sri Lanka (then Ceylon) that was characterized simply as Indian (though now they would have to be categorized as Indian, Pakistani, Bangladeshi, Nepali and Sri Lankan), which he first offered to the then British Indian government. They, however, showed no interest and so he simply left the country with it and through the auspices of Denman Ross, a patron and trustee, the Museum of Fine Arts, Boston was able to acquire it; thus the first major collection of Indian art was initiated in a museum in U.S.A. The story of the Indian collections in the British Museums is much older, of course, and much of it was taken out of the subcontinent without any hindrance by the colonists, both private and official. The biggest haul was the Amaravati sculptures that now are well looked after in the British Museum.[27]

Coomaraswamy's work was augmented by Stella Kramrisch, known for her studies of Hindu temple art. Kramrisch lived in Calcutta for thirty years and also gathered a substantial collection of Hindu sculpture which was eventually transferred to the Philadelphia Museum of Art.[28] Similar associations between scholars, universities, and museums marked the growth of other collections of Hindu sculpture in the West. At the same time, collecting Hindu sculpture became part of a milieu in the Western art world that connected interest in antiquities with Indian sculpture. In time, foundations became involved. The Nathan Rubin–Ida Ladd Family Foundation made generous gifts to the Michael C. Carlos Museum at

Emory University and also to the University of Chicago. As the major auction houses became involved in Asian art in the twenty-first century they offered access to a variety of resources and collections in digitized formats on the internet.

As museum collections of Hindu art became increasingly normative, interest in ritual settings developed. This was the case in the mid–twentieth century when the Metropolitan Museum of Art and the Philadelphia Museum of Art, each acquired parts of entire temples. In 1956, New York City, the Metropolitan Museum secured a *gūḍha-maṇḍapa*—a prayer and meeting hall from the Jain religion in the Gujarat that had been dedicated in 1596.[29] In the case of the Philadelphia Museum of Art in a more ambitious project initiated in 1940, a *maṇḍapa* (pillared hall) was acquired from a sixteenth-century stone temple in Madura which was touted as "The only Indian stone temple ensemble in America...."[30] The temple is *Vaiṣṇava* and was originally dedicated to an infant form of *Krishna* called *Madana Gopala*.[31] In order to help complete the aesthetic experience of the structure the museum installed a series of eight frieze slabs which were placed between the columns.[32] Completing the exhibit are three deities placed at the end of the hall and housed in museum display boxes.

Visitors to the temple can experience the beauty of sixteenth-century Hindu stone art and also have the experience of the antiquity of the shrine. However, the displays that they encounter emphasize artistic and aesthetic traditions and the role of museums in making them available to the public. What is missing are the smells and sounds of recurrent *pūjās* that emphasize the presence of the deity, the chanting of Brahmin priests as yoghurt, *ghī*, and other substances are poured over *mūrtis*, and the flashes of color from flower garlands and the garments of worshippers. Here, the deities, encased in display boxes, are not dressed for worship. The museum crowds who come to see them may jostle for space in an attempt to secure a photograph, but the excitement of the crowd is missing from a living temple where devotees seek *darśan*—a glimpse of the resident deities whose energy fills the temple space.

While the majority of museums that display Hindu images in the United States have retained the traditional approach of viewing *mūrtis* aesthetically, some have attempted to re-create the environments within which sacred objects are worshipped. This has been the case with the Newark Museum which houses one of the most important collections of Tibetan Buddhist artifacts. Because of the influence of Tibetan immigrants in the United States the museum began to reconsider the meaning of its collection,

The Newark Museum received its first large Tibetan collection two years after opening, and by 1935 it had grown into one of the world's most important collections of Tibetan material. In that year, the idea emerged of creating an altar setting for the great liturgical objects of the collection. Funding from the Federal Emergency Relief programme (sic) made it possible—not the least of the imaginative cultural benefits the New Deal brought to America. The altar was conceived as an engaging and comprehensible way of presenting unfamiliar Tibetan objects, but it very quickly attracted the affection and respect of visitors, and especially of local Buddhists. Mongolians settled in New Jersey after World War II, while after the Dalai Lama's exile in 1959 the museum built up strong relations with the Tibetan diaspora in the U.S. The Dalai Lama himself visited in 1979 and 1981. Originally intended as a way of displaying objects so that their intended function could be more easily understood, the "altar" gradually took on a sacred character....[33]

The museum acquired the assistance of a skilled *lāmā*, the Venerable Ganden Tri Rimpoche, who had been artistically trained in Sikkim. He presided over a ceremony to deconsecrate the original altar in the collection and spent two years in creating a new altar room that would be appropriate for worship.[34]

While this example is Buddhist, rather than Hindu, it shows the interest in some museums in reversing the earlier trends of displaying sacred objects only from the perspective of aesthetics and historical significance. Other museums in the West have also attempted similar transformations, creating Zen gardens and meditation places, offering a different level of experience that is more conducive to the display of sacred images. In Mumbai, the Prince of Wales Museum celebrates a Buddha Day.[35] In England the Birmingham Museum and Art Gallery proudly displays the Sultanganj Buddha, a 2.3 meter high *Gupta* period Buddha, holding an annual Buddha festival (Wesak) "...which has been celebrated ever year in the gallery by a group of local Buddhist monks and lay people, a celebration organized jointly by the museum service and the West Midlands Buddhist Council."[36]

These examples not only demonstrate a willingness by some museums to explore the trajectory of embodiment but also show shifts in the purposes of museum displays. However, examples of these attempts are minimal and are scattered globally. In the United States, where second-generation Hindu Americans see images in temples and in museums, the collision of trajectories reifies their experience as the sons and daughters of Hindu immigrants who understand embodiment and their peers who are removed from it. Without more wholesale change in the transformation of museum displays to incorporate Hindu images, and to place them in purified, consecrated settings, the dual effect of colliding trajectories is likely to continue.

Authenticity as a Criterion
for Museum Displays

As centers of cultural authority in their mission to protect, preserve, and display artifacts, museums depend on their ability to determine and validate authenticity. Since both museum and privately held collections of *mūrtis* are most apt to center on the rarity of individual pieces and the cultural context out of which they came, authenticity is also linked with provenience. Iconic pieces of antiquity with religious significance such as the Narmer Palette in the Egyptian Museum in Cairo, and the stele of Hammurabi in the Louvre, are reminders of the power of museums to solicit material culture, and to afford objects that would be otherwise unobtainable. In these exceptional cases, as in others, the museum establishes standards for determining authenticity.

However, in the context of its original cultural trajectory, the assumption that a Hindu *mūrti* is "authentic" is a misnomer theologically. *Mūrtis* are recognized as receptacles that house divine energy. The most perfect among them—those crafted through the lost wax process revealing intricate detail, and the stone *mūrtis* that are frequently housed in temple complexes—fully become the living god. However, even more crudely manufactured *mūrtis* can also be understood as sacred residences.

Yet, when a *mūrti* enters the art market and reaches the display floor of a museum, these criteria become irrelevant. They are subsumed beneath a canopy that highlights historicity, authenticity, and aesthetics. For *mūrtis*, authenticity is redefined in the same way it would be for other antiquities, accessing the "fit" of the piece within the period and iconic style that it represents. While *mūrtis* were never created with this trajectory in mind, when on display, they are made to conform to it.

In the Western art world, authenticity is frequently also connected to originality and, if possible, to the artists and sculptors who executed each piece. Signed art and sculpture commands enhanced value. Museums struggle with these questions, employing scientific techniques to establish that pieces bearing the signature are authentic. Thus, where provenance is the most important criteria in determining authenticity, other even more complex relationships between art and science have been necessary.

This was the case with a collection of china in England attributed to the Duke of Buckingham. Morgan Wesley describes the circumstances,

> (A) ... pair of vases ... was discovered by Gordan Lang (1942–2010), Honorary Keeper of Ceramics at Burghley House in Lincolnshire, while cataloguing the collections during a pre-inventory in 1981. Inside one of these small jars was a slip of

paper with the inscription 'Duke of Buckinghams (sic) China' in eighteenth-century script and written with chestnut brown ink, prompting immediate interest in the miniature vases....[37]

The authentication process that evolved from this discovery involved three areas of concern, (1) connoisseurship: visual authenticity and cultural context; (2) documentation: historical authenticity and communication of knowledge; and (3) scientific analysis: physical authenticity and technical accuracy. These areas of analysis came together in a complex process,

> The issue of authenticity within the field of ceramics is moulded (sic) into the form of a dialogue, conducted between defined structures of information. It is a construction of the combined knowledge of the various connoisseurs, scholars, and scientists who are expert in the discipline. It is, paradoxically, also an area of study that fixates on the unknown and undiscovered, yet focuses intellectual and market value on the specific point of attribution—that is, the factual nexus of time, place and product of a ceramic work. It is within this conversation between data and intuition that any examination of the notions of authenticity and attribution must begin.[38]

In this context, connoisseurship is a process of observation, based on familiarity with the type of objects in question, coupled with a knowledge base of material culture. Experts are required who have long histories of familiarity with specific, detailed aspects of material culture and who are able to fit objects into both a chronological and aesthetic continuum. Accordingly, the process also depends on the acquisition of primary source material and access to other objects that may be compared and contrasted with those in question.[39] In most cases, the information upon which connoisseurship depends is not published. Rather, it exists within an often hidden realm of antiquities experts, curators, and collectors.

Much the same process has also been applied to the study of Hindu images. While texts may describe *mūrtis* that are typical of the "golden" age of Hindu art in the *Chola* and *Gupta* empires, they are often ill-equipped to describe less refined pieces and the type of *mūrti* that would more likely be in common use during later periods. In these instances, the role of connoisseurs is invaluable and often provides the only tangible way of dating *mūrtis* and ascertaining the region within which they were produced.

Considerations of authenticity in Western art also involve the question of replicas. While copies of iconic works normally command less value than originals, in some genres of material culture the lines between original and copy are blurred. This is the case with *mūrtis*. Always unsigned, and the products of anonymous *sthapatis*, determining original pieces from later copies within the same genre can be extraordinarily difficult.

However, as was the case with the *Pathur Natarāja* (an image of *Shiva* that had been acquired by the British Museum), images can be linked to specific periods in history and, on occasion as was the case with this image of *Shiva*, to specific temples.

The contemporary concern with originality as a means of defining authenticity not only deviates from the Hindu tradition of *mūrti* manufacture, but also with some genres of Western art including the Renaissance and post–Renaissance periods,

> In these latter traditions, the replication and copying of an established model is not perceived as an inferior process but has validity in its own right. These represent very different approaches to the making of an artwork which possesses authenticity. From a traditional woodcarver in Essex, to the commissioning of copies of great works of design by the Victoria and Albert Museum in the nineteenth century, to numerous examples of contemporary art and design, many kinds of artworks continue to privilege both the copying and replication of earlier work and the notion of art as a continuous and collaborative process, albeit from very different perspectives.[40]

In much the same way, the replication of Hindu *mūrtis* is not considered as an affront to authenticity. Rather, in the context of Hindu iconography, all images of god are considered to embody the sacred in their own right. While canonical assumptions about proportion, symbolism, expression and a host of other iconographic variables are described in the *Śilpa Śāstras*, these standards are not adopted by all Hindu image makers. Rather, authenticity is redefined in terms of the auspicious nature of the image. That too, is reassessed regionally by diverse groups of devotees.

While *śāstras* are technical treatises, they stress the need to make proportions of images perfect, especially in the case in which a sculpture or painting represents a god. Only where proportions are made appropriate for the depiction of an image will that image be considered auspicious, and will then be seen to convey the right meaning to traditional audiences.[41]

Who Owns God: Competing Trajectories of Art and Sacred Presence in the Courts

As museums evolved as public "collectors" of sacred objects, removing them from their ritual contexts, stolen artifacts flooded receptive markets in the West. Following the call for repatriation of stolen art by UNESCO in 1970, museums in the West began to identify stolen *mūrtis*, igniting collisions between museums and private collectors, in conflict with temples and ritually produced Hindu *mūrtis*. Richard Davis describes a collision of these trajectories. A tenth-century image of *Shiva Nataraj* (*Pathur Nataraja*) was buried in order to protect it from invaders. It was subsequently disinterred in 1976, and found its way into the international art market. Passed through a series of private collectors, the *Pathur Nataraja* eventually found its way to the British Museum. When a museum conservator determined that it had been stolen, the image was seized by the police as "contested property."[42] By 1991, the government of India had decided to pursue the return of the image. The court case that followed, "…would consume forty-four court days and involved legal costs far above the market value of the bronze in question…."[43]

Davis recounts how, at that point, the image presented a "juristic personality" (249) concluding,

> Later in the case the Indian side introduced still another plaintiff, Śiva. The god Śiva, acting as a "juristic person," would claim ownership of the Śiva Natarāja image that had originally resided in the Visvanāthasvāmi temple. Śiva's participation in the case gained publicity and engendered the best headline" "Sueing (sic) Śiva Dismays Dealers" Becket 1988. And rightly so, for when Hindu gods begin suing in British courts this is newsworthy.[44]

Ultimately the temple's case prevailed. The temple celebrated the return of the *Pathur Nataraja* to his rightful place in the temple where, dressed, bathed, and anointed, he once again became the center of this sacral space.

This conflict, while dramatically representing a highly sought after, valuable and highly revered image of *Shiva*, also captured the collision of competing cultural trajectories, framing the fight in a globalized context in which antiquities freely move across borders. The case also illustrates the history of museums as bastions of cultural authority. In this case, museum collections also served as reminders of the earliest encounters of the West with Hindu images and their transformation from objects of presence into antiquities, valued for their history, aesthetic qualities, and monetary value.

Museums and Conflicting Trajectories:
The Case of *Swaminarayan,*
the RSS and the Brooklyn Museum
in a Depiction of *Kali*

With the rise of Indian economic strength, the escalation of trade, and the growth of nationalist movements in India, the trajectories of symbolism and embodiment collided. In June 2016, in a Swaminarayan mission in Surat, a picture was released of the central deity dressed in military attire and holding the national flag. The image wore "...a white shirt, tucked into baggy khaki shorts and black shoes—the RSS's uniform."[45] Reactions were instantaneous. Followers of the Swaminarayan sect, including leaders of the Congress party were upset. Several devotees tried to enter the school premises but were stopped by security guards.[46] The temple denied any ill intentions. The dress had been given by a local devotee. The priest, Swami Vishwaprakashji claimed, "We have a common practice of presenting the God's idol in various dresses."[47]

While the controversy appeared to be grounded in politicizing a sacred image by virtue of dressing him in a uniform of India's twenty-first-century conservative political party, the *Rashtriya Swayamsevak Sangh* a competitor of the governing *Bharatiya Janata* Party, there was far more under the surface of the conflict. The issue was explosive because it reduced the presentation of an image perceived as an embodiment of deity, to a set of symbols which instead of connoting transcendence, pointed to a political party and the ideology of one faction within the nation state. The conflict became a dichotomy between sacred and profane. Rival parties, including the governing BJP and the Congress Party rejected the deity's dress undoubtedly because of the negative feelings that this form of reductionism would take. The incident also demonstrated the lines that are drawn between the trajectories of symbolism and embodiment and the sensitivity that any conflation of the two trajectories causes.

In an article in *Hinduism Today*, published in the West for transnational Hindus, the editor drew similar boundaries when he described the *Ganesh* festival suggesting, "In recent history, missionaries and others from the Western religions have told the Indian people over and over again that their gods are not real beings, but merely symbols of spiritual matters and unfortunately many have begun to believe this and look at their gods in this way."[48] To the author, the trajectory of symbolism was clearly a product of the West and did not belong in a context in which a deity was concerned. Moreover, he squarely placed the blame for this confluence on missionaries as an arm of colonial presence.

The emotional reaction to conflated trajectories has also been carried into the art world when the perspectives of museums have collided with the feelings of first-generation Hindu Americans. In 2014, the Brooklyn Museum unveiled a large mural of the goddess *Kali* created by an Indian émigré, Chitra Gaṇesh. Gaṇesh described the mural as containing "...iterations of feminine power" and as exploring "...themes of femininity and multiplicity using inspiration from the collection of objects of the Brooklyn Museum."[49] Moreover, the Museum conveyed *Ganesh's* perceptions that, "There are more than 150 prayer flags displayed above the mural designed to invoke institutions or temples…. The flags each have a silkscreen image affixed on them and are made from her mother's old saris and other materials from India."[50]

Reactions to the museums display were most vocally expressed by Rajan Zed, who had also criticized Urban Outfitters for producing socks with the image of *Ganesh* on them.[51]

One wonders why such displays of artistic images, even from an Indian artist, caused such vehement reactions among Hindu Americans in much the same way that the uniform on *Lord Swaminarayan* had evoked in India. Moreover, if artistic images of deities are the issue then why, as Kajri Jain suggests in *Gods in the Bazaar*, has Indian calendar art become such a pervasive part of Hindu culture?[52] The answer lies in the conflation of trajectories of symbolism and presence much more than in the commercialization of deities or their use to support political agendas.

If the Brooklyn Museum's display of a large mural empowering women and depicting the goddess *Kali* had been displayed in India it is doubtful if it would have invoked much reaction. However, its unveiling by a major museum in the United States was another matter. The mural became an unwitting statement by the museum that representations of the goddess were art and could be publicly displayed in the same manner as other art forms. Symbolism had overpowered embodiment and the goddess had been transformed from presence to a representation.

Part 2: Art, Agency and Idolatry

Perceptions of Idolatry in the Biblical Tradition and in Renaissance Art

At the root of conflicts like this are long-standing perspectives in the trajectories of embodiment and symbolism focused on the ability of a material object to convey agency and presence. The discussion is complex since the history of art in the West has been dominated by ambiguous discussions about agency and idolatry, affecting the way that religious and secular forms of anthropomorphic art were perceived. This ambiguity was the result of a confusing array of biblical attitudes about idolatry.

The biblical injunction against idolatry was launched in an environment of competitive religion where the dangers of syncretism were seen as acute. The biblical record not only included an injunction against worshipping idols in the Ten Commandments but additional warnings about images. Some, such as the encounter of Moses with the golden calf, were polemics against the inroads of Egyptian religion. Moses was presented as the progenitor of true religion in the midst of counter religion, rejecting image worship and leading his people out of Egypt to a place where the formless, imageless Yahweh could be worshipped.[53]

However, scriptural injunctions and religious praxis in the day-to-day lives of people are entirely different things. Writing from the perspective of biblical archaeology, William G. Dever has demonstrated that the scriptural injunctions against idolatry represented one voice of biblical tradition while in actual practice images were widespread.[54] Dever describes the proliferation of Canaanite fertility images in Israel.

Whether Dever is correct or not, it is clear that image worship prevailed in ancient Israel even though the biblical record spoke so harshly against it. This ambivalence about image worship suggests that the question of idolatry had a variety of meanings including perceptions of betrayal as well as a spectrum of ontological positions,[55]

> ... it is difficult to discern whether the biblical authors gave credence to the existence of other gods or not; "It is entirely possible that the Bible admits the existence of other gods and merely forbids their worship—a standpoint called "monalatry" by scholars; it is also possible that the Bible not only forbids the worship of other gods but also denies their very existence."[56]

While ontological arguments about the existence of other gods varied, questions of loyalty and betrayal as the primary perceptions of idolatry continued.

Halbertal and Margalit further suggest that perceptions about idolatry were governed by three subordinate concerns. The first was the role of similarity in which the image can either be understood as a sign or as a fetish where the image does more than point to another level of reality but also participates in it. In the case of a fetish the role of the image is increased and "...is an object to which people attribute powers that it does not have."[57] In this case a substitution has occurred and the fetish not only represents the god but is understood to take its place.

A second type of representation is metonymic, something that stands for, or points to a greater level of reality. Thus, a flag points to the larger reality of the nation state and stands for it. Halbertal and Margalit conclude that the Bible permits this, citing the example of cherubim in the holiest of holies in the Hebrew temple. The cherub stood for the power of Yahweh but were allowed in the temple because they were not an anthropomorphic image of the deity.[58] Some scholars have viewed the worship of the golden calf in the same way, suggesting that as a metonym it was acceptable.

Finally, the third category of representation is conventional and includes the role of metaphor. Both language and art fall into this category in which,

> There is no real distinction between a linguistic picture and an actual picture. Thus if the linguistic expression is taken at its face value, then the picture too should be permitted; and if the linguistic expression is interpreted metaphorically, why shouldn't the picture also be considered a candidate for metaphorical interpretation?[59]

All three assumptions, the role of similarity, metonym, and metaphor, appear in the biblical tradition and, together, present an ambiguous picture about Hebrew attitudes to images. Much later, this ambiguity, coupled with the rise of Renaissance art in Europe, created a crisis about the question of how anthropomorphic art should be perceived. Did it have agency? Can art convey presence, and in the light of biblical tradition, if it does, is this idolatry? The debate became particularly difficult when applied to a painting or sculpture since each was both a visual image and also an object. Moreover, with the rise of Renaissance interest in ancient Greece and the creation of statues with Greek aesthetics, these questions engendered continuing debate. Perceptions of embodiment were well known among Greeks and Romans who dressed the statues of their gods and "... also employed in their temples their personal dressers or *vesitores*."[60] Complicating the debate even further was the veneration of relics in the European Middle Ages continued the practice of recognizing divine agency in sacred objects.[61]

Michael Wayne Cole and Rebecca Zorach conclude that this debate persisted for four hundred years,

> If we were to look for a new art historical designation for the period from 1400 to 1800 CE, we could very well refer to it as "the age of idolatry." To be sure, this was not the first time that artists and writers had concerned themselves with the "idol": idols had long been a preoccupation of theologians and had been common motifs in European art since the middle ages. It would be difficult, nevertheless, to find another moment in the history of the West when the idea of idolatry seemed so vivid and the danger of it so widespread.[62]

Caroline van Eck demonstrates how this debate was accelerated in 1686 in France when Louis XIV attempted to increase his ability to rule by divine right through the creation of a monumental statue. The sculpture was erected in the Palace of Victories with all of the pomp and circumstance that a Roman emperor would have required. The event caused such an outcry that it caused diplomatic problems when German, Dutch, and Spanish effigies of slaves were sculpted under the mighty figure's feet. As if that wasn't enough, when one of the monarch's supporters, the Duc de la Feuillade, not only saluted the sculpture but in the manner of Roman subjects, prostrated in front of the image, there was an outpouring of resentment. Louis was accused of idolatry, prompting an attorney, Francois Lemee, to defend the monarch. The issue in question that became politicized was agency, the effect of the image on those who gazed upon it and the potentially destructive nature of that process.

Van Eck describes this event with particular attention to Lemee's defense encapsulated in a text, *Traite des Statues*, where the author attempted to recast the question of idol worship. While purporting to condemn the treatment of an image of the king as if it were a god, Lemee, "...spends much more time trying to understand and excuse such behavior than in refuting it."[63] This argument, rooted in the assumption that statues and paintings could legitimately express agency opened the door for a new appreciation of art removed from accusations of idolatry. Moreover, the debate that the agency of a work of art could be either creative or destructive not only changed public opinion but secularized long-standing biblical perspectives about the nature of religious experience. During the Enlightenment, philosophers separated art from the domain of religion, the vestiges of this revision were also carried into the conversation. Statues were assumed to have agency, but as Lemee argued, this was appropriate and without the danger that the French public had assumed when the image of Louis was treated as a god. The biblical ambiguity about idolatry had continued, but was augmented by another set of equally ambiguous questions about anthropomorphic art and agency.

In a secularized environment, the role of agency was also assumed to be threatening because it evoked the primitive. David Hume argued that giving objects agency was part of primitive religion.[64] In the same manner, the critics of Louis XIV, saw monuments and statues as potentially threatening to the fabric of civilization. Philosopher Ottaviano de Guasco (1712–1781) in a sophisticated form of Enlightenment rationalism, even recast the view that Egyptian religion was a debased counter religion arguing "...that hieroglyphs were the first, universally understandable, iconic language. They were used by priests in Egypt to write down their religious prescripts, so that they could be understood by the illiterate masses, but became the object of idolatrous adoration because of their very iconicity."[65]

Carrying this same view to sculpture, Guasco saw sculpture as related to primitive beginnings when aniconic forms were seen as infused with divinity.

Ironically, during the same period, in India, questions about embodiment had deeply affected art, but in an entirely different way generated by a different cultural trajectory. Perceptions about the presence of the deity had created a central role for imagination as a means of accessing the deity. This understanding of imagination had also become increasingly ritualized.

Alfred Gell's Anthropology of Images— A Middle Ground Between Symbolism and Embodiment

A challenge to the dominant academic perception that sacred objects were to be understood by their beauty and form came from Alfred Gell, a British anthropologist who had done field work in Melanesia and also among tribal populations in India. Writing in the 1990s, Gell's *Art and Agency* moved into a terrain that had hitherto been unexplored.[66] Gell's prose is dense and his argument is challenging with significant numbers of critiques challenging Gell for not differentiating between aesthetic and religious experiences and for showing little historical awareness.[67] However, beyond his supporters and detractors Gell's approach emerges as one of the few, viable attempts within Western rationalism to come to terms with sacred objects in a way that moves beyond aesthetic experiences.

For Gell, the key to understanding the dynamics of embodiment rests in the concept of agency. In the posthumous publication of *Art and Agency*, Gell defined agency as" ... the source, the origin, of causal events, independently of the state of the physical universe.[68] This suggested that there were characteristics, beyond the physical construction of an object or an image, which not only could be perceived but which could have a significant effect on the observer. Through their ability to employ agency, Gell saw art objects as *indexes* which "...fascinate, compel, and entrap as well as delight the spectator."[69] Indexes were, "...a 'natural sign' ... from which the observer can make a causal inference of some kind, or an inference about the intentions or capabilities of another person."[70]

Gell illustrated the concept of index by describing the role of the sacred *Mukula* tree in *Ndembu* rituals in what was then The Democratic Republic of Congo. Referring to a case study by Victor Turner on rituals of affliction among the *Ndembu*, Gell argued that the *Mukula* wood is an index.[71] When the tree secretes sap, it resembles menstrual blood and is understood by the *Ndembu* to cause reproductive problems among women. Accordingly, "After being worshipped, the tree is ritually cut down, and its wood is carved into figurines resembling babies.... These figurines assisted the afflicted women in regaining their fertility, via further ritual procedures."[72] For Gell, the tree is an index which "...imposes form on the index in its subsequent, carved, state...."[73]

While Gell's argument about *Mukula* wood did not go so far as to find an embodied spirit, it did open a level of inquiry seeing ritual objects as connected to the human psyche beyond the observable, physical characteristics of the thing. As an index, the *Mukula* tree had the ability to express agency and to affect those who venerated it. While this characteristic of the tree was most observable in the carved figurines it was also present in the wood itself. This assumption has significant parallels in iconography, confirming the relevance of Gell's approach to Hindu perceptions of sacred objects. *Viśiṣṭadvaita* philosophy, for example, asserts that the infinite is fully present in the finite. From this perspective, the deity is already present in the stone or the bronze before it is carved or cast in iconographic form. Like the wood of the *Mukula* tree, the raw material is not different in essence from the final, cast bronze and can act on those around it. In this sense, the *mūrti* and the *Mukula* tree are each an index that can draw the observer in, holding their attention by possessing an essential spirit of mystery and transcendence.

Gell's assumptions about the nature of an index rely on the role of passive agency. In the same way that the majority of Hindus do not expect a *mūrti* to consume milk, or to behave in an active manner similar to humans, so the passive nature of the image contributes to its ability to function as an index. Unlike the role of an active agent which attracts human attention by imposing its will on others, so *mūrtis* as passive agents drawing their adherents in through a process of interaction that Gell called intersubjectivity, an intense, symbiotic relationship between image and observer. Intersubjectivity is relational, since, "The god in iconic form, becomes "a manifestation of the social other."[74] The concept of the social other implies a level of connectivity to human affairs yet at the same time is "the other," existing beyond the ordinary. This quality is applicable to Hindu deities which are attributed with social lives, receiving food, cleansing through bathing, finding pleasure through entertainment, and affecting the lives of their devotees. However, in a ritual context they are also the other, affecting devotees in ways they cannot see. This is the case with the child *Krishna*—the butter thief—who repeatedly put his hand in the butter pot to steal what he could in an act typical of children. However, when his mother, Yasoda, opened his mouth to catch him in the act, to her surprise she saw the entire universe.

In Hindu ritual traditions of *pūjā* and *sevā* the role of a deity as a social other also involves passive agency which, in this case, is a visual relationship. Gell describes the relationship as "ocular exchange" since the devotee sees the image and, at the same time, the image "sees" the devotee.[75] In positing this he cites the Hindu practice of *darśan*. Drawn from a Sanskrit root meaning "to see," *darśan* is rooted in the premise that deity is readily accessible in a visual process that is reciprocal. Not only is the devotee looking at the deity, but god is also seeing the devotee.

However, *darśan* is a concept that is explicitly drawn from the trajectory of embodiment and linked to the perception that seeing is not only a human quality but also divine. Gell challenges this, using previous work on *darśan* by Indologists as a place to begin, raising the question whether the icon can actually see. Prefacing his discussion with the assumption that devotees are aware that images are material objects and that they cannot act in the same way as biological organisms, he affirms the role of passive agency and intersubjectivity,

> The question is, what do idols see when they look? What the devotee sees is the idol looking at him or her, performing an act of looking, mirroring his or her own. It is not mysticism on the devotee's part which results in the practical inference that the image "sees" the devotee, because we only ever know what other persons are seeing by knowing what they are looking at.
>
> But the inference that if idols can look, they can see, is not drawn explicitly.... It is projected from judgement (sic) by a further consequence of the mirror–effect. This is the logical regression set up by seeing and being seen. Eye-contact, mutual looking, is a basic mechanism for intersubjectivity because to look into another's eyes is not just to see the other, but to see the other seeing you.... Eye-contact prompts self-awareness of how one appears to the other, at which point one sees oneself "from the outside" as if one were, oneself, an object (or an idol). Eye-contact seems to give direct access to others minds because the subject sees herself as an object, from the point of view of the other as a subject.[76]

In this sense Gell's argument approaches embodiment but does not fully embrace it, rejecting mysticism. Instead, he argues that eye contact is always a two-way process which creates self-awareness. In *darśan*, the devotee experiences the gaze of the deity but also sees the way in which he or she appears to the god. In other words, as the subject of the encounter the devotee also becomes its object.

This is perhaps the most critical point of Gell's argument. Eye contact between two humans produces an active level of agency—each partici-pants "sees" and each also gains a level of self-awareness by virtue of being seen. But, when a devotee gazes at a sacred object Gell suggests that this is also a form of agency, but passive. Much like the *Mukula* tree whose wood is perceived to influence fertility, the tree exhibits passive agency since it does not act. It becomes an index since the wood provokes belief and action when the tree is cut down and fertility figures are carved from it. But the devotee who acquires a *Mukula* wood figurine exhibits active agency. Both active and passive forms of agency are necessary parts of an intersubjective process of ritual exchange in which the devotee gives ven-eration to the wood, and by inference to the tree from which it came, and at the same time receives the benefit of fertility.

Gell's approach walks a fine line between the claims of ontology and psychology. Suggesting that the role of an image is passive in the same way that a doll would be passive for a child, Gell concludes that "Because idols (like dolls) are wholly 'passive' others they exhibit 'passive agency,' the kind of agency attributable to social others who or which, by definition, are only the *target* of agency, never the independent source."[77] He further concludes that. "The idol may not be biologically a 'living thing' but, if it has 'intentional psychology' attributed to it, then it has something like a spirit, a soul, an ego, lodged within it."[78] The passive presence of an image awakens the ability of the devotee to see beyond form, establishing a recip-rocal, intersubjective relationship between devotee and *mūrti*. This dynamic is visible in the *Mūrti Sthapana* ceremony in temples, celebrated for the installation of a deity. The first part of the ritual moves beyond where Gell is not willing to go, stressing ontology,

> There are two ways to understand the *Murti Sthapana* ceremony. The first is as a contract. An agreement is established between the Deity and a temple congrega-tion: the Deity agrees to "descend" into the sacred image, and the congregation agrees to care for the Deity in the form of service, *sevā*. The ceremony is literally the bringing and awakening of the Deity within the stone or metal image.[79]

However, the second part includes assumptions akin to Gell's passive agency,

> The other view is more theological. By definition God is all-pervading and omni-present and so the idea of establishing the breath of the Deity within an image is impossible, God is already there! The purpose of the ceremony is not to establish the Deity within the image, but to awaken the mind of the participants, through the power of ritual, to the presence of divinity within the sacred image. At the begin-ning of the ceremony people see only stone or metal, but at the end they see God! The real installation takes place not in the stone or metal image, but in the minds and hearts of the participants. This is the power of ritual. The culmination of such

a ceremony is when the "eyes" of the image are actually opened. In some instances, a sculptor will chip away at the eyes of the image and "open" them up. More commonly, a chief guest will be invited to remove a covering from the eyes of the image with a golden coin or similar object. The first thing the newly infused Deity will see is an image of Him or Herself as a mirror is held before the newly "awakened" image.[80]

While the deity is already present in the stone or bronze from which images are crafted, devotees cannot see this presence and need the completed, resident *mūrti* in order for the intense relationship to commence. The *sthapathi* who casts the *mūrti* and constructs the temple, and the devotee who is the recipient of their work exhibit active agency. The deity remains passive, but the intersubjectivity between god and worshipper becomes reciprocal. Both active and passive parts of the relationship occur and are each an essential part of the ritual exchange that takes place between deity and devotee.

Part 3: Art and Ritualized Imagination in the Hindu Tradition

The role of the imagination in Hindu thought, and as a component of image worship, reflects the essential differences between cultural trajectories of symbolism and presence. In the West, imagination is an ambiguous term. On one hand it is seen as a positive attribute and associated with an ability to see a range of possibilities. However, in other areas imagination is understood as frivolous and not grounded in reality. Akin to dreams, which are often viewed as peripheral to human existence, imagination is restricted, rarely evoked when conversations turn to pragmatic matters, and often entirely dismissed.

Yet, in Hinduism, imagination is an essential part of image worship. It is, Sthaneshwar Timalsina concludes: "The power of visualization, or imagining something as living and breathing, is essential to worshipping images in the Hindu traditions. In the absence of this imaginative process, images are merely stones."[81] Moreover, he suggests that ritualized imagination is essential,

Contrary to Western traditions, Indian traditions give centrality to imagination. Imagining, following Hindu philosophies, is a power that can constitute and transform reality. We observe this role of imagination in the ritual of visualization where a deity image is mentally construed and receives ritual offerings. This prominence of imagination is also crucial in viewing an image as living and breathing. The very beginning of image worship has utilized this primacy of imagination. In this sense, ritualized imagination functions as an engineering capacity of the cognitive faculty of imagination.[82]

Ritualized imagination includes the process of visualization which is well known both in the Hindu tradition and in Tibetan Buddhism where *lāmās* recreate mental images of *bodhisattvas*, bringing to life and energizing these figures in their minds. In Hinduism, visualization is referred to as *mānas pūjā*, offering gifts of food and caring for a deity as a mental process. *Mānas pūjā* can be done both with an image and also as entirely a mental exercise in which the acts of worship are completely done in the mind. Both rely extensively on the ability of the devotee to exercise imagination and to evoke the deity with concentrated mental energy.

Pichhavais and the Role of Ritualized Imagination in a Hindu *Bhakti* Tradition

In 1973, art historian Robert Skelton published a catalogue of *pichhavais* (temple hangings) entitled *Rajasthani Temple Hangings of the Krishna Cult.*[83] *Pichhvais* were used to create a pleasing devotional atmosphere in *Pushtimarg* temples which were construed as *"havelī"* or home for different manifestations of the child god *Krishna*. They had been largely unknown in the West until the display by the American Federation of Arts and the personal collection of Karl Mann. Both men had distinguished careers, Mann as an artist and Skelton as former keeper of the India Department at the Victoria and Albert Museum and a noted art historian. The temple hangings were presented as devotional art with a full description of the tenets of the *Vallabha Sampradaya* from which they had come with careful scholarly attention to detail. However, what was most notable about Skelton's presentation, was its emphasis on aesthetics. He concluded,

> The whole tenor of worship in this sect is directed toward the development of aesthetic enjoyment and the word *rāsa* (primary meaning: sap or juice) which denotes this, among other meanings, is also applied to the deity himself and alludes to his ineffable bliss. With this concentration on visual display and aesthetic enjoyment in the presentation of the deity to his devotees, it is not surprising that the larger and more spectacular of these cloth hangings have excited appreciation for their aesthetic qualities alone.[84]

Skelton's publication marked the entry of *pichhavais* into the art world and their place in the context of religious art. However, with this emphasis on aesthetics and symbolism, what this early scholarship missed was the role of ritualized imagination as an integral part of the five-hundred-year-old tradition of *pichhavais* production. As integral parts of worship, *pichhavais* hang behind a *swarūp*, an image that carried the full presence of the deity and were created through a ritualized process of creation. *Pichhavais* were not considered to be art in the Western sense since their purpose was not to create a display that would be aesthetically pleasing to the deity's observers, as much as to create a backdrop that, like the *swarūp* itself, could be inhabited by the god as a purified, sanctified space.

The process of ritualized imagination in the production of *pichhavais* emanates from the earliest beginnings of the sect in the sixteenth century in Rajasthan. The role of artists was not only to create an aesthetic experience, but instead to participate in a mystical tradition that combined craft and spirituality. Each stage of the artist's work was governed by a teacher, analogous to the tradition of *guru* and student (*chela*), who together worked to create a rarified mindset that could access the deity through the painting.

Ritualized imagination played an important role in each stage of the process. Artists were trained to approach their craft akin to a process of meditation. Visualization of the deity was essential. Color was added to the temple hanging not only to create a pleasing appearance but to incorporate natural substances in which the deity's presence was already apparent. *Pichhavais* artists never relied on commercial products but instead ground their paints from natural substances. Desmond Peter Lazaro describes color as a sacred quality. For example, the "yellow pigment," *godhūli*, is,

> ... a sacred colour a gift from the Holy Cow. This gift recalls the Puranic account of Prithvi, the mother goddess, who seeks refuge in the form of a cow to flee from the advances of the first king Prithu. The cow, a symbol of Krishna, then gives "earthly" light in the form of a color *gougli* (sic). It is believed that the colour is extracted from the urine of a cow; therefore to venerate the colour is to venerate Krishna himself.[85]

The creation of a *pichhavais* extends beyond symbolism and is connected to the trajectory of embodiment, with a symbiotic relationship to the *mūrti*. The process of executing the *pichhavais* is not done for the pleasure of an audience but rather relies on the process of creating a highly refined imagination in which the artist visualizes the deity, creating a mirror image of his presence on the cloth. The *pichhavais* cannot be fully understood apart from the *swarūp* in front of it. Both are part of an integral relationship in which the *swarūp* is fully present. In Nathdwara, the central temple of the tradition, crowds press against each other for a view of *Shri Nathji* in all his splendor. Pilgrims speak of the god's radiating presence throughout Nathdwara, emanating from the central shrine. All of this is not just the result of an aesthetic experience, but from the assumption of embodiment in which *swarūp* and *pichhavais* are part of a sacred presence.

Ritualized imagination includes the transformation of the physical properties of color and cloth into a sacred object. Unlike the role if imagination in Western art forms, here it is analogous to a process of unveiling in which each stage of the work unpeels another layer of separation between artist and deity. The relationship between *guru* and resident artist is a critical part of the process in which imagination is part of a path governed by lineages of master artists, each of whom were full participants in a tradition that emphasizes *darśan*—visual experience that contains the full presence of deity.

Ritualized Imagination and Sound and Dance

Ritualized imagination not only affects schools of religious art but is also intimately tied to sound. The entire process may include *mantra, image,* and *maṇḍala*.[86] Image worship both incorporates geometric projections of sacred space (*maṇḍalas*), images crafted as receptacles for divine energy, and vocalization (*mantras*) specifically designed to evoke the energy of the deity that has come to reside in the *mūrti*, "While mantras are recited, they are also viewed as an image. In order to see the mantras, specific phonemes are mentally placed in different centers of the body (whether in the body of the deity or in the body of the practitioner), and the viewer actively imagines a direct correlation between the phonemes and the corporeal limbs."[87]

It is at this point that the cultural trajectories of symbolism and embodiment move in entirely different directions. In both biblical and Enlightenment thought, where religion is associated with anthropomorphized forms of monotheism, imagination is a source of error and illusion. By depending on the imagination the devotee creates a level of reality that is not present, engaging in a form of error that misses the biblical word and fails to confront deity. However, in Hindu thought, the sensory world is false to begin with. Only through imagination in conjunction with *mūrtis, maṇḍalas,* and images, can the true nature of things be seen and understood. Moreover, the role of embodiment is a form of presence, moving beyond symbol or metonym, confronting the worshipper not with reason or empirical knowledge but with a level of presence that defines a reality that would otherwise be invisible. This aspect of imagination is readily apparent in the *Rās Līlā* in North Indian *bhakti* tradition where both ritualized imagination and visualization are used to evoke the presence of *Krishna. Rās Līlās* take a number of forms.

The *Rās Līlā*—Ritualized Imagination in Dance and Drama

The *Rās Līlā* is an important part of the wider North Indian *Vaiṣṇava bhakti* tradition that connects embodiment with imagination in a form of impromptu and seasonal rituals. On one hand the *Rās Līlā* is a drama, performed in the forests of Braj, associated with *Krishna* and his consort, *Radha*. On the other, it is an impromptu circular dance that is performed in any locations and frequently both in India and abroad in temples. In both cases imagination is key to the significance of the rite, "The Vaisnavite tradition, then, is totally unembarrassed about the role imagination plays in the religious life. If the worship of images sounds like playing with dolls, let it. It is the spirit, the affection, the bhava ... that counts, and it is the dramatic situation that makes this flow of emotion possible."[88]

In both of its forms, John Stratton Hawley suggests that as a drama the *Rās Līlā* is analogous to temple traditions where *Krishna* is not only fully present but has much the same function as an actor on a stage, connecting the audience with a hidden form of reality that becomes visible in the flow of emotion.[89] As a dance the *Rās Līlā* is impromptu, yet its dependence on imagination is also a requirement that each dancer understands. Here, imagination is not the stuff of frivolity or fancy but instead a gateway to a rarified, hidden level of experience. Each of the female dancers who moves in a circle looks for *Krishna* who, she believes, appears only to her. Although cast in the context of romantic attraction between *gopīs* and deity, the dancers seek sight of him as a form of transcendence that makes all other visual experiences meaningless. *Gopīs* leave their families and their responsibilities looking in the forests of Braj for *Krishna*.

Dancing under the stars the *Rās Līlā* captures a mystical level of awareness in which the community of dancers evokes him but his manifestation is always personal, appearing to each *gopī* at the same time but convincing each that he is only there for her. As the circle dance accelerates to a crescendo of emotion and movement, *Krishna* not only appears on the periphery but also in the center. *Pichhavais* that depict the *Rās Līlā* often symbolize this central appearance of the deity by an empty circle within the circle of dancers. It is empty because it is the *Krishna* beyond form, an expression of the ineffable nature of the deity that moves beyond the dance.

As a drama, the *Rās Līlā* employs the same connections with imagination as a way of perceiving embodiment. Traditionally celebrated in the forests of Braj during the monsoon months, the play relies on actors who are understood as *swarūps*, a term which in *Pushtimarg* is understood as the most complete form of embodiment of deity in an icon.[90] Both image and actor in the *Rās Līlā* have a similar function. Through a process of ritual production the image is crafted as a receptacle that will house a resident deity. On a stage the actors perform much the same function. In both cases, again, imagination is critical but not a cursory form of fancy. Hawley suggests that imagination and reason work together in a symbiotic process of rarified awareness,

> Everyone knows that images do not actually eat the food that is offered in temples. As I was reminded in a Brindavan tea stall, if God ate food such as we eat, there would scarcely be any way to satisfy him! Rather, he allows the game of feeding him for our benefit. It is symbolic action and would have value but for the belief, the mood with which it is infused. God dines on our love, not our food. And so it is with the plays. People do not believe in the svarūps in the way that children believe in Santa Claus; they know perfectly well that these are normal children. In fact they must be local children, born in Braj, to qualify for their roles—hence, entirely unmystified, completely normal. The mystery is quite the other way around. These are plays in which children enact the naturalness of childhood in order to stir the imagination of adults; the best Krishna is the one who acts most like himself, a child unbridled.[91]

In this sense, in temples, in the *Rās Līlā* drama, and in the circle dance, devotees are aware of the demands of the physical world. They know that *mūrtis* and *swarūps* are castings in the same way that they are fully aware in the forests of Braj that the actors are the sons and daughters of people they know. However, imagination is not uniform and schemas of interpretation abound. For instance, *Pushtimarg* devotees often talk about the ways in which their *lālans* (a devotional term used to describe a *swarūp* worshipped at home and the principal image of a devotee) play tricks on them often in the physical context of the ritual. Similarly, in the drama children "stir the imagination of adults" who may experience the drama as transformative, encountering *Krishna* in the same way as *gopīs* in the circular dance. In this sense it is irrelevant if the actors are understood to literally become the dark Lord or if *Krishna* becomes the actors on a stage. What the imagination requires is the assumption that he can be fully present in microcosm or macrocosm in a level of transcendence that goes beyond symbol and meaning in a level of embodiment so powerful that *gopīs* and those who worship him are absorbed in his presence. But this also begs a further question, what happens when ritualized imagination becomes grounded in a temporal reality that eviscerates the connections between art and religion?

Conclusion

The ambiguity and confusion that museum displays of Hindu images create within the transnational Hindu community are not only the product of the collision of the trajectories of embodiment and symbolism in a globalized world, but also emanate from the history of museums as cultural repositories in which sacred objects have been removed from their ritual contexts. As the Hindu temple institutionalized the trajectory of embodiment in India, so the West formally established the trajectory of material symbolism in the museum. Bolstered by torrents of Enlightenment philosophy that separated the spiritual from the material, museums were initially developed as instruments of colonialism. Reifying nationalism, interpreting European cultural histories, and casting developing nations as lesser civilizations, museums became the vanguard of dominance of the Western world and its ideology drawn from assumptions about capitalism and material culture.

The British Museum and the Louvre led the West in these pursuits, gathering collections of antiquities from all over the world and proudly displaying artifacts from a globalized British Empire that preserved and protected cultural remains. The Louvre gathered collections from Egypt, Mesopotamia, Greece, Rome, and other parts of the ancient world installing them in a former palace, reflecting the ambiance of power. Within this context sacred objects were displayed as art. In the Neues Museum in Berlin, the bust of Nefertiti, part of the divine family of Akhenaten, was proudly put on view. In Paris, the stele of Hammurabi, the first law code and predecessor of the Ten Commandments, was installed alongside art and artifacts. In Cairo, the Egyptian Museum, first constructed in 1835 on a model of Western museums, proudly displayed the gold funerary mask of Tutankhamen, created to protect the pharaoh's mummy and never intended for public display.

Museums showcased artifacts that throughout the nineteenth century would on a variety of levels of ambiguity have been perceived as forms of idolatry. While motivation for these displays was also to preserve parts of the ancient world, at the same time there is little doubt of the alternative motive for showcasing empire. This is evident in the early history of World's Fairs in the United States which became open air museums, achieving much the same ends as displays housed in permanent structures. In Chicago, in 1893, the Columbian Exposition did this by placing Western exhibits of technology, warfare, and invention in the center of the theme park. On the periphery of the sprawling "White City," developing nations opened their exhibits, in sight of the core industrial nations, but clearly the purpose of the exhibition had a lesser position. The World's Parliament of Religions, appended to the Columbian Exposition, did not even appear on the fair grounds and was showcased in the Art Institute of Chicago, far away from the exhibits of the Christian industrialized nations where power was concentrated and proudly displayed.

The Western art world in conjunction with museums thus managed to separate the trajectories of symbolism and embodiment. Visitors to museums could see for the first time exhibits of Hindu deities showcased in glass but removed from their ritual context. Catalogued by period, style, and name of the deity, museum exhibits rarely presented the deity clothed or in a setting that would have been conducive to worship. To the West, they were cast in much the same vein as older aesthetically pleasing collections of artifacts—vestiges of lesser civilizations.

Museum displays presented obvious flaws. Exhibitions could only showcase sacred objects as artifacts of civilizations and could not house them in the context for which they were designed as forms of embodied presence. As globalization accelerated in the 1990s and as fresh infusions of Hindu immigrants entered the United States, these flaws became more noticeable. Hindu communities raised objections when gods were taken out of their ritual context. Hindu publications, intended to reach transnational populations in the West, objected to expressions of symbolism as the dominant means for interpreting the role of images. In a hybridized Western environment, where both the trajectories of material symbolism and embodiment could now be found in close quarters, the forces of accelerated globalization had produced confusing arrays of interpretation.

FIVE

Transnational Hinduism and Shifting Trajectories

Characteristics of Transnational Hindu Populations

Hindu populations in the West are part of a globalized environment in which the mainstays of tradition—caste, village life, the extended family and the lasting influence of the trajectory of embodiment—are in flux. In the United States and Europe these communities experience the loss of sacred geography and observe disparity and ambiguity in the way that sacred images are defined. At the same time they also experience a highly networked, layered form of religion that is adaptive as it attempts to meet the needs of the dominant first generation and the growing numbers of second- and third-generation Hindu transplanted communities. The adaptation of cultural and religious practices is a phenomenon of the immigrant experience irrespective of the origin of the migrant. The universal is, however, also characterized by particular manifestations within Hindu communities.

The Loss of Sacred Geography

India's sacred geography is an expression of the trajectory of embodiment. The subcontinent is filled with places where deities were born, spent their childhood, lived out their lives, and performed superhuman feats. Every corner of the subcontinent is identified with a theophany. *Krishna* was born in Mathura and spent his childhood in the forests of Braj. Later, as an adult, he migrated from Mathura to Dwarka and established his kingdom. Haridwar, at the foothills of the Himalayas is revered for the footprints of *Vishnu*. Kashi, is the holy city of *Shiva* who is its primary resident. Rameswaram, in southern India is tied to the exploits of the god *Rama* who initiated the movement of his army from there to rescue his consort, *Sita*, held captive in Sri Lanka by the demon, *Ravana*. Hindus know these stories intimately and connect with each place in the most personal of ways. The subcontinent is alive with a multiplicity of stories of these and other gods who are not only identified by their adventures but by the very places within which they happened.

> The language of embodiment is the narrative of sacred places. Place and deity are conjoined in the same manner as *mūrtis* and deity are one in the same. Diana Eck concludes,
> The landscape not only connects places to the lore of the gods, heroes, and saints, but it connects places to one another through local, regional, and transregional practices of pilgrimage. Even more, these tracks of connection stretch from this world toward the horizon of the infinite, linking this world with the world beyond. The pilgrim's India is a vividly imagined landscape that has been created not by honing in on the singular importance of one place, but by the linking, duplication, and multiplication of places so as to create an entire world.[1]

Sacred images of the gods not only contain their presence but also embody the heart of this landscape. To connect with an image of *balkrishna* is to move into Braj where every hill and river front is associated with the child *Krishna*. To perform *pūjā* or *sevā* to a bronze image of *Krishna* is also to be transported to the forests where devotees wait to see him.

However, for second- and third-generation transnational Hindus in the West, this sacred geography is not lived but is a reference point for a belief system and for ethnic and cultural identity. It is a land far removed from their experience and a place that they may periodically visit but never reside within. Geographical and experiential separation modifies perceptions. The environment they inhabit results in a level of separation from any sacred landscape which relegates it to a place their parents and grandparents may have experienced but a domain outside their immediate purview. Their understanding is mediated through the stories of their elders' firsthand experiences. Intimacy is diluted by time and by space. Their world experience is not that of parents or grandparents.

This loss of an important part of Hindu tradition has informed controversies that on the surface appear to be about academic concerns but in reality point toward the separation from sacred space. For example, in a controversy in 2005, the *Vedic Foundation* in Texas and the *American Hindu Education Foundation* challenged textbooks on a number of fronts including caste, the role of women in India and the Indo-Aryan migration theory. The migration theory had been developed by nineteenth-century Orientalists and had become standard fare in academic courses about Hinduism. It argued that nomadic Aryan peoples moved from central Asia to north India around 1500 BCE. The theory disputed suggestions that indigenous Dravidian peoples authored the *Vedas*, the central scriptures of Hinduism. American anthropologists and historians of religion found themselves in heated discussions with Hindus who argued that the *Vedas* could not have been written outside India. For them, India's geography also defined sacred texts.

In 2016, tensions erupted again, this time focusing on editors' decisions to replace the designation "Indian" with "South Asian." The regional designation had been used in scholarly works in history, and the social sciences since the mid–twentieth century to describe the peoples of the Indian subcontinent and the nation states of Pakistan, Bangladesh, Sikkim, Bhutan, Nepal and Sri Lanka. However, the reaction among immigrants in the United States was not about the accuracy of the term but rather the loss of the designation "Indian" and its connections to sacred geography.

A high school freshman, Vidhima Shetty, told the review committee that using the term "South Asian" would be akin to asking her to change her name.

> Names are what define us as people; they represent character and personality. The board is confusing our cultural terms with geographical terms. By removing India as a term from the textbooks this leaves Indian-American children with no ethnic or cultural identification to turn to. When we acknowledge ourselves as South Asians, us Hindus are forced to re-identify ourselves as something we are not.[2]

The debate revealed the changes that the transnational Hindu community had already internalized, replacing the language of sacred presence and geography with the rhetoric of ethnic identification and heritage. At the same time it also reflected political polarization in India and the attempt by the Indian government of Prime Minister Modi to create a strong Hindu nationalist movement.

The difference between the language of identity and the rhetoric of sacred geography and embodiment is considerable. Pilgrims speak of the healing power of sacred rivers and the majesty of the mountains that are associated with the presence of deity. Visitors to Mount Kailash in Tibet speak of the abode of *Shiva* and in many cases the power of the waters of Lake Manasarowar. In like manner pilgrims in the forests of Braj talk about the presence of *Krishna*. David Haberman writes of his experience near a pond, Prema Sarovar, in the heart of Braj where geography and theophany became one in the same as an image of *Radha* and *Krishna* appeared,

> I walked out onto the meditation platform on the northern side of the pond and sat down to rest. I looked into the water. It was a dark green color and appeared to be very deep. Something about it attracted me. I stared into its depths, lost in silence. Suddenly, I became aware that I was no longer alone. I started and turned around. Standing behind me was Maya…. She spoke, instructing me with a firm voice, "Look into the pond. Fix your eyes on the surface of the water."
>
> I did as she said. The first thing I noticed was the reflection on the surface of the pond. The slightest breeze created ever-changing patterns of shapes and colors. The visual designs, momentarily appearing and disappearing, were something like an impressionist painting viewed up close … "you must use the eyes of the body given to you by Yamuna Ji," Maya insisted. A shiver ran up my spine. I wondered what she was referring to….
>
> She instructed me to return my gaze to the surface of the pond. My attention went back to the creation and destruction of the random patterns produced by the crests and valleys of the ripples. I shifted my focus back and forth between these two scenes, I was not certain what I was supposed to be looking at, when Maya bent over and whispered something into my ear. Suddenly, a third scene appeared, neither in the crests nor in the valleys but out of the plain created by the oscillating motion of the two. A whole new world became visible.
>
> I was looking at a dense forest of flowering trees in which stood a woman and a man. She had a golden complexion and was dressed in a blue sari; he was of a dark color and wore a yellow dhoti. She had flowers braided into her long black hair; he wore a garland of flowers behind his neck and had a peacock feather stuck in his hair.[3]

Haberman's experience described the power of place in the context of India's sacred geography. The rhetoric of place is that of embodiment as the land itself becomes the bearer of divine presence. His vision in the pond was not isolated from the space that contained it but, instead, maintained a symbiotic relationship with it. The place became the guide to the perception of a deeper level of reality and a vision of the mother goddess.

India's sacred geography is punctuated by myriads of festivals, each connecting the land to the embodiment of deity. In the *Kumbh Melā* festival held every 12 years in Haridwar, Allahabad, Nashik, and Ujjain, pilgrims experience the confluence of rivers where they can immerse themselves in sacred waters. The festival, has been celebrated for over 2500 years and, in 2013, attracted 120 million people. These and other ritual occasions help define a living sacred geography. Villages become microcosms of the same experiences, marked through animistic practices in which rocks, rivers, and trees are also understood as components of the wider sacred geography. The rivers are understood to contain sacred presence in the same way that a bronze or stone *mūrti* embodies the deity.

One has only to listen to the voices of second- and third-generation Hindu children in the West describing their perception of images to understand the absence of the trajectory of embodiment. In 1997 when the Smithsonian Institution conducted a series of conversations with Hindu children in the United States about *pūjā,* responses from the children were illuminating. One respondent concluded,

> People ask, "Why does the god Ganesha have an elephant's head?" Well, the elephant is considered one of the wisest animals, and Ganesha is a very wise god. His big ears mean he listens a lot. His mouth is generally covered, which means he doesn't speak too much. He is very wise because he doesn't talk too much and he listens. So the elephant head is a simple way of reminding us of this. Each idol provides a focus so that you can concentrate on that one aspect of religion. You aren't praying to the idol, it is just a path to God. Some people need something to focus on, others don't. It's there if you need it.[4]

To the student, praying to an "idol" could be helpful, but was not necessary. The image remained a symbol that provided "a path to God" but was little more than that. In keeping with Western tradition, the elephant was a good listener as suggested by his large ears and therefore was understood to be quite wise. In the same way the student suggested that she was not praying to the "idol" (incorporating a Western term with negative connotations).

Conflict Vetween Trajectories in American Popular Culture

While the respect of second- and third-generation Hindu Americans for their parents and grandparents tends to mitigate conflicts between trajectories within families, conflict periodically has emerged publicly. An example of such confluence and conflict emerged in 2014, when an art exhibit in Buenos Aries displayed a Barbie doll dressed as the goddess *Kali.* Rajan Zed (who, as described in Chapter Four, had also criticized a mural at the Brooklyn museum), organized a protest,

> Calling the depicting of Barbie doll as goddess Kali as highly inappropriate, Zed had urged the artists to not include Barbie-ized goddess Kali in the show as it trivialized the highly revered deity of Hinduism. Goddess Kali, who personified Shakti or divine energy and considered the goddess of time and change, was widely worshipped in Hinduism.[5]

Zed's efforts were successful and the artist cancelled the exhibit. While figures from other religious traditions were also used in the same exhibit,

Hindus felt that the display was particularly offensive. Underneath the discontent, the event attempted to conflate both cultural trajectories, making Barbie and *Kali* one in the same. In the West, dolls are highly symbolic and have a long history of use as symbolic forms of material culture. In particular, Barbie has evolved as a cultural image in which she "...is treated as a symbol of consumer culture and a barometer of attitudes toward women."[6] Barbie became such a powerful symbol that the imagery was also critiqued as sexist, "The whole point of the Barbie doll is that she owns things and buys things," said Professor Motz, who published a study of Barbie in 1983. She said that the doll, if copied to scale as a life-size woman, would have a torso measuring 33 inches at the bust, 18 inches at the waist and 28 inches at the hips—a feminine ideal that, she pointed out, is "almost not possible anatomically."[7] What the discussion overlooked was the powerful nature of *Kali* as a mother goddess whose presence was potentially destructive and needed to be appeased rather than viewed as a "sex symbol."

While discussions about Barbie broach controversial discussions about sexism, femininity, and American culture, they are far apart from conversations about embodiment. Beyond the culture wars in the West about the ability of Barbie to be seen as a cultural image or mass-marketed symbol of American capitalism and greed, the consensus was that the doll was symbolic. When she was depicted as the goddess *Kali*, not only were the symbols of Western commercial culture offensive but the cultural trajectory of a *mūrti* as embodied presence was overlooked.

Tanisha Ramachandran argues that the commercialization of images of Hindu gods is not as much of a problem as is the depiction of deities in polluting contexts.[8] While she is undoubtedly correct, commercial venues may become problematic when they extract deities from the context of embodiment. This was the case with the debate about Barbie when presented as *Kali* and the mural depicting the goddess in the Brooklyn Museum. In both cases the environment in which the deity was presented was not polluting. The museum display was public while Barbie was offered commercially. While Hindus may not always be offended by commercial images of deities, their removal from the context of embodiment and immersion in art or marketing environments can provoke conflict. What is at stake in these debates, which are often initiated by first-generation immigrants, is the erosion of the cultural trajectory of embodiment in in the West.

At times, the absence of an understanding of embodiment has been conflated with the arrogance of empire in India during the British period when missionaries cast aspersions on Hinduism. An article in *Hinduism Today*, written in 2005, years before the Brooklyn Museum debate, attempted to correlate the damage done by missionaries with Western assumptions that material culture was symbolic, "In recent history, missionaries and others from the Western religions have told the Indian people over and over again that their gods are not real beings, but merely symbols of spiritual matters—and unfortunately many have begun to believe this and look at their gods in this way."[9] In the article, the two parallel words of nineteenth- and early twentieth-century empire and twenty-first-century globalized Hindu culture both remained in place. This was ironic given the motivation for expatriate Hindus who left the arrogance of empire behind only to find similar aspersions about their culture in Western attitudes toward sacred objects. In both cases, the divide between the trajectories of symbolism and embodiment was unyielding.

Networking

While social and religious networks matured in British India, extending well beyond traditional Hindu networks based on caste (*jāti*) and religion, they have taken an expansive role in connecting Hindu communities in the age of globalization. Social and religious networking expanded to meet a variety of needs of a burgeoning Hindu transnational community. Whereas, expatriate Hindu communities in the nineteenth century were small and self-contained within themselves, the immigrant community size exploded in the twentieth century throughout the United Kingdom, the United States, the Middle East, Canada, Australia, and Southeast Asia. At the same time advances in technology and travel made communication with the homeland easier and cheaper.

Jonathan Friedman's premise that socially shared experience is an important dynamic in a globalized world has clear applications to Hindu communities outside India.[10] Online forms of Hinduism make borders and geographical distance irrelevant. The *Shri Vaishnava* tradition, once a bastion of Tamil orthodoxy that traced its orthodoxy to the eleventh-century philosopher, Ramanuja, has been associated with northern and southern forms in Kanchipuram and Srirangam in Tamilnadu. However, with increasing Hindu transnationalism, the shared experiences of this ritual community have looked to electronic forms of networking. Online e-classes are now offered by the *Shri Vaishnava* community, with additional support both from radio and television. A *Shri Vaishnava* Digital Fund raises money for publications and in 2016 had already completed two books.[11]

Similarly, an internet search for another form of shared experience, *satsaṅg* (religious gatherings among devotees), produces a host of networking opportunities. *Satsaṅgs* may regularly meet online or communally. As shared experiences, as Vasquez and Marquardt suggest, they may bridge messages of universal salvation and existential needs.[12] This is often in the context of multiple functions. Prema Kurian concludes that *satsaṅg* groups meet periodically in the United States where they conduct *pūjā*, chant *bhajans*, and discuss sacred texts.[13] While such group activity is not as common in India were family worship is prevalent,[14] it is a mainstay of transnational Hinduism and dependent on fresh levels of networking.

Global religious networks also provide collective identities. Judit Bokser-Liwerant describes them as—"…patterns of similarity and dissimilarity constructed in order to build social boundaries: social construction and the maintenance of trust and solidarity among the members of a collective (to) become its central core."[15] If Bokser-Liwerant is correct, in an age of accelerated globalization, trust and solidarity are the hallmarks of religious networks that, much like the secret Chinese societies in the nineteenth century, provided important ways of retaining cultural identity. Moreover, globalized networks have evolved during a time of "conflicting epistemologies" when ways of knowing are changing and competing with one another, negating the possibility that any single cultural trajectory or perspective can become normative.

Transnational religious networks can also be both local and international at the same time.[16] They also can appear to be primarily assimilative but may reflect global movements.[17] These variables make religious networks particularly important and difficult to understand since they may be fulfilling a variety of functions simultaneously. This has also been the case with globalized forms of terrorism such as ISIS or the Islamic Brotherhood that have used advances in technology to foster patterns of religious identity cross culturally.

Finally, networking in an increasingly globalized world offers opportunities to voice multiple levels of identity freed from fixed notions of community identification. This presents opportunities for persons with a vested interest in the trajectory of embodiment to share experiences and perspectives. It also encourages members of the second and third generations to explore the symbolic meaning of sacred images. In both cases, each trajectory is also integral to patterns of identity. Second- and third-generation Hindu Americans often define themselves as millennials and share common perceptions of material culture with their peers. This is in contrast with first-generation immigrants, who may bring *mūrtis* with them from India, and continue patterns of embodiment that they learned as children.

First-generation networks in the West also include a cadre of entrepreneurs who have founded temples and who are deeply committed to the trajectory of embodiment. United by common perspectives about the nature of Hindu *mūrtis* and the need for temples as residences for the gods, they are the voice of established tradition. Interlocking networks of priests, *gurus, goswāmīs,* and temple designers also evoke the same trajectory. Yet, second- and third-generation transnational Hindus have been remarkably absent in the design or management of temples in the West. Their networks are layered in a way typical of the millennial generation that they represent with a heavy participation in all forms of social media, the formation of temple youth groups, and family networks.

Layering and Networking

In an increasingly globalized world accelerated contact between different cultural trajectories has produced a layered, highly networked tradition where alternate points of view remain equally visible, often held by different parts of the same communities. In this context a new immigrant, no matter what period in which they arrived, is always first generation while their children and grandchildren form the second and third generations.

On one hand, priests, *gurus,* temple leaders, and many first-generation immigrants may perceive images through a traditional lens of embodiment. On the other hand, large numbers of second- and third-generation children, acculturated in non–Hindu environments, may see them as symbolic. The two trajectories do not represent opposing points of view and are not a dichotomy. Rather, they are expressions of culture and belief that for centuries have been isolated but have now been brought into the same terrain by advances in communication, travel, and the resulting effect on immigration. The combined result of these approaches is a globalized Hinduism defined by layers of interpretations that are no longer separated by distance. As a result, transnational forms of Hinduism are increasingly pluralistic, accommodating and affirming multiple levels of interpretation in order to meet the needs of a religiously diverse population.

The layering of cultural trajectories of embodiment and symbolism in the West is a product of the ability of each trajectory to align itself with people of similar beliefs. Networks conjoin populations with similar perspectives beyond national borders. Manuel Castells concludes that before the advent of a fully globalized world, networks "...were the domain of the private life, while the world of production, power, and war was occupied by large, vertical organizations, such as states, churches, armies, and corporations that could marshal vast pools of resources around the purpose defined by a central authority."[18] However, as cultures become increasingly globalized, these limitations are removed as decentralized networks move beyond borders, quickly adapting to change, and enabling different cultural trajectories to coexist among the same population. In the United States, this process is influenced by the strength of the first generation which continues to be the dominant South Asian population. In 2010, 87.2 percent of Indian-American adults were foreign-born, the highest percentage among the six largest Asian-American groups; 37.6 percent of those had been in the U.S. 10 years or less. One consequence of so many Indian Americans having arrived so recently: Only 56.2 percent of adults were U.S. citizens, the lowest share among the six subgroups studied in detail.[19]

This remarkable statistic has had important ramifications for the development of the Hindu religious landscape and may be a primary reason for the continued proliferation of Hindu temples in the United States. It also suggests that processes of Westernization and assimilation may move at different rates among first, second, and third generations. Members of the first generation often have continuing business interests and family ties in India, many owning property both in the United States and in South Asia, and have a fully transnational existence. Markedly different from earlier patterns of migration, this form of globalization provides multiple opportunities for maintaining forms of Hinduism while living in America. At the same time, it suggests that patterns of assimilation and cultural identity for second- and third-generation Hindu Americans are quite different. Hindu children in the United States have a primary identity as Americans and, only as family opportunities provide, can forge a second identity in concert with traditions in the homeland. For some, where families provide opportunities for frequent travel to India, speak Indian languages in the home, and teach traditional patterns of religion and culture, a bi-cultural identity is standard. Yet for others, in families who have resided in the United States for a long time, who have moved parents and grandparents to North America, and who now identify with the cultural institutions in the Unites States, bi-cultural opportunities for their children may be diluted.

Layering and Religion

To some extent, religious traditions are already adept at layering. Most have experienced layered traditions brought about through periods of orthodoxy and heterodoxy, as well as periods of intense change through movement across borders. The early transition of Buddhism outside India, across the Silk Road into western China is an example. In China, Buddhists affirmed a larger *Mahayana* tradition replete with complex cosmologies that the earlier *Theravada* tradition did not have. At the same time through contact with forms of Taoism, Chinese Buddhism adopted multiple levels of tradition in the same culture exhibiting a cumulative presence. While variations in tradition eventually produced sects, Chinese Buddhism became layered in the process with successive levels of interpretation and understanding as new traditions replaced older ones and as heterodox forms of faith achieved their own level of orthodoxy.

However, the layering of theological and ritual traditions in the developmental history of religions is quite different from the layering of cultural trajectories of entire civilizations in an age of accelerated globalization. Within Hindu history, for example, it is not difficult to find examples of theological and ritual differences in the same community. These differences are compounded by complex sectarian, familial, caste, temple, and village traditions and have been part of the religious landscape for centuries. Yet, despite this complex layering of tradition, cultural trajectories remained intact. Few Hindus in traditional settings in India, for instance, would question the cultural trajectory of purity and pollution which has a far broader part in Hindu civilization than any sectarian tradition could ever encompass. Hindu perceptions of pollution are dependent on caste, sources of ritual contamination, as well as cultural perceptions of sacred space. Yet, in a transnational environment, where the trajectory of Hindu purity exists alongside societal perceptions of cleanliness, the result is a layered perspective that can exist in the same space. Affluent Hindu homes in the United States often exhibit both trajectories conforming to societal values of cleanliness and opulence, reflecting the American Dream. Yet, within these houses shrine rooms offer different understandings of purity. Shoes are removed before entering and any meat products, which would pollute the environment, are removed.

In transnational Hindu communities in the West different generational perspectives about purity may exist in the same family, community, or temple. In temples, priests wash before performing *pūjā*, avoid contact with devotees, and retain the same standards that they would in India. Members of the first generation who have recently arrived from India may retain caste related standards of purity even though the caste system does not survive in the West. By contrast, their children, who have never experienced the constraints of caste-based traditions, while conforming to their parent's expectations about purity inside the home, align their perspectives with other millennials once outside.

Differences about purity and pollution between Hindus in India and in the West often focus on the role of the kitchen in extremely complex alignments of caste (*jāti*) and patterns of familial life, as well as cultural perceptions in which the kitchen is analogous to the temple as the locus of purity. In India, where Indian hospitality is a predominant part of the culture, visitors may experience a cordial welcome and be fed lavish meals. But few will ever enter the family's kitchen which is a center of ritual purity and easily defiled. Yet, among second- and third-generation families in the West, this is not seen as a priority and there are few ways of maintaining the same standards. American practices of social gatherings in the kitchen, the role of meat in diets, and the absence of any religious prohibitions that prevent persons of differing ritual status from eating together cannot be maintained. Moreover, even when Hindu families in the West practice vegetarianism at home, their sons and daughters participate in the wider culture where segregated patterns of dining would not be understood. Among transnational Hindu families layering becomes an essential part of lifestyle as Hindu and Western cultural trajectories about purity find a way to coexist.

Layering is also complicated by the period of time in which the first generation entered the United States. In some older Indian communities immigrant families can still be found who entered the country prior to the 1965 immigration reforms, although these numbers are quite small. However, after the passage of the amendment to the Immigration and Nationality Act, a new first-generation entered the county, establishing families. As the flow of South Asians into the United States accelerated, parents and grandparents in India frequently came to live with their families creating an older presence with first-generation values. Many second-generation Hindu Americans are now finishing college and graduate school and entering the professions.

The effect of the expanding second generation among all immigrants to the United States is staggering. Alejandro Portes and Ruben G. Rumbaut conclude,

> During the last half century a large new second generation has emerged, formed by children of immigrants born in the United States or brought at an early age from abroad. Many of its members are still in school but a large number also entered adulthood during the 1990s and the first decade of the new millennium. During the 1990s the prior record of twenty-eight million native-born citizens of foreign parentage, reached by Europeans in the 1940s, was surpassed. Immigrants and their offspring contributed a full 70 percent of the country's population growth since 1990.[20]

For South Asians as well as other immigrants, the difference between layering and earlier patterns of assimilation is the rapidity of the change where cultural trajectories that once shaped entire civilizations now assume a layered existence in a globalized world. The economic, cultural, and social processes of globalization places people from vastly different backgrounds and perspectives in the same place at the same time in an environment that accelerates change. What prevents globalized layered traditions from generating chaos are networks that keep layers of tradition alive.

Layered Traditions vs. Diaspora

Two Different Models of Interpretation of Transnational Hindu Communities

The creation of a globalized, layered Hinduism challenges traditional perceptions of a "Hindu diaspora" which has been common in studies of overseas Indian populations. Unlike the layered model that includes diverse centers of authority in transnational Indian communities, this model assumes that India is a singular center of cultural and religious authority emulated by residents of the diaspora. To be Indian was defined by the microcosm of individual experience including family, city, or village. The model further assumes that diasporan communities establish their own levels of authenticity through sustained contact with the homeland. In *New Roots in America's Sacred Ground*, Khyati Joshi frames her discussion of Indian religion in the United States in these terms,

The reader will recall that "authenticity"—the degree to which a practice or a person was genuinely "Indian"—involved an inevitable reference to one's understanding of how things are done in India. In addition to functioning as an emotional touchpoint for identity and authenticity, India was literally only a plane flight away, albeit an expensive one, for the second-generation Indian Americans who came of age in the 1980s and 1990s.[21]

Joshi sees "transnational experiences" as forms of immersion that help second- and third-generation Indian Americans understand the cultural and religious authority within the homeland.

While the diaspora/homeland model may well have accurately characterized the Hindu American community during the 1980s and 1990s when the second generation were still children, its relevance is beginning to wane. This has resulted from the rapid growth of transnational forms of Hinduism and shifts in perceptions of authenticity. The development of *Bochasanvasi Akshar Purushottam Sansthan* (BAPS) as a vibrant form of *Swaminarayan* Hinduism exemplifies these changes. BAPS temples now proliferate the American religious landscape, each becoming an established center of tradition in its own right. When leaders of the faith developed a plan to create temple *Akshardham*, in Robbinsville, New Jersey that would become the largest institution of its type, the tradition cast a global footprint with multiple centers. *The Times of India* reported, "The biggest Hindu temple in India, the Sri Rangaswami temple in Srirangam, Tamil Nadu, covers 155.92 acres. Now, the Bochasanvasi Akshar Purushottam Sansthan (BAPS) has envisioned an Akshardham temple at Robbinsville in New Jersey, U.S. that will be spread over a mammoth 162 acres."[22]

Akshardham is the sixth stone temple constructed by BAPS in North America, frequently eliciting comments about its complete authenticity.[23] However, it is equally clear with the construction of the Robbinsville temple that if a world record is to be set for the largest Hindu temple, Yogiji Maharaj (the late spiritual head of the global BAPS tradition) had no qualms about constructing it outside India. However, the *guru's* interest in constructing a large number of Hindu temples internationally was not only about setting records based on size, but was also dictated by function and the religious needs of the widespread global migration of Gujaratis.

The term, "diaspora," has posed a number of difficulties. It is derived from biblical religion and has little relevance for Asian faiths.[24] Yet another difficulty with the diaspora/homeland model is that second- and third-generation Hindu Americans are Millennials and incorporate the American values associated with their age groups. As a cohort, secular millennials have rejected single sources of authority such as religion. South Asian millennials may participate in religious gatherings but often because of family loyalty. However, for many, this allegiance to family structures is not linked to Indian values nor to sources of authority in the Indian subcontinent. For example, a college student in a retreat setting in Pennsylvania commented that he would vote for a presidential candidate because his father asked him to. The student's decision to align his vote with his parents was not based on his father's ties to India, or on the perceptions of American presidential candidates in India. Instead, the decision was explained in terms of family loyalty which is a dynamic that is also apparent among other immigrant groups. At the same time, the distinction between age and generation is complex. Intricate family alignments which may include intermarriage between first- and second-generation persons and the presence of the "1.5 generation" born in India but brought up in the West, makes any fixed definition of generations difficult.

In other instances, the authority of Hindu religious leaders in India does not readily transfer to the increasingly significant cohort of second-generation Hindu Americans. When American Hindu youth gravitate toward Hindu spiritual leaders from India, acceptance is greater among *gurus* who tend to relax orthodox values and show acceptance of Western lifestyles. This has become evident in a number of Hindu traditions in which *gurus, goswāmīs* and other religious leaders have achieved popularity in the West through their involvement with youth. This shift in values was evident in a *Pushtimarg* retreat in 2016 where participants enthusiastically supported a conversation with a visiting *goswāmī* and his wife. The conversation was bolstered by the *goswāmī's* self-disclosure that he was a business man and had completed an MBA degree. At the same time the couple encouraged conversations with his wife who in traditional settings in India might have been left out of the conversation.

Similarly, the *Swaminarayan* tradition regularly recruits second-generation leaders who relate well to high school and college students. The *Anoopam Mission* in Coplay, Pennsylvania is a sectarian movement which created a theologically liberal alternative to the larger BAPS tradition. Its *guru,* Guruvarya Param Pujya Sahebji, developed a cadre of young professionally trained second-generation leaders who would easily relate to the vibrant youth tradition within the *Swaminarayan* movement. These leaders, removed from more stringent levels of orthodoxy in India, have an easier rapport with second-generation Hindu Americans than spiritual leaders from India. At the same time they have formed a layered, highly networked institution in which traditional patterns of worship and service to the deity are maintained while also meeting the needs of Hindu youth that are quite different.

Finally, a globalized model of transnational Hinduism suggests that as generational ties with the homeland weaken over time, immigrant traditions develop their own centers of tradition. While Indian culture is always an important point of reference it does not stand alone as a voice of orthodoxy. As a result, globalized Hinduism affirms multiple centers of tradition, each with its own layers of interpretation, and each part of a wider, more diversified form of religion than the diaspora/homeland model could provide.

Networking and the Earlier Influence of British India

The appearance of globalized, transnational Hindu networks is not just the product of the internet age and has historical antecedents in British India both in the interconnections achieved through empire, and in the formation of religious networks in India. The age of globalization in which networks proliferate both online and among ethnic and religious associations owes a great deal to this beginning.

Over an almost 300 year period (1600–1874) the British constructed its East India Company which was a visible extension of empire in India, but also included South Asia within the globalizing network of communications. Empire was,

> ... a "series of historically contingent networks," "bundles of relationships," or "webs" that "connected disparate locations into circuits of exchange and debate" as part of a broader process of "imperial globalization" ... these webs not only linked with its colonies but also forged connections among various sites of colonization, allowing "cultural traffic" from diverse points of origin to mingle.[25]

Britain achieved these global relationships through the use of newspapers, undersea cable and telegraph, for the first time providing English people with both the knowledge and the ability to communicate with its colonies in distant parts of the globe. The network of empire, with its technological infrastructure (railroad, telegraph, shipping, etc.) facilitated movement and communication as well as the establishment of overseas Indian communities in the United Kingdom, Malaysia, Singapore, East Africa, South

Africa, and other places. The British Indian army garrisoned overseas engaged in both world wars. Hindu students, trained in the United Kingdom, were the backbone of what became the nationalist movements and the rise of an "Indian middle class" that was urbanized and outward looking. Western education was also a ticket to status outside of tradition. All these elements set in motion the emigration patterns of the twentieth century as South Asians formed an international community.

At the same time, the expansion of empire had profound implications for residents of the United Kingdom who sought travel and adventure, often winding up in the civil service or military in India. The international shipping operations of the East India Company employed a variety of people whose lives were shaped by opportunities in both the British Isles and in India in multiple layers of networking.[26] An example was artist and engraver Patrick Begbie. Begbie was known in both Scotland and England, producing copper plate images of eighteenth-century urban life. Hoping to expand his clientele, Begbie signed on a number of "Indiaman" ships, through the East India Company, as purser, including two voyages on the same ship—the Earl of Hertford. While on board he completed charts, drew panoramas of the coasts he observed, and maintained the ship's accounts. When, in 1782, after only a year at sea, the Earl of Hertford was lost off the coast of southern India, Begbie may have used the advantages of empire to forge a new livelihood, joining the British army in West Bengal.[27] While records of Begbie's career are scant, indications are that as a British subject in India he was adept at networking, moving from the East India Company's service to the British army.

The records of the East India company are full of similar exploits that for the first time brought British citizens to India and, once there, enmeshed them in the networks of the company, the army, and social organizations that connected them with their home. At the same time, the development of a British education system in India also resulted in an increasing number of associations and indigenous networks. In Calcutta, the *Society for the Acquisition of General Knowledge* was formed in 1838 and by 1843 included a cadre of 200 intellectual Indian members.[28] Other associations that emanated from colleges and universities included the work of Ram Mohun Roy who "…gave Calcutta its leading school, its first Indian newspapers, and the Brahmo Samaj, an organization for religious reform which played an important part in Bengal's renaissance."[29] In major cities in nineteenth-century India similar practices followed. The growing list of organizations and networks created a need to both evaluate and, where possible, control the growth and precipitated the passage of the Indian Societies Registration Act of 1860. As Britains in India organized their professional and social lives in networks, Indians did likewise. As a result, Indian communities organized around patterns of religious identity, ultimately leading to the nineteenth-century Hindu Renaissance which became the seedbed for a budding nationalist movement. Not surprisingly, nationalism had its inception in Bengal, the region with the most extended, direct interaction with British administrative structures.

Networking in India incorporated British values about the nature of religious and cultural societies, producing the beginnings of an Indian middle class whose understanding of religion was motivated by perceptions of social justice, reform, and the dominance of Western values.

Not the least of these was the trajectory of symbolism and meaning which became incorporated in a world view that was coupled with the rise of scientific education. The Anglicization of Indian intellectuals was a necessary aspect for the further development of trade and the ability of the privately owned East India Company to extend its reach ever deeper into the subcontinent. This created the beginnings of middle class urban groups seeking status and advancement within British administration. These efforts were supported in 1854 with the declaration of English as an official language, creating a pathway for Anglicized Indians to succeed. While these efforts ultimately resulted in the nationalist movement and, in 1947, the expulsion of Britain from India, they embedded the widespread use of networks as an effective tool for connecting persons with like-minded points of view.

Networks had evolved both within India and among overseas Indian communities but also in Europe, as residents of the United Kingdom sought fresh opportunities for employment in South Asia. This global pattern was actually two parallel flows of people that did not intersect for some time. The process in India had a number of key periods including the formation of the East India Company in 1600, the spread of British temporal control throughout the eighteenth century, and the mutiny of 1857 in which Indian soldiers in the British army rebelled, resulting in the nationalization of the East India Company followed by direct rule of the British crown. In the Societies Registration Act of 1860 the British sought to increase the number of private associations which contributed to its attempts in creating a university system to sculpt a society in its own image. All of this resulted in the beginnings of an internal series of networks in India that would eventually carry over among global populations in the late twentieth and early twenty-first centuries. Among

Hindu sects that experienced this history, devotees found new ways of expanding networks through regional movements within the Indian subcontinent.

A Case Study—Networking in Transnational Forms of Pushtimarg and the Coexistence of Different Cultural Trajectories

Pushtimarg ("the way of grace") is one of the oldest and most prolific forms of the fifteenth- and sixteenth-century north Indian *bhakti* movement.[30] As a sectarian *Vaiṣṇava* tradition with recent entry into the global religious landscape, it also provides a significant example of the symbiotic nature of networking and the symbiotic role of lay entrepreneurs and tradition. The transnational presence of the sect illustrates the process of layering among overseas Hindu communities, and the ways in which these processes have developed tiered communities in which the cultural trajectories of embodiment and material symbolism coexist. *Pushtimarg* is also particularly well suited for this analysis because of its strong association with the trajectory of embodiment. Formed in the early sixteenth century through the teachings and religious practices of Vallabhacharya (1479–1532 CE), this *Vaiṣṇava* tradition founds its home among the princely states which became bastions of Hindu independence. As the sect developed, it created internal networks based on the lineage of the founder, his son, and their descendants (*goswāmīs*).

A form of images called *swarūps*, which were understood as the highest form of embodiment, became the focal point of the tradition. The word, *swarūp*, means "his own" and is understood as a form of the deity that is the most present and the most fully embodied. The sect distinguishes *swarūps* from *mūrtis* and focuses devotion, through a ritual practice called *sevā*, on these images. *Sevā*, or service, incorporates the requirements of Hindu *pūjā* but also is an expression of intimacy and devotion, recognizing the presence of the deity in iconographic form. *Pushtimargiyas* are required to perform *sevā* daily, often incorporating food prepared especially for the deity. *Swarūps* are treated as the most important members of families and are lovingly cared for and passed down from one generation to the next.

Pushtimarg relies on a juxtaposition of music, art, and iconography to create a ritual path for access to the deity creating internal networks of highly trained priests, musicians, and artists who served its temples.

Beginning in the 1980s and extending into the early twenty-first century, these networks became increasingly important abroad. In temples (*havelīs*) vocalists and instrumentalists offer *rāgas* suited for the time of the year corresponding to rainy, cold, spring, and summer. Each season is correlated with poetry and music especially designed to evoke the presence of god during that time. The poetry is the product of the *Aṣṭachāp*, a group of eight who followed Vallabhacharya, founder of the faith. *Braj Bhāsha*, a soft, poetic form of Hindi is used for each song (*kīrtan*) that helps set the mood. In *havelīs* in Rajasthan and the Gujarat, temple hangings called *pichhavais* are employed behind the deity, each crafted to contain the presence of the deity.

Through these means whether in home ritual (*sevā*) or in a temple, music, art, and season come together to create an atmosphere in which a glimpse (*darśan*) of *Krishna* as an embodied deity is possible. Adherents understand that their ability to "see" god may only last for a fraction of a second. Yet, within this carefully articulated focus on embodiment, the image is understood as a manifestation of the divine.

Historical Background

From its inception in the fifteenth and sixteenth centuries the *Vallabha Sampradaya* emphasized embodiment, as manifested in the image of *Shri Nathji* discovered by Vallabha. The image was buried on Mount Govardhan with an arm protruding that local Hindus worshiped as a snake deity. Recognizing the arm as part of a larger figure of a child form of *Krishna, Shri Nathji*, Vallabha established a pattern of worship that attracted devotees from the region which was revered as Braj, *Krishna's* homeland.

The sect was developed by Vallabha's second son, Vitthalnath (*Śrī Gusāīmjī*) who established lineage, and the networks that evolve from it, in Rajasthan and the Gujarat. Vitthalnath had seven sons and each was given a *swarūp* of the infant *Krishna* which were installed in a variety of locations throughout Rajasthan and the Gujarat. The original form of Śrī Nāthjī was eventually transferred to a small village in Mewar (Rajasthan) following the cultivation of economic relationships between the descendants of Vallabha (who were identified as *goswāmīs*) and the ruling *Mahārāṇas* of Mewar. The religious network evolved when each of Vallabha's grandchildren established a central location for their *swarūp* and an administrative district or *gaddī* within which they exercised control. Beginning in the sixteenth century, *gaddīs* became independent theocracies. Each provided a steady source of devotees through *Pushtimargiya* families who supported the enshrined *swarūp* of *Krishna*. In addition, income was received through a *manorath* system in which the *darśans* (public viewings) of the *swarūps* were funded by prominent families, creating networks of laity within the tradition.

In the sixteenth and seventeenth centuries the central *gaddī* of Nathdwara grew in prestige and power with the lineage holder identified as the *Tilkāyat* who exercised the central ritual authority of the tradition and an important level of influence throughout the network. Other temples in Rajasthan (identified as homes or *havelīs*) also grew in status including the central *havelī* at Kankroli, also in Mewar. Still others in contiguous states of Marwar and Bundi developed close associations between the governing *Mahārājas* and members of the *Vallabhkul.*

The faith was also supported through alliances with the ruling *Mahārāṇas* and *Mahārājas* of princely states in larger networks of patronage. In Mewar, *Pushtimarg* became the adopted faith of the ruling *Mahārāṇas* who saw the economic benefits that could be obtained from a form of the *bhakti* tradition that attracted large number of devotees. Mewar's alliance with the British in 1818 insured the independence of he kingdom in return for tribute to the East India Company and a level of prestige. Similar arrangements were forged between the company and the princely state of Bundi. In such insulated locations the sect was able to prosper, creating networks of artists, musicians, and ritual specialists.

As the network of temples (*havelīs*) increased in the sixteenth and seventeenth centuries in Rajasthan and the Gujarat, the tradition formed other networks of sacred geography. Sites where Vallabhacharya had spiritual experiences throughout the subcontinent became shrines (*baiṭhaks*). As places of frequent pilgrimage the sect was able to expand its networks beyond the princely states in significant numbers. 84 *baiṭhaks* were associated with Vallabha, 28 with his son, Vitthalnath, and 30 additional places with Vitthalnath's seven sons.[31]

The sect's insulation in the princely states and the system of patronage that it had enjoyed was weakened when in 1857, Britain assumed direct rule of a substantial percentage of the subcontinent. *Mahārājas* and *Mahārāṇas* became vassals of the British Empire. Later, following Indian independence in 1947, the protection the sect had once enjoyed collapsed further when the newly formed Indian government began to investigate and regulate the wealthiest temples in the country including Nathdwara. As a result, through the passage of the Religious Endowments and Charities Act in 1951, the ability of the *Vallabha Sampradaya* to retain the independence and strength of its major *gaddīs* was severely decreased.

All of this began to change in the mid–twentieth century with increases in emigration from India that propelled Gujaratis and Rajasthanis into overseas networks in East Africa and the British Commonwealth as *Pushtimarg* was carried abroad. Three waves of Indian immigrants came to Britain following Indian independence. The first, from the 1950s through the 1970s but was curtailed by the passage of the Immigration Act of 1972. A second period from the 1970s through the 1990s saw further reductions in immigration with the restriction on education subsidies under the Thatcher administration. In a third period, beginning in 2002, the Blair administration facilitated increases in immigration reaching over 17,000 in 2005.[32] At the same time, in 1965, immigration reforms in the United States created new opportunities for South Asians. Gujarati emigres found employment overseas in a variety of locations including areas of older migration such as the Caribbean and regions with rapid growth such as Dubai.

As the age of globalization accelerated, *havelīs* were erected in major urban centers in the United States in a new network of tradition in the global Hindu network. The emergence of *Pushtimarg* in the United States was not foreseen by the *Vallabha Sampradaya* and represented a new form of networking that reached beyond the *gaddīs* and the four-hundred-year-old networks that had supported the tradition. Following the purchase of property in central Pennsylvania for a temple in 1988 and the development of *havelīs* in New York, Texas, and New Jersey, the central leadership of the sect in Nathdwara (Rajasthan) began to reassess the possibilities of a global footprint and fresh avenues of networking. *Goswāmīs*, who had managed the *gaddī* system as an effective means of sustaining the tradition, also began to envision a new transnational presence and symbiotic relationships with their devotees overseas. This was significant since in *Pushtimarg, dikṣā,* or initiation to the tradition, can only be administered by members of the *Vallabhkul* (the lineage of Vallabhacharya) in a ritual identified as *Brahmsambandh*.

As the transnational network of *Pushtimargiyas* grew in the United States, Britain, Australia, Dubai, and East Africa, the association between lay entrepreneurs and *goswāmīs* helped support the construction of *havelīs*, emphasizing the central role of *swarūps* and the trajectory of embodiment. In urban Houston, Indira Betiji, a highly charismatic *goswāmī,* assisted in the creation of a *havelī* in the American southwest. First established in the garage of a member of the *Pushtimarg* community, and later in a free-standing temple, affectionately dubbed "The Texas Nathdwara," Gujarati entrepreneurs and *goswāmīs* developed a symbiotic relationship that was the beginning of a highly networked tradition that supported perceptions of embodiment. In 1992, when the Vraj temple was dedicated in Schuylkill Haven, Pennsylvania devotees proclaimed that the *havelī* contained the official presence of *Shrī Nathji* in the Western hemisphere. In 1992, after prolonged negotiations with the *Tilkāyat* of Nathdwara (the spiritual head of the tradition) the transnational *Pushtimarg* community was legitimized through official recognition of the Vraj temple in Pennsylvania as the seat of *Shri Nathji* in the West. The *havelī* became the only temple outside Nathdwara to sport a golden cupola over the central sanctuary which became a symbol of the embodiment of the deity inside. The *havelī* was dedicated and the *swarūp* of *Shri Nathji* brought to life in front of a crowd of 22,000 devotees. Helicopters brought priests from New York, New Jersey, and Texas to the dedication further cementing the evolving transnational *Pushtimarg* tradition in place.

Pushtimarg Networks

Following the dedication of Vraj, a series of networks developed among *goswāmīs*, first-generation immigrants, and *havelīs* both in the United States and in India. As the same time, the second generation also grew, developing their own social and religious networks which supported the American trajectory of symbolic meaning. As a burgeoning, transnational religion *Pushtimarg* in North America became defined through tiered communities with an expanding number of electronic networks that contained both trajectories and symbiotic relationships between the generations that held them.

Networks of *goswāmīs*, supporting the central tenets of embodiment began to redefine their roles in the new overseas network in global terms. With the inability of the Indian economy to provide ample sources of employment and the relaxation of immigration restrictions in the West, large numbers of Gujaratis left India. Many were highly skilled professionals while others had received educations in India that emphasized the benefits of entrepreneurial approaches to business.

In order to meet the needs of their devotees, *goswāmīs* became global travelers, moving between *Pushtimarg* communities in the United Kingdom, Dubai, and the United States. As part of their entry into a globalized world, some also entered professions, maximizing their role as religious leaders and also as an upwardly mobile class of business people.

Utilizing the social media as a way of communicating with their devotees, some also created websites and developed electronic networks.

An example of the networked presence of this new level of networking is Pushtimarg.com, developed by *Goswāmī* Anandbhava, who descends from the seventeenth generation of lineage holders of Vallabhacharya. Anandbhava is a resident of Bhavnagar, Gujarat, and is connected to a central *havelī* in Kamvan. In addition to his spiritual functions, he is also an architect, securing his role in both hemispheres and providing him with an ability to easily access followers in both realms.[33]

Pushtimarg.com has a transnational presence with Anandbhava's articles published in both Gujarati and English. Addressing theological topics that pertain to the fast-paced, Westernized life of his followers, Anandbhava urges his followers to adopt the path of surrender. The website also maintains an international footprint, with commentaries directly related to India but at the same time also discussing events in the United States. An event at the *Vallabha Priti Seva Samaj* in Houston is included alongside devotional gatherings in India. At the same time, Anandbhava is a frequent traveler to the West, meeting his devotees in a variety of settings including London.

Other *goswāmīs*, such as Hariray, have developed blogs, as yet another form of electronic networking.[34] Like Anandbhava, Hariray is part of the seventeenth generation of descendants of Vallabhacharya and is attached to a *havelī*—the *Shri Pushtidham Haveli* in Surat. Educated in Ahmedabad, he is a traditional *goswāmī* who studied with *Pushtimarg* scholars.[35] Hariray's website also includes events in India and in the West, travels between India and the United Kingdom, and can be reached via Instagram, Twitter, and Facebook. His blog and global network often contain injunctions to his devotees about ritual and reinforces the trajectory of embodiment. He describes the intimacy that characterizes the ritual,

> In this form of worship that is by doing Sevā to the svarūp (Idol) as if the svarup is his own Son, just as we take care of our son and protect him from heat/cold so also this Svarup is to be protected from heat/Cold (sic) etc. Just as we offer food to our child in the same way while doing Seva the person has to offer food to the Svarup.... Just as we pamper our child from Morning to Night by giving him the best food, clothes or whatever he wants. So also the Svarup has to be pampered as our own child and attend to his needs.[36]

As transnational networks have developed so the *gaddī* network has become peripheral overseas. Taking its place are symbiotic associations of *goswāmīs* and their lay followers who together define the ritual life abroad. Lay followers of the tradition needed *goswāmīs* to initiate them into the sect. At the same time the descendants of Vallabhacharya have retained an important function as *gurus* and spiritual guides. Visits to the West are an important part of this relationship, and not only nurture the association between *gurus* and laity but also strengthen the electronic networks that connect them. For the *goswāmīs*, the ability to service their transnational communities provided global recognition, as well as income produced from the *guru dakṣiṇa* (offerings to *gurus*) that accompany these visits.

Since the establishment as *havelīs* as the central residence for a *swarūp* required the authorization of a *goswāmī*, networks also began to link different avenues of authority including *goswāmīs* and temple developers. American *havelīs* have become transnational institutions often recruiting multiple *goswāmīs* to assist them. Layered networks between *goswāmīs* and Gujarati entrepreneurs also became a path toward the successful establishment of a *havelī* in the West. Each level of networking, from the electronic blogs of *goswāmīs* to the networks started by American *havelīs* exist among the same clientele, connecting layered patterns of devotion in India with the transnational community abroad. Together, these layered networks also became a way of perpetuating the cultural trajectory of embodiment which was also a necessary part for the establishment of a *havelī*. Working together, networks of *goswāmīs* and American entrepreneurs have assisted *havelīs* to acquire *swarūps*, arranging for their installation in a ritually sanctified space, and insuring the location of priests and ancillary workers.

Lay *Pushtimarg* leaders also found support in their own networks. Some are internal and are used to help supply *havelīs* with personnel and components necessary for the maintenance of tradition. In one instance, the Vraj *havelī* in Pennsylvania and the Texas Nathdwara in Houston shared priests (*mukhiyās*) from the same family. Temple leaders in the United States also participated in a broad pan-Hindu network of temple executives through annual conferences. This group, the *Hindu Mandir Executives Conference*, and its parent organization the *Vishwa Hindu Parishad* of America helps to address mutual problems, share resources, and find common ground beyond independent sectarian traditions. At the same time it offers a number of online publications, electronic networks for youth, and a forthcoming helpline.

As *goswāmīs* and Gujarati lay entrepreneurs found increasing benefit from symbiotic layers of networking, at the same time members of the second generation also began to network in two different ways. The *Vallabh Youth Organization* worked to perpetuate embodiment and the tenets of *Pushtimarg* among members of the millennial generation. However, a second tier of youth networks also developed independently in some *havelīs*. Functioning as a way of affirming the Indian heritage of its members, these networks were interrelated with others scattered throughout the social media.

In 2009, The *Vallabh Youth Organization* (VYO)—an international network of *Pushtimarg* youth organizations, was created by a young charismatic member of the *Vallabhkul, Goswāmī* Vrajrajkumarji. Established as an attempt to instill the values of the faith among members of the millennial generation, the VYO became an international organization. In 2016 it advertised a global membership of 30,000 members with associations in sixteen Indian centers, in the United States, the United Kingdom, and other locations around the world. The VYO also achieved the status of a registered Non-Governmental Organization (NGO), marking its ability to cross borders with ease, engage in international charitable work, and to create a global venue for the faith.[37] The tradition maintains a high level of activity with a daily blog that reaches its global following.[38]

In the United States, the strategy of the VYO has been to build a vibrant overseas network of youth, directing this enthusiasm into the founding of a *havelīs*, a process which depends on mutually interactive layered networks of youth and devotees. This process has been successful in a number of locations including Boston, Richmond, and Dallas. In other cities, including Raleigh and Charlotte, North Carolina active VYO networks have worked to the same end.

To much the same end, the Vraj temple in Pennsylvania has launched a highly networked series of *Pushtimarg* centers on the east coast and in the mid-west. Similar to the educational efforts of the VYO, each center will be staffed by trained teachers, offering classes in *Pushtimarg*, and networked in a way that offers them mutual aid and support. These efforts are intended to offset the shift in values that second-generation *Pushtimarg* children experience, when, growing up as Americans they adopt the dominant values of the culture including the Western trajectory of symbolic meaning.

These efforts launched by layered networks of *goswāmīs* and lay leaders in the West, were accompanied by parallel networks of *Pushtimarg* youth, often emphasizing different cultural trajectories than their parents. The existence of both perspectives of embodiment and symbolic meaning within the overseas tradition is not a dichotomy and does not represent a source of conflict. Rather, through layered networks the transnational tradition is able to meet the needs of both first and second generations.

The absence of conflict is the product of close relationships and strong family bonds and the recognition that the layering of tradition, through which both groups can find accommodations, is an important part of the development of transnational Hinduism.

Throughout its five hundred year history, both in India, and in transnational locations, *Pushtimarg* has depended on networking. The initial formation of the faith through the seven sons of Vitthalnath established lineage, as a primary means of organizing and expanding the faith in a system of networks called *gaddīs*. Each *gaddī* became the spiritual center of a *swarūp* of the child *Krishna* which was understood as the highest form of embodiment possible. *Gaddīs* had an important impact on ritual and became associated with strong patterns of devotion among *Pushtimarg* families. In princely states the networks of *gaddīs* thrived, supported by ruling *Mahārāṇas* and *Mahārājās* who, in turn, formed alliances with the British East India Company. *Gaddīs* supported networks of priests, artisans, musicians as well as influential devotees who supported worship through the *manorath* system. In the late twentieth and early twenty-first centuries, when many Gujaratis moved abroad looking for economic opportunities, these networks, which had been weakened when Britain ruled India directly after 1857 and by independence in 1947, were weakened. However, transnational patterns of migration created new opportunities for layered networks among first- and second-generation devotees. Second- and third-generation *Pushtimargiyas* have adopted a Western cultural trajectory and often do not perceive patterns of embodiment like their parents. The two trajectories of embodiment and symbolism exist in a parallel form, each meeting the needs of a different generational population.

Concluding Remarks

This text has focused on one aspect of transnational Hinduism, the erosion of the trajectory of embodiment among second- and third-generation Hindus in the West. It has shown how the trajectory evolved with the Hindu temple for more than two-thousand years, and the ways in which it is maintained in temples and among first-generation Hindus in the United States. However, at the same time, the trajectory is collapsing among the sons and daughters of Hindu immigrants in the West. Reifying these changes with the growing popularity of Hindu art in the West, images are not viewed as embodied figures but as aesthetic and historical artifacts. This transition is supported by the erosion of the traditional craft of ritual production in India and the mass production of factory produced images both in India and China.

Accompanying such a loss of tradition are more difficult considerations about changing patterns of Hindu identity beyond India. The erosion of the trajectory of embodiment is but one of a series of changes that have accompanied the movement of Hinduism abroad. Separated from caste in the West, Hinduism exists with a truncated version of ancient patterns of purity and pollution. Transnational Hinduism also exists apart from indigenous patterns of animism in India and what Robert Redfield called the "Little Traditions" of Hinduism.[39] Changes in patterns of the extended family are also evident as second- and third-generation Hindu families are increasingly adopting American and European models of the nuclear family. Finally, while Hindu temples have demonstrated a remarkable pattern of resilient growth in the United States and in Europe, they are removed from traditional systems of governance and increasingly modeled on socio-religious patterns of religious identity in the West. In the United States temples become non-profit tax exempt institutions and develop systems of governance similar to other parts of the American denominational system.[40]

While all of these changes are significant, the erosion of the trajectory of embodiment would seem to present one of the greatest challenges to Hindu identity. While perceptions of presence are maintained in temples through priests it is often compromised in Hindu homes where children often adopt American values related to material culture. Moreover, many second- and third-generation Hindus do not practice *pūjā* in their homes, leaving the demands of tradition to their parents and grandparents.

Yet, paradoxically, despite these changes, when asked, many second- and third-generation Indian Americans consider themselves to be Hindu, prompting the question about what Hindu identity is in a globalized world.

Globalization theorists approach these questions through the lens of hybridization. Vasquez and Marquardt suggest that earlier paradigms of syncretism and assimilation are inadequate to understand the barrage of changes in transnational forms of religion, often encapsulating opposite behaviors in the same context.[41] Homi Bhabha concludes that in a globalized world hybridity "...renders problematic binary oppositions and exclusionary difference because it constructs artifacts and identities that are "neither One nor the Other but something else beside in between.""[42] While these insights are quite helpful, the question of Hindu identity in the diaspora is still problematic since even in India it has never had a single point of reference.

Brent Nongbri concludes that the term "Hindu" first emerged in the eighteenth century when British officials attempted to identify the people of the Indus River.[43] Earlier observers had labeled the tradition as "the religion of the Hindoos" and that of the "Banians."[44] While these terms were the products of colonial regimes that looked at religion based on what they had experienced in Europe, the reality was that there was no single term of self-identification that "Hindus" employed to describe their way of life. There was also no word for "religion."

Perhaps the only term that connected the diverse parts of what the English colonials identified as Hinduism was *dharma* which has connotations of truth and order but is not synonymous with "religion" in the West. Later, in attempts to avoid the term "Hinduism" as a colonial construct, nineteenth-century Hindu reformers applied a Vedic phrase, *sanātana dharma* ("eternal duty"), to their practices.[45] Ironically, in the popular jargon of these Westernized reformers, the phrase became a substitute for "religion," presenting a flat image with little hint of the highly pluralistic nature of Indian piety.

The problem that has confounded the West in its numerous attempts to understand "Hinduism" is that there is no single, unifying thread that binds it together in ways that are parallel to the concept of religion in the West. Hindu history does not include ecclesiastical councils that have spoken on behalf of the entire faith. Nor have there been spiritual leaders who have claimed a single voice for all of India. Instead, religious authority is a mosaic encompassing a wide variety of symbiotic traditions. It is found in familial traditions, in the Sanskritized voices of priests, in sectarian paradigms and diverse temple practices, in both canonical (*śruti*) and non-canonical (*smṛti*) forms of scripture and in villages where governance is administered through a complex web of caste and local control affecting every aspect of life. In this sense "Hinduism" is not what the word implies and any attempt to define it or to find an overall unity within it is doomed to failure.

Yet, despite this ambiguity, the term "Hinduism" remains popular in the West both among immigrants and their children. There is little doubt that the faith of second and third generations is hybridized, defined by the layering of cultural trajectories, and the binary opposition from the voices of their parents and peers. Yet, given the ambiguity of the term "Hindu" and its failure to connote the inherent diversity of the tradition, any consideration of success or failure in the West is futile.

What has emerged "beyond India" in the twenty-first century is in many ways a continuation of the ritual and theological diversity that confounded British observers in India, albeit in a postmodern context. The cultural trajectory of embodiment which for millennia in India bridged sectarian and different ritual practices exists in parallel in the West with the trajectory of symbolism. The process is visible but not a source of opposition or conflict. First-generation devotees share stories about embodiment while their sons and daughters explore their Hindu identity using perceptions of symbolic meaning. In the end this is an important reminder that religions exist beyond the terms that seek to define or limit them and that they are dynamic aspects of the human search for transcendence. While outside observers will continue to describe the total matrix as "Hindu," the reality will be far more complex. Hybridized second-generation traditions in concert with more orthodox forms of sectarian tradition will redefine themselves in adaptive forms of Indian religious presence in a changing religious landscape.

Glossary

Abhaya (***mudrā***)—a hand gesture meaning without fear, common among both Hindu and Buddhist images in which the palm is raised outward with the arm bent at the elbow. The *abhaya mudrā* also symbolizes protection.

Abhicārikā Mūrti—an iconographic form of an image in which it is shown in a posture depicting the defeat of enemies.

Ācārya—"Great Teacher," referring to the great historical religious teachers in the Hindu tradition and for spiritual leaders as well.

Ācamanīya—to sip water; part of a *pūjā* ceremony in which water is offered to images for face washing.

Advaita—non-dualism. One of the traditional systems of Hindu philosophy often associated with the teacher Shankara.

Agastīya—one of four figures identified with the writing of the *Śilpa Śāstras* which are treatises that describe art, architecture and the ritualized production of images. Agastīya is understood as an ancient sage who crossed the Vindhya range of mountains from north to south spreading *Vedic* knowledge to South India. As a mythologized figure he drank the entire ocean.

Agatīya Sakalādhikāra—a treatise on iconometry attributed to Agastīya.

Ajā—the unborn, eternal.

Ālwārs—*Vaiṣṇava* saints in the Hindu *bhakti* movement during the fifth through tenth centuries CE.

Āmalaka—a stone finial that is placed on top of a Hindu temple.

Angula tāla—a subdivision of a *tāla* which is a unit of measurement in the ritual production of Hindu images. *Angula tāla* is often defined as a finger width.

Arghya—part of a *pūjā* ceremony in which the deity is presented with water in which flowers, saffron and sandalwood have been placed.

Arya Samaj—a religious movement during the nineteenth-century Hindu Renaissance led by Swami Dayananda.

Āsana ("seat")—one of the stages of *yoga* comprising physical postures and positions. *Āsana* is an introductory stage in *yoga*, enabling practitioners to sit for long periods of time focusing on the breath. *Āsana* is also a stage in *pūjā* ceremonies in which a seat is presented to a deity. It may also be used in secular contexts to refer to anything offered as a seat.

Atmiya Samaj—a reformist Hindu association founded by Ram Mohan Roy in the nineteenth century which did not allow image worship.

Āvāhana—a *mudrā* or hand gesture with both palms placed up side by side, often used to evoke a deity. Also, part of a *pūjā* or worship ceremony in which the deity is evoked.

Avatār—an incarnation of a Hindu god in another form. *Avatār* is usually associated with Vishna and his ten incarnations but also applies to other gods.

Ayādi Lakṣaṇa Vidhi—a perception in which images are understood to represent the vital, inner rhythm of life.

Balkrishna (*Bālakṛṣṇa*)—a child form of the Hindu deity *Krishna*, often represented crawling on the floor while holding butter in his left hand.

Ban Yātrā—a traditional pilgrimage in the forests of Braj in the Hindu *Pushtimarg* tradition.

Bāṇa liṅga—a naturally formed stone found in the Narmada River in Madya Pradesh, India that is understood to contain the creative powers of the deity, *Shiva*.

Bera—a Hindu image or *mūrti* often associated with differentiated forms of *Shiva*.

Bhāgavata Purāṇa—a major treatise in the Hindu tradition elevating the god *Krishna* as the "*Para-Brahman*" (ultimate reality). He is seen as the ideal goal for devotion (*bhakti*).

Bhajan—devotional songs popular in the Hindu *bhakti* traditions.

Bhakti—an attitude of devotion and a historical movement in Hinduism associated with the popular appeal of a tutelary deity. Many North Indian *bhakti* traditions are associated with the popular god, *Krishna* and *Rama*.

Bharatiya Janata **Party**—a political party in India advocating Hindu nationalism.

Bhāva—a feeling or mood. It is associated with the Hindu *bhakti* traditions. *Bhāva* conjoins perception with imagination, becoming a means of looking into an image or natural phenomena, and perceiving its sacral nature. It is used extensively in dance, literature, and devotional sense to refer to inner feelings / mood of the devotee.

Bhoga—food that is offered to a deity and then given to devotees as *prasād* (grace).

Bindi—a cosmetic dot worn on the forehead by Hindu women. The deeper significance of the *bindi* is the perception that it marks a universal center often represented in the *maṇḍala*.

Bodhisattva—a future Buddha that is an important part of *Mahayana* Buddhist cosmology; a compassionate spirit who defers full spiritual release to assist others in receiving enlightenment.

Brahman—in Hindu monistic thought (*Advaita*) the singular form of ultimate reality that is beyond speech and thought.

Brahmo Samaj—a Hindu reform tradition championed by Ram Mohan Roy that was opposed to image worship, championing principles influenced by Christianity.

Brahmsambandh—an initiation ritual performed by a *goswāmī* (descendent of Vallabhacharya) in the Hindu *Pushtimarg* tradition.

Braj—in Hindu mythology a forested area adjacent to the Yamuna River where *Krishna* was born and grew up. Braj is located south of New Delhi, north of Agra, and includes land in Rajasthan and Uttar Pradesh. Cities such as Mathura and villages like Gokul and Brindaban within Braj have special significance in the life of *Krishna*.

Bṛhatsaṃhitā (**"expanded or greater collection"**)—referring to an encyclopedic treatise of hymns and verses attributed to Varahamihira who wrote in the sixth century CE.

Cārvāka—a materialistic school of Indian philosophy that rejects the *Vedas* as well as the mainstays of Hindu philosophy including *karma* and *mokṣa*. The *Cārvāka* School held that only direct perception matters and was an atheistic school of philosophy.

Catuṣṭāla (**"four *tālas*"**)—four units of measurement for Hindu images as described in the *Śilpa Śāstras*.

Chennai—a southern city in India formerly known as Madras.

Chola—an ancient dynasty in South India that began before 200 BCE and lasting until its demise in 1279 CE. The *Chola* dynasty was best known for their bronze statues and grand temples.

Dakṣiṇa (**"skill"**)—payment (given to a *guru* for performing ritual services). *Dakṣiṇa* is payment for the skill with which service was delivered and is usually used for religious services offered by priests, *Brahmins* and *gurus*.

Damaru—a double-headed drum held by the god *Shiva*.

Darśan (**"seeing"**)—reflecting a mode of worship common in Hindu image worship and especially in *bhakti* traditions. Seeing the deity is understood as a reciprocal process in which devotees are also seen by the god and is an important part of traditions such as *Pushtimarg*. With reference to philosophy, *darśan* means "insight." There are six different *"darśans"* or philosophical schools of Hinduism.

Dāsya bhāva—a mood connected with the worship in which the devotee feels like a servant of the deity who is lord and master.

Devadāsī—maid servant of the god. *Devadāsīs* worked as singers and dancers in temples. Some "ritually married" the deity.

Devārāma—devotional songs.

Devī—a Hindu (mother) goddess.

Dharmabhūtāñjana—a teaching developed by the Hindu philosopher Ramanuja that both consciousness and perception are object oriented.

Dīkṣā—initiation in Hindu sectarian traditions often administered by a *guru*.

Dochakuka—in Japanese tradition the practice of adapting a global institution to local conditions.

Dwarka—a pilgrimage center on the coast of Gujarat. In Hindu mythology, a "Golden city" founded by *Krishna* after leaving Mathura.

Dvitāla—two *tālas* or units, of measurement for Hindu images.

Ekatāla—one unit of measurement for Hindu images.

Gaddī—a term meaning cushion which has also been used to signify a royal seat. In *Pushtimarg*, one of the seats of the *Vallabha Sampradaya* in Rajasthan, the Gujarat and Uttar Pradesh where a patrilineal descendent of Vitthalnath's seven sons (*Goswāmīs* or *bālaks*) serves one of the original images (*swarūps*) associated with the tradition.

Ganesh (Gaṇesh)—a popular elephant-headed deity of Hinduism. In *Śaiva* mythology he is also known as *Gaṇapati*, Lord of Hosts. As Vighneshwar, he is worshiped as the "Remover of Obstacles."

Gaṇesh Chaturthi—a Hindu festival of the elephant-headed deity *Ganesh* celebrated in the mid–monsoon season.

Ganga-Daśamī—a Hindu summer festival marking the descent of the sacred river Ganges to the earth.

Garbha Gṛha—the inner sanctuary of a Hindu temple that houses a resident deity.

Godhūli—cow-dust time; a reference to the time cows come home in the evening from grazing all day.

Gopī—milk maids and women cow herders associated with the Hindu god *Krishna*.

Gopuram—large ornate gateways that are important parts of classical South Indian Hindu temple architecture.

Goswāmī—in the *Pushtimarg* tradition, descendants of Vallabhacharya (1479–1532). *Goswāmīs* are considered *gurus* in *Pushtimarg* and are responsible for initiating devotees into the tradition.

Goswāmī & Gosāī—"Lord of Cows." During the time of the Mughal Emperor Akber, *Vaiṣṇava* religious leaders were often given honorary title of *Goswāmī* and *Gosāī*, both meaning "Lord of Cows."

Govardhan—a mountain located in the Mathura district of Uttar Pradesh in India. It is associated with *Krishna* who in Hindu mythology lifted the mountain to protect his devotees from the wrath of *Indra*.

Gūḍha-maṇḍapa—a type of large enclosed hall in ancient Hindu temples.

Gudimallam Liṅga—an aniconic image associated with the deity *Shiva* located in the village of Gudimallam in the state of Andra Pradesh, South India. The Gudimallam *linga* is considered to be one of the earliest *liṅgas* extant.

Gujarat—a state in western India.

Gupta—an ancient empire in northern India from 320–550 CE. The *Gupta* period is considered to be "golden" in Indian history due to its cultural and artistic achievements.

Guru—a Sanskrit term for "teacher" used primarily for spiritual or religious teachers.

Guru dakṣiṇā—a monetary gift given to a *guru* or priest following a ritual service.

Harappa—an ancient city in southern Pakistan associated with the Indus Valley civilization. 2500–1900 BCE.

Haridwar—an ancient pilgrimage city in Uttarakahnad, India, on the banks of the river Ganges.

Havelī—a large mansion or house in northwestern India that was especially popular in the Mughal period. In *Pushtimarg*, temples are often referred to as *havelīs*, reflecting the centrality of home worship or *sevā* within the tradition. However, *Pushtimarg* temples are more properly referred to as *Nandālaya*, the home of *Krishna's* foster father Nanda.

Homa—a *Vedic* fire ceremony.

Indra (**Indra**)—the *Vedic* god of rain and storms and the king of deities in the *Vedic* pantheon. *Indra* remains an important deity in Hinduism and also appears in Buddhist and Jain scriptures.

Iśvara—god in the form of a personal deity in the Hindu tradition. *Shiva* is also often referred to as *Īśvara* or *Maheśvara*, signifying a great god.

Jagannath (**"Lord of the world"**)—a form of *Vishnu* or *Krishna* worshipped in different regions in India including Odisha. The largest and most ancient temple of *Jagannath* is at Puri on the coast of the Bay of Bengal.

Jaimini—a Hindu sage associated with the *Mīmāṃsā* School of philosophy which emphasizes the authority of the *Vedas* and *Vedic* ritual.

Jain—an ancient Indian religious tradition that champions *ahiṃsā* or non-violence.

Jaipur—the capital of Rajasthan state in India.

Janatā Bhāva—a mood in Hindu *bhakti* traditions in which *Krishna* is perceived as a divine being.

Jaṭā Bandham—matted hair tied in a bun. A form of stylized hair in iconography associated with *Shiva*.

Jaṭā mukuṭam—Matted hair fashioned and decorated as a "tall crown." A form of stylized hair in iconography associated with *Krishna* and other deities.

Jāti—endogamous groups that share a common occupation and level of purity and pollution in the Hindu caste system. *Jāti* is distinguished from *varṇa*, the four-fold system of priests, soldiers, merchants, and laborers which is the scriptural definition of caste.

Jayavarman II—the founder of the *Khmer* Empire in Cambodia in the ninth century.

Kali (*Kālī*)—a mother goddess and consort of *Shiva* in the Hindu pantheon. *Kālī* is often presented with a fierce countenance and has an important role in the tantric tradition. In Hindu mythology *Kālī* killed the demon *Mahiṣāsura*.

Kanchipuram—a city in Tamil Nadu (South India) that contains some of the oldest and most sacred temples for both *Vaiṣṇavas* and *Śaivas*. Kanchipuram is an important pilgrimage site.

Kankroli—a city in Rajasthan, Western India. It is often associated with the historical development of the Hindu *Pushtimarg* tradition and houses the *havelī* for *Shri Dwarkadhishji*.

Kashi Vishwanath—chief deity of Kashi (also called Varanasi or Banares). Kashi is in the Indian state of Uttar Pradesh in North India on the banks of the Ganges River. The Kashi Vishwanath temple is one of the most important pilgrimage sites for the deity *Shiva*.

Kasyapa—a *Vedic* seer in Hindu mythology recognized for his great knowledge and spiritual insight. He is understood to be one of seven original sages and the father of both gods and demons in Hindu mythology.

Kaudinya Brahmins—Hindu priests who migrated to Cambodia during the fourth through eighth centuries CE.

Keśa Bandham—a form of highly stylized, tied and decorated hair in the iconography of *Krishna*.

Kirīṭa Mukuṭam (**"tall crown"**)—a form of highly stylized and decorated hair in the iconography of *Krishna*.

Kīrtan—a genre of song popular in the *bhakti* or devotional tradition containing narrative poetic lyrics.

Krishna (*Kṛṣṇa*) (**"black" or "dark"**)—a popular Hindu deity who is understood as an incarnation (*avatār*) of the god *Vishnu*. *Krishna* is especially popular in the North Indian *bhakti* movement.

Kumbakonam—a town in the state of Tamil Nadu (South India) known for its early Hindu temples.

Kumbhābhiṣekam—a ritual in which the spire on top of a Hindu temple is bathed with sacred waters, sanctifying the temple. Also called *Mahā Kumbhābhiṣekam* which connotes the importance of this great ritual of dedication.

Kumbh Melā—a large Hindu festival is held in rotation (in unequal time periods) between four sacred cities across North India. The festival comes back to the same city every twelve years.

Ladkhan **temple at Aihole**—an ancient *Śaiva* temple in the state of Karnataka, India.

Lake Manasarowar—a sacred lake in Tibet near Mount Kailash which is considered to be the abode of *Shiva*. Both the mountain and the lake are also considered sacred in the Bon, Jain, and Buddhist traditions.

Lālan—in *Pushtimarg* a term of endearment used for the baby or toddler form of *Krishna* images worshipped in the home. *Lālans* are sources of intense reverence both for the families and the individuals who worship them daily.

Lāmā—a monk in Tibetan Buddhism.

Līlā (**"divine play"**)—often associated with the deity *Krishna*. A *līlā* may also be a formal drama. In Hindu *bhakti* or devotional traditions, the theological meaning of play is associated with the nature of the cosmos which is generated from the *līlā* of the deity.

Liṅga—an aniconic, phallic form associated with the creative nature of the god *Shiva*.

Madhu Parka—a drink made of honey, curds, and *ghee* (clarified butter) used for ritual occasions during *pūjā*.

Mādhurya bhāva (**also identified as** *sṛṇgāra bhāva*)—a mood in the Hindu *bhakti* traditions in which feelings toward a deity, often *Krishna*, are expressed with deep love with feelings of sweetness.

Mahā Kumbhābhiṣekam—a ritual for the dedication and empowerment of a Hindu temple conducted by pouring sacred water on the spire above the inner sanctuary. See also *Kumbhābhiṣekam*.

Mahabalipuram—an ancient city in India now in the southern state of Tamil Nadu. Mahaballipuram contains a number of shore temples built during the *Pallava* dynasty in the third through seventh centuries CE.

Mahārājā (**"great king"**)—the ruler of a Hindu state in India before independence. *Mahārājās* may also be identified as Mahārāṇas. The term is also used in the *Pushtimarg* Hindu tradition for heads of the *Guru-Ghar* or *Vallabhkul* (the families of descendants of the founder of the tradition, Vallabhacharya).

Mahārāṇa—a ruler of a Hindu kingdom in Rajasthan, Western India. During the period of British rule in India these heads of state were referred to as princes rather than kings coupled with their jurisdictions being identified as princely states.

Mānas Pūjā—*pūjā* through meditation; worshipping a deity in the Hindu tradition through thought and prayer as distinguished from the physical act of *pūjā* which involves awakening, feeding, dressing, and anointing a deity in iconography form.

Maṇḍala—sacred space for invoking deities through sacred design or letters; a geometric design used in Hindu, Jain, and Buddhist religious art to define sacred space.

Maṇḍapa—a porch and hall in a Hindu temple with pillars and canopy.

Mandir—a Hindu temple.

Maṇikhambh Līlā—an aspect of the child *Krishna* who observed his reflection on one of the polished pillars in his house while he attempted to find butter.

Manorath—a system of fundraising in *Pushtimarg* in which individuals and families sponsor a *darśan* or period of unveiling of the deity. *Manorathis* frequently subsidize the noon meal (*darśan*) in *Pushtimarg* temples (*havelīs*) or *rājbhog*. Since the laity are not allowed in the inner sanctum, they "pay" for the rituals to be performed on their behalf. *Darśans* or periods of worship in a temple (*havelī*) are associated with food offerings. In like manner *manoraths* are also associated with food. While the laity can't cook in the *havelī*, they "pay" the temple staff to do it for performing additional work on behalf of the *manorathī*, or the person who wants to perform the offering.

Mantra—an incantation often focused on the experience of the sound rather than literal meaning. *Mantras* are used by Hindu priests to evoke a deity and for other ritual purposes. *Mantras* have to be pronounced in an exact manner in order to be effective.

Mathura—a city in the state of Uttar Pradesh in North India with ancient roots. Mathura is associated with the birth and childhood of the god *Krishna*.

Mauryan—an early empire in India between 322 and 187 BCE.

Māyā ("**illusion**")—in the monistic system of *Advaita* Hindu philosophy, *māyā* is understood as a pervasive characteristic of a *karma* driven universe in which ultimate reality (*Brahman*) remains hidden and beyond thought and language.

Māyā Śilpa—one of the four authors of the *Śilpa Śāstras*. Maya was credited with four texts, the *Mayamata*, *Maya Śilpa*, the *Maya Śilpa Śatikā*, and the *Śilpa Śāstra Bilhanam*.

Mehrgarh-Nausharo—an archaeological site in southern Pakistan near the village of Nahsharo with occupation during the period of the Indus Valley Civilization (circa 2500 BCE).

Mewar—a Rajput kingdom in Rajasthan, India with a history of resistance to Mughal rule. Mewar became the center of the *Pushtimarg* Hindu tradition in the seventeenth century when an image of *Krishna* sought refuge in the small village of Sinhar which became identified as Nathdwara, the central residence of the image of *Shri Nathji*. Mewar is the only state that never married its princesses to the Mughals. The *Mahārāṇa* (king) of Mewar was considered one of the foremost Indian monarchs.

Mīmāṃsā—a Hindu system of philosophy centered on the importance of the *Vedas*.

Mohenjo Daro—an ancient city in southern Pakistan associated with the Indus Valley civilization.

Mudrās—symbolic hand gestures used in *yoga*, religious rituals, and seen in Hindu and Buddhist iconography.

Mukhiyā—head priest in the *Pushtimarg* tradition. The term is also used to refer to a chief in a village.

Mūrti—a Hindu image used for devotional purposes. *Mūrtis* are traditionally made of bronze, stone, and a group of five precious metals called *Pāñcaloha* (gold, silver, copper, brass, and lead). They can also be made from (unfired) clay, ceramic, or wood.

Mūrti Sthāpana—a synonym for *Prāṇ Pratiṣṭhā*; a ritual of installation of a Hindu deity in a temple.

Nagijit—according to Hindu tradition Nagajit was one of the authors of the *Śilpa Śāstras*.

Nāyaṇmārs—*Śaiva* saints who were part of the *bhakti* movement during the sixth through eighth centuries CE.

Nataraga (Naṭarāja) **"lord of the dance"**—a form of the Hindu god *Shiva* associated with dance.

Nathdwara ("Gateway of God")—a town in Rajasthan associated with the Hindu god *Shri Nathji,* who is recognized as a form of *Krishna* as a child who in Hindu mythology lifts Mount Govardhan in order to shelter his devotees from the deity *Indra.* When the deity was given safe refuge in the village of Sinhar in the Hindu state of Mewar in the late seventeenth century, the name of the village was changed to Nathdwara in honor of the deity.

Navatāla—the traditional system of measurement for Hindu images based on nine *tālas* or units.

Navnit Priya (Navnīt Priya) **"he who loves butter"**—an iconographic form of the child *Krishna* with a butter ball in one hand.

Nitya **("permanent")**—rituals such as *pūjā* that are performed daily in Hindu temples or homes.

Pādya—part of a *pūjā* ceremony in which the deity's feet are washed.

Pāñcaloha—a traditional blend of five metals including gold, silver, copper, iron, and lead specified in the *Śilpa Śāstras* for the creation of images or *mūrtis.*

Pāñcarātra Paramansaṃhitā—an ancient text describing ritual worship.

Pāñcatala—a measurement of five *tālas* in the *Śilpa Śāstras* for the construction of images.

Pāñca-dhātu—a synonym for *pāñcaloha.*

Pāsha—a noose held in iconographic forms of deities, often seen in images of *Ganesh,* symbolizing binding.

Paśupati—a name associated with *Shiva* who is seen as the lord of animals.

Pichhavai—temple hangings in the *Pushtimarg* Hindu tradition that are used as backdrops behind the deity.

Prāṇ Pratiṣṭhā **("to establish life")**—a ceremony for the dedication of a Hindu temple in which the deity is formally brought to life inside the central sanctuary.

Prāṇa—breath; an important component of Hindu teachings about *yoga* which require concentration on the breath. *Prāṇa* is also understood as a life force.

***Prasād* (sanctified or consecrated food)**—food that has been offered to a Hindu deity and then presented as grace to the devotees who offer worship.

***Prema Sarovar* ("lake of love")**—referring to the love between *Krishna* and his consort *Radha*—a sacred pond in Vrindaban, India.

***Proto-Shiva* (*Śiva*)**—a figure discovered on Indus valley seals depicting a person seated in what appears to be a yogic position wearing a headdress and once thought to be an early image of the Hindu deity, *Shiva*. This theory once held to be true is no longer accepted.

Pūjā—a system of worship in Hinduism focused on the care of a tutelary deity in iconographic form. *Pūjā* includes awakening, bathing, anointing, dressing and entertaining a deity in a home or temple.

Puruṣa—a term appearing in a *Vedic* hymn (*Ṛg Veda* 10:90) depicting a male cosmic figure whose arms and legs form the four *varnas* (social classes) in the caste system: *brahmins* (priests), *kṣatriyas* (soldiers), *vaiśyas* (merchants), and *śūdras* (laborers).

Pūrva Mīmāṃsā—a system of Hindu philosophy that argued that image worship was of minor importance. *Pūrva Mīmāṃsā* philosophy looked to the *Vedas* for its primary source of authority.

Pushtimarg—a Hindu *bhakti* sect or *sampradāya* founded by Vallabhacharya (1479–1532). *Pushtimarg* was formed in a region called Braj and later spread all across north and western India. Its main centers were founded in Rajasthan and the Gujarat in the fifteenth through seventeenth centuries and has become a transnational tradition.

Pushtimarg Kendra—a program of religious schools started in the United States to teach *Pushtimarg* religious tradition.

***Pushtimargiya* (*Pushṭimārgīya*)**—a devotee of the *Pushtimarg* tradition.

Radha Vallabha Sampradaya—a sixteenth-century north Indian *bhakti* or devotional tradition founded by Harivamsa.

Rajaraja—Rajaraja I ruled the *Chola Empire* from 985 to 1014 CE.

Rājbhog—a meal in the *Pushtimarg* tradition served at the noon *darśan* or unveiling of the image of *Krishna*.

***Rama* (*Rāma*)**—a Hindu god who is the central character in the epic *Rāmāyana*. *Rama* is an *avatār* or incarnation of the deity *Vishnu*.

Ramanuja—a Hindu philosopher (1017–1137 CE) who formed the *Viśiṣṭadvaita* system of thought which qualified the *Advaita* system of non-dualism incorporating the worship of images. Ramanuja was also an important source of authority for the *Shri Vaishnava* tradition.

Rameswaram—an important *Śaiva* temple in the southern India state of Tamil Nadu that is also a pilgrimage center.

Rammohun Roy—(1772–1833) a reformer in the early nineteenth-century Hindu Renaissance movement who became the leader of the *Brahmo Samaj* which attempted to create a revisionist form of Hinduism by employing Christian values including the rejection of image worship.

Rās Līlā—a circular dance in the Hindu *bhakti* traditions in which *Krishna* appears and reappears to each of the cowherdesses (*gopīs*) in the circle. The term is also used to describe religious dramas enacted in Braj associated with *Krishna*.

Rāsa—an aesthetic and an emotion associated with the Hindu *bhakti* tradition and often with the worship of the deity, *Krishna*.

***Rashtriya Swayamsevak Sangh* (RSS)**—a conservative nationalist Hindu political party. The *Bharatiya Janata Party* evolved from the RSS.

Sabara—a third-century Hindu philosopher known for his commentary on the *Mīmāṃsā Sutra* (*Sabara Bhāṣya*). *Mīmāṃsā* is an early school of philosophy that interpreted the *Vedas*.

Sādhu—a Hindu holy man or renunciant.

***Śaiva* (*Śaivite*)**—a sectarian designation used to refer to the followers of the deity *Shiva* or his consorts.

Sakhya bhāva—a mood in the Hindu *bhakti* traditions associated with friendship, often with *Krishna*.

Śaligrāma—an aniconic image found in sacred rivers used by *Vaiṣṇavas* in the Hindu tradition who perceive it as a form on the conch of the deity *Vishnu*.

***Sanātana Dharma* ("eternal duty or truth")**—an indigenous name for the Hindu tradition. The term "Hindu" was a corruption of the word "Sindhu" referring to the Indus River.

Sanchi—an ancient site in Madya Pradesh, India associated with the early Buddhist tradition. Sanchi includes a Buddhist *stupa* (reliquary) erected during the *Mauryan* period in the third century BCE.

Sapta Tāla—seven *tālas* or units of measurement in the *Śilpa Śāstras* for the construction of images.

Śāstra—a treatise in the body of non-canonical Hindu literature or *Smṛti*.

Satsaṅg—a devotional gathering of adherents of a Hindu tradition for religious conversation. *Satsaṅg* has become particularly popular in the West among transnational Hindu populations.

Saṭṭāla—six *tālas* or units of measurement in the Hindu system of measurement for iconography.

***Sevā* ("service")**—*sevā* is an important ritual in the Hindu *Pushtimarg* tradition which is centered in the home where a resident form of *Krishna* (*swarūp*) is cared for daily.

Sevak—servants in *Pushtimarg* temples.

Shaiva Siddhanta—an ancient *Śaiva* philosophy that became an important part of the *bhakti* or devotional movement within Hinduism.

Shankara—an Indian philosopher (circa eighth or ninth centuries CE) who developed the *Advaita* school of Hindu monism. Shankara taught that reality was illusory because of a pervasive pall of illusion (*māyā*) which arose from the ill effects of *karma*.

Śilpi—a *sthapati*, a craftsperson who makes images (*mūrtis*).

Siddhānta—in Hindu thought the development of a philosophical tradition.

Śikhara—a bulbous spire erected on top of a Hindu temple.

Śilpa Śāstra—a corpus of treatises on iconography that have become authoritative in the creation of Hindu images or *mūrtis*.

Śilpa Śāstra Bilhaṇam—One of four texts of *Śilpa Śāstra* attributed to the quasi-historical author Maya.

Sita (Sīta)—a Hindu goddess who is the consort of *Rama*.

Shiva (Śiva)—a Hindu god associated with the destruction of the universe ending a cosmic cycle. In *Śaiva* theology creation and destruction are symbiotic parts of a never ending cycle of regeneration of the cosmos. *Shiva* is part of the *trimūrti* including *Brahma* and *Vishnu*.

Smārta—a caste defined tradition of Hindu *Brahmins* in the priestly class (*varna*).

Smṛti—a classification of Hindu scripture that is non-canonical and distinguished from *śruti* or the canon. Literally, "that which is learned."

Snāna Jala—water for bathing a Hindu deity in iconographic form during *pūjā* or worship.

Śrī Gusāīmjī—a term of endearment in *Pushtimarg* used for the second son of Vallabha, Vitthalnath.

Sri Lanka—the island nation off the southern tip of India.

Shri Nathji (Śrī Nāthjī)—the central form of *Krishna* as a seven-year-old child in the Hindu *Pushtimarg* tradition.

Shri Vaisnava—a Hindu sectarian tradition in South India influenced by the teachings of Ramanuja (1017–1137 CE) who developed the philosophy of *Viśiṣṭadvaita* or qualified non-dualism which opened monistic thought to the role of image worship.

Sri Vari—One of the temples in Tirupati in the state of Andra Pradesh dedicated to the deity *Padala Venkateswara Swamy*.

Sri Ventateswara—an important *Vaiṣṇava* Hindu temple in Andhra Pradesh, India.

Srirangam—an important *Vaiṣṇava* Hindu temple in Tamil Nadu, India. The temple is the largest in India and is constructed in an area of 156 acres.

Sṛṅgāra—a *rāsa* or emotion identified with romantic love.

Śruti (**"that which is heard"**)—the *Vedas* as the canon of Hindu scripture.

Sthapati—workers who create images (*mūrtis*) of deities in the Hindu tradition.

Sucindram—an important Hindu temple and pilgrimage site in Tamil Nadu, South India.

Sur Das—a blind sixteenth-century poet highly revered in the Hindu *bhakti* or devotional tradition for his poetry related to *Krishna*.

Sūr Sāgar—the most important work of the blind poet Sur Das who wrote devotional poetry praising *Krishna*. Sur Das was part of a group of eight poets known as *Astachap* who made important contributions to the *Pushtimarg* school.

Svāgata—part of a *pūjā* ceremony in which the deity is asked if he (she) has arrived safely.

Swarūp—in the Hindu *Pushtimarg* tradition an image which is the most complete form of a deity; usually associated with *Krishna*.

Svayambhū (**self-generating**)—a term that is used to describe images in the Hindu tradition that were naturally formed.

Swami Dayananda Saraswati—a leader of the *Arya Samaj*, a reformist tradition during the late nineteenth-century Hindu renaissance. Dayananda advocated a return to the authority of the *Vedas*.

Swamimalai—a town in the Thanjavur district of the state of Tamil Nadu. Swamimalai is known for its traditional practices of image manufacture through the process of ritual production.

Swaminarayan—a sectarian *Vaiṣṇava* Hindu tradition formed in the early nineteenth century through the teachings of Nilkanth in what is now Gujarat state. The *Swaminaryan* tradition is a *bhakti* or devotional movement that has achieved a globalized presence in the West in addition to its role in India.

Tabla—a pair of single-headed, barrel-shaped small drums of slightly different size and shapes

Tāla—a unit of measurement for Hindu images specified in the *Śilpa Śāstras*. The *Śāstras* are ambiguous on the dimensions of the *tāla*, some associating it with the hand and others with the face. In an alternative meaning *tāla* is also identified as a beat in Indian classical music.

TamilNadu—a southern state in India.

Tarjanī Mudrā—a gesture in Hindu and Buddhist iconography in which the index finger is extended in sign of warning or vigilance.

Thākorjī (**also commonly spelled Thakurji**) (**"Ruler/Master/Lord"**)—an honorific, affectionate title or term of endearment for an image of *Krishna* in the Hindu *Pushtimarg* tradition.

Ṭhākur Pañcāyat—a practice among *Vaiṣṇavas* in West Bengal of convening a council meeting of deities in iconographic form.

Tilkāyat—the senior member of the descendants of Vallabhacharya (*Vallabhkul*) in *Pushitmarg* and the spiritual head of the central temple of the tradition in Nathdwara, Rajasthan. The term *Tilkāyat* also refers to an honorific vermilion mark on the forehead in a group of peers and was first given by the Mughal emperors to the most senior member of the *Vallabhkul*.

Tiruvacakam—a text of *Śaiva* hymns attributed to a Tamil author, Munikkavasagar.

Trimūrti—the Hindu trinity including the deities *Brahma*, *Vishnu*, and *Shiva* associated with the creation, preservation, and destruction of the universe in a cyclical pattern of cosmic regeneration.

Tritāla—three *tālas* or units of measurement in the *Śilpa Śāstras* used for the construction of images. In an alternative meaning *tritāla* may refer to a musical scale of three beats.

Ugra (**angry or highly agitated**)—an iconographic form of a Hindu image in which the deity is shown as protective.

Ulakku—a Tamil measuring unit.

Utsava—a Hindu festival.

Uttar Pradesh—an Indian state located in the northern part of the country.

Vaiṣṇava—also termed *Vaiṣṇavite*. Hindu devotees of *Vishnu* or one of his incarnations including *Krishna*. In *Pushtimarg*, *Vaiṣṇava* is often used as a means of identification.

Vallabha Sampradāya—a North Indian *bhakti* or devotional tradition founded by Vallabhacharya (1479–1532) and centered on the worship of *Krishna* as a child often depicted as seven years old but ranging in age from one to eleven.

Vallabhkul—the descendants of the sons of Vallabhacharya.

Vātsalya bhāva (**parental love**)—a mood in Hindu *bhakti* traditions in which the devotee takes on the role a parent. The *vātsalya rāsa* is central in the *Pushtimarg* tradition which worships *Krishna* as a child.

Vedānta—a school of Hindu philosophy codifed by Shankara in the eighth century. *Vedānta* emphasizes monism and the singular nature of reality which, in a *karmic* universe, cannot be perceived because of the pervasive nature of *māyā* or illusion. *Vedānta* was understood as the ultimate or final development of *Vedic* philosophy.

Vigraha—a form of Hindu sacred art in which a deity is sculpted, molded, cast, painted, or drawn.

Vijayanagar—a Hindu empire in southern India from the fourteenth through seventeenth centuries. (1336–1646 CE)

Vīra (**brave**)—an iconographic form of a Hindu deity represented as a hero.

Viral—in Hindu iconometry one of twelve divisions of a *tāla*.

Vishnu (*Viṣṇu*)—a Hindu deity associated with preservation of the universe and connected to *Brahma*, the creator, and *Shiva* the destroyer. *Avatārs* or incarnations of *Vishnu* include the popular deities *Rama* and *Krishna*.

Vishwa Hindu Parishad—a nationalist, social, and political Hindu organization in India that seeks to bring together disparate Hindu organizations under one umbrella group in India's secular democracy. The *Vishwa Hindu Parishad* has also developed an American presence.

Viśiṣṭadvaita—a philosophy of qualified non-dualism attributed to Ramanuja (1017–1137 CE).

Visvanathasvami—an important *Śaiva* temple in the Indian state of Kerala.

Vivekananda (1863–1902)—a monk and disciple of the nineteenth-century mystic Ramakrishna who achieved prominence through his speeches at the World's Parliament of Religions in 1893 in Chicago. Vivekananda represented the *Vedānta* tradition of Hindu philosophy and was responsible for helping to establish Hindu religious centers in India, the UK, and in the United States.

Vraj—a Gujarati translation of the Hindi term "Braj" used to refer to the rural area around the city of Mathura in North India. In the United States Vraj also refers to the seat of the *Pushtimarg* tradition in the United States located in Schuylkill Haven, Pennsylvania.

Yantra—a geometric design used for worship of a deity in the Hindu tradition.

Yātrā—a Hindu pilgrimage.

Yavai—in Hindu iconometry one of eight divisions of a *viral*.

Chapter Notes

Introduction

1. Diana L. Eck, *India: A Sacred Geography* (New York: Harmony, 2011).

2. I am grateful to Bhagwat Shah for sharing his observations of Nathdwara.

3. George Mitchell, *The Hindu Temple: An Introduction to Its Meaning and Forms* (Chicago: University of Chicago Press), 61–62.

4. Samuel K. Parker, "Ritual As a Mode of Production: Ethnoarchaeology and Creative Practice in Hindu Temple Arts," in *South Asian Studies* 26, no. 1 (2010): 31–57.

5. Richard Elliott and Kritsadarat Wattanasuwan, "Consumption and the Symbolic Project of the Self," *European Advances in Consumer Research* 3 (1998): 17–20.

6. http://www.amazon.com/Ganesh-Finger-Puppet-Ref, accessed April 17, 2016.

7. http://www.ganeshmall.com/Terra-Cotta-Ganesha-Statue-On-Slide/dp/B001SPIWI8?field_availability=-1&field_browse=8830343, accessed April 17, 2016.

8. David Knipe, *Hinduism: Experiments in the Sacred* (Long Grove, Illinois: Waveland Press), 75.

9. Raymond Brady Williams, *Christian Pluralism in the United States: The Indian Immigrant Experience* (Cambridge: Cambridge University Press), 97.

10. Kamari Maxine Clarke and Deborah A. Thomas, *Globalization and Race: Transformations in the Cultural Production of Blackness* (Durham, North Carolina: Duke University Press, 2006).

11. B. Kumaravadivelu, *Cultural Globalization and Language Education* (New Haven: Yale University Press, 2007).

12. Roland Wenzlhuemer, *Connecting the Nineteenth Century World: The Telegraph and Globalization* (Cambridge: Cambridge University Press), 14.

13. "The Sacred Image: Shri Murti," http://sanskrit.org/the-sacred-image-shri-murti/, accessed January 1, 2017. For further discussion of aniconic images see Diana L. Eck, *Darśan: Seeing the Divine Image in India* (New York, Columbia University Press, 1998), 32–36.

14. Molly Oshatz, "From "Meh" to "Amen," *First Things*, http://www.firstthings.com/web-exclusives/2015/06/can-the-nones-go-from-meh-to-amen, accessed April 17, 2016.

Chapter One

1. Personal Interview, Shivani Desai, Cedar Crest College, 2015.

2. Richard Davis, *Lives of Indian Images* (Princeton: Princeton University Press, 1999), 30.

3. Caroline Walker Bynum, "The Sacrality of Things: An Inquiry into Divine Materiality in the Christian Middle Ages," *Irish Theological Quarterly* 78, no. 1 (2012): 4.

4. Alejandro Portes and Ruben G. Rumbaut, *Immigrant America: A Portrait* (Oakland, California: University of California Press, 2014).

5. Milton Gordon, *Assimilation in American Life: The Role of Race, Religion*

and National Origins (New York: Oxford University Press, 1963).

6. *Trinidad, Daily Express*, September 22, 2010, http://www.trinidadexpress.com/news/Ganesh_murtis__drink__milk_-103591304, accessed July 1, 2916.

7. http://www.milkmiracle.com/, accessed July 1, 2016.

8. I am indebted to Mrs. Kinnari Desai for sharing her experiences. Personal interview, Allentown, Pennsylvania, October 25, 2016.

9. Narrenaditya Komaragiri, "Amazing Secrets of Tirumala Temple Revealed by Head Priest Ramana Deekshithulu," *Tirumalesa* (October 2, 2016). http://www.tirumalesa.com/amazing-secrets-of-tirumala-temple-revealed-by-head-priest-ramana-deekshithulu/, accessed October 2, 2016.

10. *Ibid.*

11. *Ibid.*

12. Originally reported in the *Times of India*, this decision was described in, "Indian Courts Uphold that Deities are Legal Entities," *Hinduism Today*, October 10, 2010, 3197.

13. June McDaniel, "Folk Vaishnavism and the Thakur Pancayat" in Guy L. Beck, ed. *Alternative Krishnas: Regional and Vernacular Variations on a Hindu Deity* (Albany: SUNY Press, 2005), 36.

14. Bhagwat Shah, interview.

15. Vraj Hindu temple, Schuylkill Haven, PA, January 8–10, 2016.

16. Khyati Y. Joshi, *New Roots in America's Sacred Ground: Religion, Race, and Ethnicity in Indian America* (New Brunswick: Rutgers University Press, 2006), 86.

17. John Y. Fenton, *Transplanting Religious Traditions: Asian Indians in America* (New York: Praeger, 1988).

18. Joshi, *New Roots in America's Sacred Ground*, 79.

19. Personal Interview, Anonymous, Cedar Crest College, 2015

20. *Ibid.*

21. Satguru Bodhinatha Veylandswami, "My Friend, Lord Ganesha," *Hinduism Today*, October/November/December 2005.

22. Jane Naomi Iwamura, "The Oriental Monk in American Popular Culture," in Bruce David Forbes and Jeffrey H. Mahan, eds. *Religion and Popular Culture in America* (Berkeley: University of California, 2017), 25–43, 205.

23. Henry David Thoreau, "letter to a friend," *IRWLE* 7, no. 2 (July, 2011): 3.

24. Paramahansa Yogananda, *Autobiography of a Yogi* (Los Angeles: Self-Realization Fellowship Publishers Reprint edition, 1998).

25. Abbe J. A. Dubois, trans., Henry K. Beauchamp, *Hindu Manners, Customs and Ceremonies* (New York: Oxford at the Clarendon Press, 1906), 147.

26. *Parliament Papers* 11: 975–6.

27. *Ibid.*

28. The Immigration Act of 1924 was also identified as the Johnson Reed Act and was preceded by federal immigration legislation in 1917 and 1921. State alien land acts, which prohibited Asians to own the land that they farmed, were passed in a number of states including California, Nebraska, Washington, Oregon, Texas, Minnesota, Utah, Wyoming, and a number of other states.

29. Phan Anh Tú, "The Shiva image in Champa Iconography," *Dialogue* 16, no. 2: 109–128.

30. *Ibid.* 131.

31. *Ibid.* 135.

32. Robert L. Brown, "Ritual and Image at Ankor Wat" in Phyllis Granoff and Koichi Shinohara, eds. *Images in Asian Religions: Texts and Contexts* (Toronto: UBC Press, 2004), 346–366.

33. Michael D. Coe, *Angkor and the Khmer Civilization* (New York: Thames and Hudson, 2003), 183.

34. Donald Swearer, *Becoming the Buddha: The Ritual of Image Consecration in Thailand* (Princeton: Princeton University Press, 2004).

35. Robert L. Brown, ed. "Ganesha in Southeast Asian Art: Indian Connections and Indigenous Developments," in *Ganesh: Studies of an Asian God* (Albany, NY: SUNY, 1991), 182.

36. *Ibid.* 185.

37. "Hindus," Religion & Public Life Project, Pew Research Center, 2015.

38. http://moia.gov.in/index.aspx, accessed July 1, 2016.

39. *Ibid.*

40. Manfred B. Steger, *Globalization: A Very Short Introduction* (New York: Oxford University Press, 2009) 6.

41. Manuel A. Vasquez and Marie Friedmann Marquardt, *Globalizing the Sacred: Religion Across the Americas* (New Brunswick: Rutgers University Press, 2003), 56.

42. Caroline B. Brettell and Faith Nibbs, "Lived Hybridity: Second-Generation Identity Construction through College Festival," *Identities: Global Studies in Culture and Power* 16, no. 6 (2009): 678–699.

43. Thomas Hylland Eriksen, *Globalization: The Key Concepts* (Oxford: Berg, 2007).

44. The concept of Great and Little traditions in Anthropology was first introduced by Robert Redfield.

45. Anon., personal interview, Cathedral and John Connon School, Mumbai, 2015.

46. Saranam.com

47. Phyllis K. Herma, "Seeing the Divine Through Windows: Online Darshan and Virtual Religious Experience," *Heidelberg Journal of Religions on the Internet* 4.1 (2010).

48. *Ibid.*

49. *Ibid.*

50. Literature on symbolic consumption is well established. See, for example, Grant David McCracken, *Culture and Consumption: New Approaches to the Symbolic Character of Consumer Goods and Activities* (Bloomington: Indiana University Press, Midland Book, 1990).

51. http://www.ganeshmall.com/b/ 8853785011, accessed May 17, 2016

52. http://www.dollsofindia.com/read/ ganesha-statues.htm, accessed May 17, 2016.

53. http://www.amazon.com/Sale-Ganesh-Lord-Prosperity-Fortune/dp/ B0040L9W9K, accessed May 17, 2016.

54. Michael Thompson, *Rubbish Theory: The Creation and Destruction of Value* (Oxford: Oxford University Press, 1979).

55. http://www.amazon.com/remover-obstacles-hand-made-devotion-krishna/ dp/B0045PA9LQ/ref=cm_cr_pr_product_ top?ie=UTF8, accessed May 17. 2016.

56. http://www.amazon.com/s/?ie= UTF8&keywords=golu+dolls&tag= googhydr-20&index=aps&hvadid=317148 51276&hvpos=1o1&hvexid=&hvnetw= g&hvrand=4921188949540316375&

hvpone=&hvptwo=&hvqmt=b&hvdev= c&ref=pd_sl_9r6ipq280j_b, accessed May 17, 2016.

57. https://www.nyganeshtemple.org/, accessed May 17, 2016.

58. http://www.nytimes.com/2009/07/ 14/nyregion/14temple.html?_r=0, accessed May 17, 2016.

59. http://www.livermoretemple.org/ hints/MKA2010/index.html, accessed May 17, 2016.

60. Stella Kramrisch and Raymond Burnier, *The Hindu Temple*, Vol. 2 (Motilal Banarsidass reprint, 1976), https://books. google.com/books?id=8-aS52MgIk MC&pg=PA359&lpg=PA359&dq=hindu+ temple+as+living+presence&so, 359, accessed July 1, 2016.

61. Shree Patel, personal interview, *Anoopam Mission*, Coplay, Pennsylvania, 2015.

62. Christopher John Fuller, *The Camphor Flame: Popular Hinduism and Society in India* (Princeton: Princeton University Press, 2004), 25.

Chapter Two

1. Sthaneshwar Timalsina, "Imagining Reality: Image and Visualization in Classical Hinduism," (SERAS) *Southeast Review of Asian Studies* 35 (2013): 51.

2. Matthew Gregory Wiecek, "South Asian Figurines in the British Museum: Literature Review and Analysis," (Master of Arts Thesis, Department of Archaeology, Durham University, 2012) 1, 48–49.

3. Dilip Chakrabarti, "The Archaeology of Hinduism," in Timothy Insoll, ed. *Archaeology and World Religion* (Hove, England: Psychology Press, 2001), 38.

4. Robert L Kelly and David Hurst Thomas, *Archeology, 6th Edition* (Boston, MA: Wadworth Publishing, 2013), 43.

5. Gregory L. Possehl, *The Indus Civilization; A Contemporary Perspective* (Lanham, MD: AltaMira Press, 2002), 180.

6. See Doris Srinivasan, "The So-Called Proto-Śiva Seal from Mohenjo-Daro: An Iconological Assessment," *Archives of Indian Art* 29 (1975/1976): 47–58.

7. Richard H. Davis, *Indian Image-Worship and Its Discontents in Represen-*

tation in Religion; Studies in Honor of Moche Barasch, Jan Assman and Albert I. Baumgarten, eds (Leiden: Brill, 2001), 118.

8. "Temple Architecture," Centre for Cultural Resources and Training, Government of India, http://ccrtindia.gov.in/templearchitecture.php, accessed July 1. 2016.

9. *Ibid.*

10. *Ibid.*

11. *Ibid.*

12. Diana L. Eck, *India: A Sacred Geography* (Bourbon, IN: Harmony, 2011), 211.

13. Viyanak Bharne and Krupali Krusche, *Rediscovering the Hindu Temple: The Sacred Architecture and Urbanism of India* (Newcastle Upon Tyne: Cambridge Scholars Publishing, 2012), 85.

14. *Ibid.* 53.

15. *Ibid.* 178.

16. *Ibid.* 185.

17. Eck, *India: A Sacred Geography*, 5.

18. Richard Davis, *Ritual in an Oscillating Universe: Worshipping Siva in Medieval India* (Princeton: Princeton University Press, 1991), 5.

19. Arjun Appadurai and Carol A. Breckenridge, "The South Indian Temple: Authority, Honor and Redistribution," *Contributions to Indian Sociology* 10: 187–211, quoted in, Cynthia Talbot, "Temples, Donors, and Gifts: Patterns of Patronage in Thirteenth-Century South India," *Journal of Asian Studies* 50, no, 2 (May 1991): 308.

20. K.K. Pillay, *The Sacindram Temple* (Adyar Madras: Kalakshetra Publications, 1953), 26.

21. E. Allen Richardson, *Seeing Krishna in America; The Hindu Bhakti Tradition of Vallabhacharya in India and Its Movement to the West* (Jefferson, NC: McFarland, 2014).

22. Richard M. Eaton, *Temple Desecration and Muslim States in Medieval India* (Gurgaon, India: Hope India Publications, 2004).

23. David Shulman, *Tamil Temple Myths: Sacrifice and Divine Marriage in the South Indian Saiva Tradition* (Princeton: Princeton University Press, 1980), 48, in Richard M. Eaton, "Temple desecration in pre-modern India. When, where, and why were Hindu temples desecrated in pre-modern history, and how was this connected with the rise of Indo-Muslim states?" *Frontline* (December 22, 2000), http://www.columbia.edu/itc/mealac/pritchett/00islamlinks/txt_eaton_temples1.pdf, accessed July 1, 2016.

24. Richard Davis, *Ritual in an Oscillating Universe, Worshipping Śiva in Medieval India* (Princeton, Princeton University Press, 1981).

25. *Ibid.* 121.

26. *Ibid.* 71.

27. *Ibid.* 160.

28. Richard H. Davis, *Lives of Indian Images.* (Princeton, Princeton University Press, 1997), 44ff.

29. *Ibid.* 30.

30. *Ibid.* 45.

31. *Ibid.* 46.

32. "Rammohun Roy," http://uudb.org/articles/rajarammohunroy.html, accessed July 1, 2016.

33. *Ibid.*

34. *Ibid.*

35. Satyarth Prakash, *The Light of Truth*, by Swami Dayanand Saraswati, Part 1, Chapter 11, "An examination of the Different; Examination of the Different Religions Prevailing in Aryavarta (India), http://www.aryasamajjamnagar.org/chapter eleven.htm#11, accessed July 1, 2016.

36. V. Ganapati Sthapati and Sashikala Ananth, trans., *Indian Sculpture & Iconography: Forms & Measurement* (Ahmedabad, India: Sri Aurobindo Society, Pondicherry in Association with Mapin Publishing, 2002), xi.

37. Richardson, *Seeing Krishna in America*, 24ff.

38. O.C. Gangoly, *South Indian Bronzes: A Historical Survey of South Indian Sculpture with Iconographical Notes Based on Original Sources* (Calcutta: Nababharat Publishers, 1915 reprint 1978), 2–9.

39. Julian Garcia, Munoz and Juan Carlos Losada Gonzalez, "Modern Shastras," *Proceedings of the Third International Congress on Construction History* (Cottbus, May 2009).

40. R. Vanitha and S. Mayilvanganan, "Organisation of Metal Icon Production in Swamimalai," *Indian Journal of Applied Research* 3, no. 4 (April, 2013).

41. Gangoly, *South Indian Bronzes* (Calcutta: Nababharat Publishers, revised edition), 39.

42. *Ibid.* 283.

43. *Ibid.* 282.

44. Ganapati et al., *Indian Sculpture & Iconography*, 95.

45. *Ibid.* 95–96.

46. Pandit Sri Rama Ramanuja Achari, *Hindu Iconology* (Simha Publications, 2015), www.austrailiancouncilofhinduclergy.com, accessed July 1, 2016.

47. *Ibid.*

48. Phanindra Nath Bose, *Principles of Indian Silpasastra with the Text of Mayasastra* (Lahore, Pakistan: Punjab Sanskrit Book Depot, 1926), 22.

49. Gangoly, *South Indian Bronzes*, 5.

50. S. Sundaravadivel & Co., http://southindianhandicrafts.co.in/panchalogha_utsava_vigraham, accessed July 1, 2016.

51. http://www.census2011.co.in/data/town/803698-swamimalai.html, accessed July 1, 2016.

52. Thomas E. Levy, Alina M. Levy, D. Radhakrishna Stapathy, Srikanda Sthapathy, Swaminatha Sthapathy, *Masters of Fire: Hereditary Bronze Casters of South India* (Bochum, India, 2008), 26.

53. Note: Still other regional centers of ritual production can be found in Bangalore, Mysore, Mannar, Irinjalukuda, Kerala, Tirupathi, and Andhra Pradesh. (R.M. Pillai, S.G.K. Pillai, and A.D. Damodaran, "The Lost-Wax Casting of icons, utensils, bells, and other items in South India," JOM ON-LINE, TMS Publications, October 2002).

54. R. Vanitha and S. Mayilvaganan, "Organisation of Metal Icon Production in Swamimalai," *Indian Journal of Applied Research* 3, no. 4 (April 2013): 79.

55. *Ibid.*

56. *Ibid.*

57. Levy et al., *Masters of Fire*, 26.

58. Ratnam Krishnamurti Ashok Kumar, interview by Rajendran Srinivasan, Swamimalai (Tamil Nadu), 2016.

59. *Ibid.*

60. Levy et al., *Masters of Fire*, 26.

61. Levy, *Masters of Fire.*

62. A chart can be found on the following website, https://www.epanchang.com/GowriPanchangam.aspx.

63. Pratapaditya Pal, *Indian Sculpture circa 700–1800* (Berkeley: Los Angeles County Museum and University of California Press, 1988), https://books.google.com/books?id=-fvKVDxcJoUC&pg=PA231&lpg=PA231&dq=characteristics+of+Chola+art&source=bl&ots=CDUtRuQCNX&sig=iCqn6 37, accessed July 1, 2016.

64. Owen Lynch, *Divine Passions: The Social, Construction of Emotion in India* (New York: Oxford University Press, 1990), 161.

65. *Ibid.* 11.

66. David Haberman, *Journey Through the Twelve Forests: An Encounter with Krishna* (New York: Oxford University Press, 1994), 169.

67. Bhagwat Shah, personal interview, 2016.

68. Bhaktivedanta data base, SB (Srimad Bhāgavata Purāṇa) 10–43–17, http://www.vedabase.com/en/sb/10/43/17, accessed July 1, 2016.

69. Levy et al., *Masters of Fire*, 69.

70. John Stratton Hawley, *Krishna: The Butter Thief* (Princeton: Princeton University Press, 1983), Cover flap.

71. Sur Das, "Krishna Denying He Stole the Butter," *Sant Surdas Poems* (Poem hunter.com), http://vedicilluminations.com/downloads/Bhakti-Vaisnava-Texts/sant_surdas_2004_9.pdf, accessed July 1, 2016.

72. William S. Sax, *The Gods at Play: Lila in South Asia* (New York, Oxford, 1995), 6.

73. Hawley, *Krishna: The Butter Thief*, 34.

74. See *Sur's Ocean: Poems from the Early Tradition, Surdas*, Kenneth E. Bryant, ed. Translated by John Stratton Hawley (Cambridge, Massachusetts: Harvard University Press, Murty Classical Library of India, 2015).

75. *Ibid.* 143.

76. I am grateful to Dr. John Hawley and Goswami Shyam Manoharji in Mumbai for their help in interpreting the iconography.

77. I am grateful to Kanha Vyas for this suggestion.

78. Hawley, *The Butter Thief*, 76.

79. I am especially grateful to Dr. Lindsay Welch of Cedar Crest College who tested the content of the *Balkrishna* images on a scanning electron microscope (SEM).

Chapter Three

1. Talal Asad, *Genealogies of Religion* (1993, Baltimore: Johns Hopkins University Press, 1993), 40–54, quoted in Manuel A. Vasquez and Marie Friedmann Marquardt, *Globalizing the Sacred: Religion Across the Americas* (New Brunswick: Rutgers University Press, 1993).

2. Plato, *Republic, Book VI: The Allegory of the Cave*, http://www.michaelbaur.com/teaching/PlatoCave.pdf, accessed September 1, 2016.

3. Jeremiah 10:5, *New International Version of the Bible*.

4. *New International Version of the Bible*.

5. *Ibid.*

6. *Ibid.*

7. William Dever, *Did God Have a Wife: Archaeology and Folk Religion in Ancient Israel* (Grand Rapids, Michigan: Erdmans, 2008), 289.

8. *Ibid.* 237.

9. Troels Myrup Kristensen, *Making and Breaking the Gods: Christian Responses to Pagan Sculpture in Late Antiquity* (Langelandsgade, Denmark: Aarhus University Press, Aarhus studies in Mediterranean Antiquity, 2013).

10. *Ibid.* 50.

11. *Ibid.* 3.

12. V. Tran Tam Tihn, *Isis Lactans, Corpus des Monuments, Gréco-Romains d'Isis allaitant Harpocrate* (Leiden: Brill, 1973). http://www.academia.edu/1954926/Divine_Mothers_The_Influence_of_Isis_on_the_Virgin_Mary_in_Egyptian_Lactans-Iconography_Journal_of_the_Canadian_Society_for_Coptic_Studies_3_4_2012_71–90, accessed September 1, 2016. See also Sabrina Higgins, "Divine Mothers: The Influence of Isis on the Virgin Mary in Egyptian Lactans-Iconography," *Journal of the Canadian Society for Coptic Studies* 304 (2022): 71–90.

13. Higgins, "Divine Mothers," 72–73.

14. Kristensen, *Making and Breaking the Gods*, 181.

15. *Ibid.*

16. *Ibid.*

17. *Ibid.* 47.

18. Elena Ene D-Vasilescu, "Development of Eastern Christian Iconography," *SAGE Transformation* 27, no. 3 (2010): 169–185.

19. Caroline W. Bynum, "Bleeding Hosts and their Contact Relics in Late Medieval Northern Germany," *The Medieval History Journal*, SAGE 7, no. 2 (2004).

20. *Ibid.*

21. *Ibid.* 235.

22. Jane Garnett and Gervase Rosser, "Miraculous images and the sanctification of urban neighborhood in post-medieval Italy," *Journal of Urban History* 32, no. 5 (July 2006): 731.

23. Diane Purkiss, *The English Civil War: Papists, Gentlewomen, Soldiers, and Witchfinders in the Birth of Modern Britain* (New York: Basic, 2006), 203.

24. Stephen E. Lahey, "Denying Transubstantiation: Physics, Eucharist, and Apostasy," Oxford Scholarship Online, http://www.oxfordscholarship.com/view/10.1093/acprof:oso/9780195183313.001.0001/acprof-9780195183313-chapter-4, accessed June 1, 2016.

25. Alistar E. McGrath, *Reformation Thought: An Introduction* (Hoboken, New Jersey: Wiley and Blackwell, 4th edition, 2012), 3.

26. Kilian McDonnell, "Conclusion." In *John Calvin, the Church and the Eucharist* (Princeton: Princeton University Press, 1967), 363–366, http://www.jstor.org/stable/j.ctt183ph4t.13, accessed June 1, 1016.

27. For further discussion of Pascal's dilemma and the role of the rise in Enlightenment rationalism in challenging traditional beliefs, see Jan Assmann, *Religio Duplex: How the Enlightenment Reinvented Egyptian Religion* (Cambridge, England: Polity Press, 2014).

28. John Locke, *Second Treatise*, 318–319, quoted in Karen Vaughn, *Locke on Property, A Biographical Essay*. Liberty Fund, 2015 http://oll.libertyfund.org/pages/locke-on-property-a-bibliographical-essay-by-karen-vaughn#_ftn22, accessed June 1, 2016.

29. Adam Smith, *An Inquiry into the Nature and Cause of the Wealth of Nations*, 2 vols. (London: W. Strahan and T. Cadell, 1776).

30. Emile Durkheim, *The Elementary Forms of Religious Life* (London: G. Allen & Unwin, 1915, reprint 1995, The Free Press),

232 and 238, quoted in Bjorn Schiermer, "On the Ageing of Objects in Modern Culture: Ornament and Crime," *SAGE Theory, Culture & Society* 0, no. 0: 1–24.

31. Emile Durkheim, *The Elementary Forms of Religious Life*, translated by Joseph Ward Swain (New York: Free Press, 1965), 119.

32. Bjorn Schiermer, "Quasi-Objects, Cult Objects and Fashion Objects: On Two Kinds of Fetishism on Display in Modern Culture," *SAGE* 28, no. 1: 81–102.

33. R. Sridhar "Right-Trunked Ganesha? Be Careful!" *Mumbai Mirror*, Jan 23, 2009.

34. Christopher Tilley, *Metaphor and Material Culture* (Hoboken, NJ: Blackwell, 1999), 6.

35. *Ibid.* 17.

36. S.J. Levy, "Symbols for Sale," *Harvard Business Review* 37, no. 4 (1959): 117–24.

37. Grant McCracken, *Culture and Consumption: New Approaches to the Symbolic Character of Consumer Goods and Activities* (Bloomington: Indiana University Press, 1988), 20.

38. *Ibid.*

39. *Ibid.* 32–43.

40. *Ibid.* 32.

41. *Ibid.* 36.

42. *Ibid.* 32.

43. *Ibid.*

44. Asian Education, "Detection of Fakes and Copies," http://education.asianart.org/ explore-resources/background-information/detection-fakes-and-copies, accessed June 1, 2016.

45. H. E. Allison, *Kant's Transcendental Idealism* (New Haven: Yale University Press, 2004), xv.

46. G.W.F. Hegel, *Phenomenology of Spirit*, A.V. Miller, trans. (New York: Oxford University Press, 1952).

47. *Ibid.* 72. While such parallels are important to acknowledge, Hegel's monistic philosophy was devoid of the central ingredients of Hindu *Advaitan* thinking about the role of *māyā* or illusion and the ability of *karma* to generate it.

48. George Berkeley, "A Treatise Concerning the Principles of Human Knowledge," http://philosophy.eserver.org/ berkeley.html, accessed June 1, 2016.

49. *Ibid.*

50. Graham Harman, "Tristan Garcia and the Thing-in-itself," *Parrhesia* 16 (2013): 27.

51. Martin Heidigger, *Being and Time, a Translation of Sein and Zeit*, Joan Stambaugh, trans. (Albany: SUNY Press, 1996), 67.

52. Pierre Teilhard de Chardin, *The Heart of Matter* (New York: Harcourt, Brace), 17, http://www.pdfarchive.info/ pdf/T/Te/Teilhard_de_Chardin_Pierre_-_ The_Heart_of_Matter.pdf, accessed July 1, 2016.

53. *Ibid.* 18.

54. Ursula King, *Teilhard de Chardin and Eastern Religions: Spirituality and Mysticism in an Evolutionary World* (Mahwah, NJ: Paulist Press, 2011), 43.

55. *Ibid.* 123.

56. *Ibid.*

57. *Ibid.* 33.

58. *Ibid.* 36.

59. de Chardin, *The Heart of Matter.*

60. *Ibid.*

61. William James, *The Varieties of Religious Experience: A Study in Human Nature. Being the Gifford Lectures on Natural Religion Delivered at Edinburgh in 1901–1902* (New York: Longmans, Green and Co., 1902).

62. King, *Teilhard de Chardin*, 222–223.

63. *Ibid.* 226.

64. Marcus Braybooke, "The World Congress of Faiths—An Overview," *The Interfaith Observer*, July 15, 2013, http:// theinterfaithobserver.org/journal-articles/ 2013/7/15/the-world-congress-of-faiths-an-overview.html, accessed July 1, 20116.

65. King, *Teilhard de Chardin*, 226.

66. *Ibid.* 227.

67. *Ibid.*

68. *Ibid.* 80.

69. *Ibid.* 79.

70. Paul Tillich, *The Dynamics of Faith* (New York: HarperCollins, Perennial Classics, 1957), 47.

71. *Ibid.* 48.

72. *Ibid.*

73. *Ibid.* 49.

74. *Ibid.*

75. *Ibid.*

76. Paul Tillich, *Dynamics of Faith* (New York: Harper & Row, 1957), 42–48.

77. Werner Weick, director, Carl *Gus-*

tav Jung: Artist of the Soul (New York: Mystic Fire Videos, 1997).

78. C.G. Jung, *Memories, Dreams, Reflections*, Aniela Jaffe ed. (New York: Vintage Books, 1989), 21.

79. C.G. Jung, *Mandala Symbolism*, translated by R.F.C. Hull (Princeton: Princeton University. Press, 1972), 5.

80. Judit Törzsök, "Icons of Inclusivism, Maṇḍalas in Some Early Śaiva Tantras…" in *Maṇḍalas and Yantras in the Hindu Traditions* (Leiden: Koninklyke Brill NV, 2003), 189–190.

81. See Gudrun Bühnemann, "Maṇḍala, Yantra and Cakra: Some Observations," in *Mandalas and Yantras*, 13–56.

82. Carl Gustav Jung, ed. *Man and His Symbols* (New York: Dell, 1968), 20–21.

83. *Ibid.* 77.

84. C.G. Jung, *Mandala Symbolism*, 99.

85. Desmond Peter Lazaro, *Pichhvai Painting Tradition of Rajasthan: Materials, Methods and Symbolism* (Ahmedabad, India: Mapin, 2006), 32.

86. *Ibid.* 34.

87. Peter Korn, *Why We Make Things and Why It Matters: The Education of a Craftsman* (Boston: David R. Godine, 2015), 58–59.

88. *Ibid.*

89. Daniel J. Wakin, "Selling a 300-Year-Old Cello," *New York Times*, January 13, 2012.

90. *Ibid.*

91. *Ibid.*

92. Martin Heidegger, *Being and Time*, John Macquarrie and Edward Robinson, trans. (London: Blackwell, 2000).

93. Herbert K. Goodkind, *Violin Iconography of Antonio Stradivari 1644–1737* (New York: Larchmont, 1972).

94. Douglas E. Haynes, *Small Town Capitalism in Western India: Artisans, Merchants and the Making of the Informal Economy 1870–1960* (New York: Cambridge University Press, 2012), 2.

95. *The Creation of "The Public" and the Question of Privilege* (Oakland, California: UC Press e-books collection, 1982–2004), http://publishing.cdlib.org/ucpressebooks/view?docId=ft88700868&chunk.id=d0e 7721&toc.depth=100&brand=ucpress; query=india, accessed July 1, 2016.

Chapter Four

1. *Vaishnav Kendra* conference, *Pushti Margiya Vaishnav Samaj* (Vraj), Schuylkill Haven, PA, June 2017.

2. *Vraj Youth Organization*, Schuylkill Haven, PA, January, 2016.

3. Megha Rajguru, "From Shrine to Plinth: Studying the Dialectics of Hindu Deities Displayed in the Museum Through Artworks and Their Exhibition." (Ph.D. Dissertation, University of Brighton, 2010).

4. Richard H. Davis, *Lives of Indian Images* (Princeton: Princeton University Press), 17.

5. Samuel K. Parker, "Renovation, Disposal, and Conservation of Hindu Temples and Images: The Institutionalization of Creativity in South Indian and American Art Worlds," *Museum Anthropology Review* 3, no. 2 (Fall 2009).

6. Partha Mitter, *Much Maligned Monsters* (Clarendon Press, Oxford, 1977), 3.

7. *Ibid.* 10.

8. Carol Cains, "Devotion and Idolatry: The Conflicting Purposes of a Nineteenth-Century Indian Deity Album," NVG Publications, *Art Journal* 50, http://www.ngv.vic.gov.au/essay/devotion-and-idolatry-the-conflicting-purposes-of-a-nineteenth-century-indian-deity/, accessed September 1, 2016.

9. F. Max Müller, et al., *Sacred Books of the East,* 50 Vols. (Oxford: Clarendon Press, 1879).

10. See Wendy Doniger, "War and Peace in the Bhagavad Gita," *New York Times* (December 4, 2014).

11. T.A. Gopinatha Rao, *Elements of Hindu Iconography* (New York: Garland, 1991).

12. *Ibid.* 1.

13. *Ibid.* 8–9

14. *Ibid.* 12

15. Rao, *Elements of Hindu Iconography*, 36.

16. *Ibid.*

17. *Ibid.*

18. *Benjamin Rowland, The Art and Architecture of India: Buddhist, Hindu, Jain* (London: Penguin, 1953).

19. Christopher H. Foreman, "Noted Arts Expert Benjamin Rowland Dies at Age of 67," *Harvard Crimson*, October 5,

1972, http://www.thecrimson.com/article/ 1972/10/5/noted-arts-expert-benjamin-rowland-d, accessed September 1, 2016.

20. Jitendra Nath Banerjea, *The Development of Hindu Iconography* (Calcutta: University of Calcutta, 1941).

21. P.K. Misra, *Studies in Hindu and Buddhist Art* (Chikhli, India: Abhinav Publications, 1999).

22. Paul Michael Taylor, "Collecting icons of Power and Identity: Transformation of Indonesian Material Culture in the Museum Context," *Cultural Dynamics* 7, no. 1 (SAGE publications, 1995): 101–124.

23. Caroline van Eck, *Art, Agency, and Living Presence: From the Animated Image to the Excessive Object* (Leiden, De Gruyter, Leiden University Press), 14.

24. Tapati Guha-Thakurta, "The Museumised (sic) Relic: Archaeology and the First Museum of Colonial India," *The Indian Economic and Social History Review* 34, no, 1 (SAGE Publications, 1997): 21–51.

25. British Museum, *History of the Collection*, http://www.britishmuseum.org/ about_us/the_museums_story/the_ collection.aspx, accessed September 1, 2016.

26. *Ibid.* 14.

27. Pratapaditya Pal, "Some Hindu and Buddhist Bronzes from Bangladesh," *Studies in South Asian Heritage, Essays in Memory of M. Harunur Rashid*, Mokammal H. Bhuiyan, ed. (Bangla Academy: Dhaka, Bangladesh, 2015), http://www.asianart. com/articles/bangladesh/index.html, accessed September 1, 2016.

28. *Ibid.*

29. "Architectural Ensemble from Jain Meeting Hall," Metropolitan Museum of Art, Collection Records, http://www.met museum.org/collection/the-collection-online/search/39317, accessed September 1, 2016. Later in the early twentieth century when the temple was renovated, this portion had been discarded.

30. W. Norman Brown, *A Pillared Hall from a Temple at Madura, India in the Philadelphia Museum of Art* (Philadelphia: University of Pennsylvania Press and London: Humphrey Milford: Oxford University Press, 1940)

31. *Ibid.* 21.

32. *Ibid.* 66.

33. Crispin Paine, *Religious Objects in Museums: Private Lives and Public Duties* (London: Bloomsbury, 2013), 41.

34. *Ibid.*

35. *Ibid.* 38.

36. *Ibid.*

37. Morgan Wesley, "A Dialogue of Connoisseurship and Science in Constructing Authenticity: The case of the Duke of Buckingham's China," in Megan Aldrich and Jos Hackforth-Jones, *Art and Authenticity* (New York: Sotheby's Institute of Art, 2012), 40.

38. *Ibid.*

39. *Ibid.* 40–41.

40. *Ibid.* 19.

41. Isabella Nardi, "Re-evaluating the Role of Text in Indian Art: Towards a *Shastric* Analysis of the Image of Shrī Nathji in Nathdvara Miniature Painting," *South Asia Research* 29, no. 2: 2009.

42. Richard H. Davis, *Lives of Indian Images*, 240.

43. *Ibid.* 241.

44. *Ibid.*, 249.

45. Shruti Singh, "Gujarat Temple Dresses Lord Swaminarayan in RSS Uniform," *India Today*, Ahmedabad, July 8, 2016, http://indiatoday.intoday.in/story/ gujarat-temple-dresses-lord-swaminarayan-in-rss-uniform/1/686975. html, accessed September 1, 2016.

46. "Swaminarayan Idol in RSS Dress at Surat School Kicks Up Row," *The Indian Express*, July 9, 2016, http://indianexpress. com/article/india/india-news-india/ gujarat-temple-lord-swaminarayan-rss-sevak-dress-bjp-controversy-2840929/, accessed September 1, 2016.

47. Shruti Singh, "Gujarat Temple Dresses Lord Swaminarayan in RSS Uniform."

48. Satguru Bodhinatha, "My Friend, Lord Ganesha: Hinduism's Lord of Djharma," *Hinduism Today*, Oct/Nov/Dec 2005.

49. Reuven Blau, "Hindus Upset Over Brooklyn Museum's Exhibit of Goddess Kālī," *New York Daily News*, December 18, 2014, http://www.nydailynews.com/new-york/brooklyn/hindus-upset-brooklyn-museum-exhibit-goddess-kali-article-1. 2050474, accessed September 1, 2016.

50. *Ibid.*

51. *Ibid.*

52. Kajri Jain, *Gods in the Bazaar; The Economies of Indian Calendar Art* (Durham, North Carolina: Duke University Press, 2007).

53. Jan Assmann, *Moses the Egyptian: The Memory of Egypt in Western Monotheism* (Cambridge, Massachusetts: Harvard University Press, 1997).

54. William G. Dever, *Did God Have a Wife: Archaeology and Folk Religion in Ancient Israel* (Grand Rapids, Michigan: William B. Eerdmans, 2005).

55. Moshe Halbertal and Avishai Margalit, *Idolatry* (Cambridge, Massachusetts: Harvard University Press, 1992).

56. *Ibid.* 22.

57. *Ibid.* 42.

58. *Ibid.* 48–49.

59. *Ibid.* 50

60. Caroline van Eck, *Art, Agency and Living Presence: From the Animated Image to the Excessive Object* (Leiden, the Netherlands, De Gruyter, Leiden University Press), 115.

61. Michael Camille, *The Gothic Idol: Ideology and Image-Making in Medieval Art, Cambridge Studies in New Art History and Criticism* (New York: Cambridge University Press, 1991).

62. Michael Wayne Cole and Rebecca Zorach, eds. *The Idol in the Age of Art: Objects, Devotions and the Early Modern World* (Aldershot, England: Ashgate, Saint Andrews Studies in Reformation History, 2009).

63. van Dyke, *Art, Agency and Living Presence*, 86.

64. *Ibid.* 107.

65. *Ibid.* 111.

66. Alfred Gell, *Art and Agency: An Anthropological Theory* (New York: Oxford University Press, 1998).

67. Van Dyke *Art, Agency and Living Presence*, 54.

68. Gell, *Art and Agency*, 16.

69. Robert Layton, "Art and Agency: A Reassessment," *The Journal of the Royal Anthropological Institute* 9, no. 3 (September 2003): 447–464.

70. *Ibid.*

71. Victor Turner, *Drums of Affliction* (Oxford, England: Oxford University Press, 1968), 72–75.

72. Gell, *Art and Agency*, 30–31.

73. *Ibid.*

74. *Ibid.* 117.

75. *Ibid.* 120.

76. *Ibid.*

77. *Ibid.* 129.

78. *Ibid.*

79. "Installing a Sacred Image Mūrti Sthapana/Prāṇ Pratiṣṭhā," Devasthanam, Website of the Sanskrit Religions Institute, http://sanskrit.org/installing-a-sacred-image-murti-sthapanaprana-pratishta/, accessed September 1, 2016.

80. *Ibid.*

81. Sthaneshwar Timalsina, "Imagining Reality: Image and Visualization in Classical Hinduism," *Southeast Review of Asian Studies* 35 (2013): 50–69.

82. *Ibid.*

83. Robert Skelton, *Rajasthani Temple Hangings of the Krishna Cult from the Collection of Karl Mann, New York* (New York: American Federation of Arts, 1973).

84. *Ibid.*

85. Desmond Peter Lazaro, *Materials, Methods & Symbolism in the Pichhvai Painting Tradition of Rajasthan* (Ahmedabad, India: Mapin, 2005), 55.

86. Sthaneshwar Timalsina, "Imagining Reality: Image and Visualization in Classical Hinduism," 57.

87. *Ibid.*

88. John Stratton Hawley, *At Play with Krishna: Pilgrimage Dramas from Brindavan* (New Delhi: Motilal Banarsidas reprint, 2010), 17.

89. *Ibid.*

90. *Ibid.*

91. *Ibid.* 18.

Chapter Five

1. Diana L. Eck, *India a Sacred Geography* (New York: Harmony Reprint, 2013), 5.

2. Jennifer Medina, "Debate Erupts in California Over Curriculum on India's History, *New York Times*, May 4, 2016.

3. David Haberman, *Journey Through the Twelve Forests, My Encounter with Krishna* (New York: Oxford University Press, 1993), 178–9.

4. "A Discussion with Young American Hindus," *Puja: Expressions of Hindu Devotion*, Guide for Educators, Washington, D.C., Smithsonian Institution, 1997, https://

www.asia.si.edu/pujaonline/puja/sitemap_1.html, accessed September 1, 2016.

5. "Hindus' Success: Argentine Exhibit Converting Barbie into Goddess Kali Cancelled," *Hindu Janajagruti Samiti*, October 2, 2014, https://www.hindujagruti.org/news/25434.html, accessed September 1, 2016.

6. "Barbie: Doll, Icon or Sexist Symbol?" *New York Times*, December 23, 1987.

7. "Barbie: Doll, Icon or Sexist Symbol?" *New York Times*, December 23, 1987, http://www.nytimes.com/1987/12/23/garden/barbie-doll-icon-or-sexist-symbol.html, accessed September 1, 2016.

8. Tanisha Ramachandran, "A Call to Multiple Arms! Protesting the Communization of Hindu Imagery in Western Society," *Material Religion: The Journal of Objects, Art and Belief*, 10 (2014), Issue 1.

9. Satgutu Bodhinatha Veylanswami, "My Friend, Lord Ganesh: Lord of Hinduism," *Hinduism Today*, October, November, December 2005, https://www.hinduismtoday.com/modules/smartsection/item.php?itemid=1366, accessed September 1, 2016.

10. Jonathan Friedman, "Globalization, Class and Culture in Global Systems, in *Journal of World-Systems Research* vi, no. 3 (Fall/Winter 2000): 636–656.

11. "Sri Vaisnavam," https://ramanujadasan.wordpress.com/sri vaishnava-digital-fund/, accessed September 1, 2016.

12. Manuel A. Vasquez and Marie Friedmann Marquardt, in Vasquez, *Globalizing the Sacred: Religion Across the Americas* (New Brunswick: Rutgers University Press, 2003), 56.

13. Prema Kurian, *A Place at the Multicultural Table: The Development of an American Hinduism* (New Brunswick, NJ: Rutgers University Press, 2007), 9.

14. *Ibid.*

15. Judit Bokser-Liwerant, "Globalization and Collective Identities," *Social Compass* 49, no. 2 (2002): 254.

16. *Ibid.* 253–271.

17. *Ibid.*

18. Manuel Castells, Gustavo Cardoso, Eds. *The Network Society from Knowledge to Policy* (Washington, DC: Johns Hopkins Center for Transatlantic Relations, 2005), 4.

19. Drew Disilver, "Five Facts About Indian Americans," Pew Research Center, http://www.pewresearch.org/fact-tank/2014/09/30/5-facts-about-indian-americans/, accessed September 1, 2016.

20. Alejandro Portes and Ruben G. Rumbaut, *Immigrant America: A Portrait,* 4th edition (Oakland: University of California Press, 2014).

21. Khyati Y. Joshi, *New Roots in America's Sacred Ground: Religion, Race and Ethnicity in Indian Americ* (New Brunswick, NJ: Rutgers University Press, 2006), 69.

22. Bharat Yagnik, "162-Acre Akshardham Coming Up in New Jersey" *Times of India*, July 22, 2014.

23. Mike Davis, "Traditional Hindu Temple Opening in Robbinsville, Part of BAPS Community," *Times of Trenton*, July 28, 2014.

24. John R. Hinnells, "South Asian Religions in Migration: A Comparative Study of the British, Canadian, and U.S. Experiences," in Howard Coward, John R. Hinnells, and Raymond Brady Williams, *The South Asian Religious Diaspora in Britain, Canada, and the United States* (Albany: State University of New York Press, 2000).

25. Simon J, Potter, "Webs, Networks, and Systems: Globalization and the Mass Media in the Nineteenth- and Twentieth-Century British Empire" in *Journal of British Studies* 46, no. 3 (July 2007): 621–646. Page 625 quotes Tony Ballantyne, *Orientalism and Race: Aryanism in the British Empire* (Basingstoke, England: 2002), 12, 195.

26. "East India Company Ships: The Maritime Service 1600 to 1834," http://www.eicships.info/, accessed September 1, 2016.

27. Journal At Sea of Patrick Begbie (1781), author's collection. Records of the British Army in Bengal show Begbie's name several years after the loss of his ship. While it seems likely that references to Begbie in the East India Company records and those of the army in Bengal refer to the same person there is no complete history of his career in India. Records of Begbie's death are also uncertain but indications exist that his son continued in the same pattern of life taking two trips to India.

28. Anil Seal, *The Emergence of Indian Nationalism: Competition and Collaboration in the Later Nineteenth Century* (New York: Cambridge University Press, 1971), 196.

29. *Ibid.*

30. See E. Allen Richardson, *Seeing Krishna in America: The Hindu Bhakti Tradition of Vallabhacharya in India and Its Movement to the West* (Jefferson, North Carolina: McFarland, 2014).

31. *Ibid.* 188.

32. "India, Britain and Three Waves of Migration," Blog, *Hindustan Times*, https://www.hinduismtoday.com/modules/smart section/item.php?itemid=1366, accessed September 1, 2016.

33. "Goswami Anandbava," http://en.gravatar.com/anandbava, accessed September 1, 2016.

34. "Hariray Goswami's Blog," https://shriharirayji.com/pushtimarg/, accessed September 1, 2016.

35. *Ibid.*

36. *Ibid.*

37. http://vyoworld.org/centers/, accessed September 1, 2016.

38. http://paroolmodi67.blogspot.com/, accessed September 1, 2016.

39. Robert Redfield, *Peasant Society and Culture* (Chicago: University of Chicago Press, 1956).

40. See E. Allen Richardson, *Strangers in This Land: Religion, Pluralism and the American Dream* (Jefferson, North Carolina: McFarland, 2010), 130–167.

41. Vasquez and Friedmann Marquardt, *Globalizing the Sacred,* 58.

42. Homi Bhabha, *The Location of Culture* (London: Routledge, 1994), 60.

43. Brent Nongbri, *Before Religion: A History of a Modern Concept* (New Haven: Yale University Press, 2013), 110.

44. *Ibid.*

45. *Concise Oxford Dictionary of World Religions,* John Bowker, ed. (New York: Oxford University Press, 2000).

Bibliography

Achari, Pandit Sri Rama Ramanuja. *Hindu Iconology* (sic). Simla Productions, 2015. www. austrailiancouncilofHinduclergy.com (accessed July 1, 2016).

Ackroyd, Bradley Sterling. *Hinduism in Cyberspace.* Ph.D. Thesis, University of Florida, 2006.

Allison, H. E. *Kant's Transcendental Idealism.* New Haven: Yale University Press, 2004.

Anandbava, Goswami. Blog. http://en.gravatar.com/anandbava (accessed September 1, 2016).

Anh Tú, Phan. "The Shiva Image in Champa Iconography," 109–128, *Dialogue* 16 no. 2: 109–128.

Anonymous, interview with the author, 2015.

Appadurai, A., and Carol A. Breckenridge. "The South Indian Temple: Authority, Honor and Redistribution." *Contributions to Indian Sociology* 10: 187–211.

Asad, Talal. *Genealogies of Religion.* Baltimore: Johns Hopkins University Press, 1993, 40–54.

Assmann, Jan. *Moses the Egyptian: The Memory of Egypt in Western Monotheism.* Cambridge, Massachusetts: Harvard University Press, 1997.

_____. *Religio Duplex: How the Enlightenment Reinvented Egyptian Religion.* Cambridge, England: Polity Press, 2014.

_____, and Albert I. Baumgarten, ed. *Representation in Religion: Studies in Honor of Moshe Barasch.* Leiden: Brill, 2001.

Babb, Lawrence A., and Susan S. Wadley. *Media and the Transformation of Religion in South Asia.* Philadelphia: University of Pennsylvania Press, 1995.

Bachrach, Emilia. "The Living Tradition of Hagiography in the Vallabh Sect of Contemporary Gujarat." Ph.D. dissertation, University of Texas at Austin, 2014.

Ballantyne, Tony. *Orientalism and Race: Aryanism in the British Empire.* Basingstoke, England: 2002.

Banerjea, Jitendra Nath. *The Development of Hindu Iconography.* Calcutta: University of Calcutta, 1941.

Barnard, Anne. "Reconsecration, With Bells, Saffron and Elephant." *New York Times*, July 13, 2009. http://www.nytimes.com/2009/07/14/nyregion/14temple.html?_r=0 (accessed January 1, 2017).

Barringer, Tim, and Tom Flynn, eds. *Colonialism and the Object: Empire, Material Culture and the Museum.* New York: Routledge, 1998.

Beck, Guy L., ed. *Alternative Krishnas: Regional and Vernacular Variations on a Hindu Deity.* Albany: State University of New York Press, 2005.

Bennett, Peter. *The Path of Grace: Social Organisation (sic) and Temple Worship in a Vaishnava Sect.* Delhi: Hindustan Publishing Company, 1993.

Berkeley, George. "A Treatise Concerning the Principles of Human Knowledge." http://philosophy.eserver.org/berkeley.html (accessed January 1, 2017).

Bhabha, Brent Homi. *The Location of Culture*. London: Routledge, 1994.

Bhagavata Purana, Srimad. http://www.vedabase.com/en/sb/10/43/17 (accessed July 1, 2016).

Bharne, Viyanak, and Krupali Krusche. *Rediscovering the Hindu Temple: The Sacred Architecture and Urbanism of India*. Newcastle upon Tyne, England: Cambridge Scholars Publishing, 2012.

Blau, Reuven. "Hindus Angered Over Brooklyn Museum's New Massive Exhibit of Goddess Kali," *New York Daily News*, December 18, 2014. http://www.nydailynews.com/new-york/brooklyn/hindus-upset-brooklyn-museum-exhibit-goddess-kali-article-1.2050474 (accessed September 1, 2016).

Bodhinatha, Satguru. "My Friend, Lord Ganesha: Hinduism's Lord of Dharma," *Hinduism Today*, Oct/Nov/Dec, 2005.

Bokser-Liwerant, Judit. "Globalization and Collective Identities," *Social Compass* 49 no. 2 (2002): 254.

Bose, Phanindra Nath. *Principles of Indian Silpasastra with the Text of Mayasastra*. Lahore, Pakistan: Punjab Sanskrit Book Depot, 1926.

Braybooke, Marcus. "The World Congress of Faiths—An Overview," *The Interfaith Observer*, July 15, 2013. http://theinterfaithobserver.org/journal-articles/2013/7/15/the-world-congress-of-faiths-an-overview.html (accessed July 1, 2016).

Brettell, Caroline B., and Faith Nibbs. "Lived Hybridity: Second-Generation Identity Construction Through College Festival," *Identities: Global Studies in Culture and Power* 16, no. 6 (2009): 678–699.

British Museum. *History of the Collection*. http://www.britishmuseum.org/about_us/the_museums_story/the_collection.aspx (accessed September 1, 2016).

Brown, Robert L., ed. "Ganesha in Southeast Asian Art: Indian Connections and Indigenous Developments," in *Ganesh: Studies of an Asian God*. Albany: SUNY, 1991.

Brown, Robert L. "Ritual and Image at Ankor Wat," in Phyllis Granoff and Koichi Shinohara, eds. *Images in Asian Religions: Texts and Contexts*. Toronto: UBC Press, 346–366.

Brown, W. Norman. *A Pillared Hall from a Temple at Madura, India in the Philadelphia Museum of Art*. Philadelphia: University of Pennsylvania Press, 1940.

Bryant, Kenneth E., ed. *Surdas*. See *Sur's Ocean: Poems from the Early Tradition*. Translated by John Stratton Hawley. Cambridge, Massachusetts: Harvard University Press, 2015.

Bühnemann, Gudrun. "Mandala, Yantra and Cakra: Some Observations" in Gudrun Bühnemann, *Mandalas and Yantras in the Hindu Traditions*. Boston: Brill, 2003, 13–56.

Bynum, Caroline W. "Bleeding Hosts and Their Contact Relics in Late Medieval Northern Germany," *SAGE Journals. The Medieval History Journal* 7, no. 2 (2004).

Bynum, Caroline Walker. "The Sacrality of Things: An inquiry into Divine Materiality in the Christian Middle Ages." *Irish Theological Quarterly* 78, no. 1 (2012): 3–18.

Cains, Carol. "Devotion and Idolatry: The Cconflicting Purposes of a Nineteenth-Century Indian Deity Album," NVG Publications, *Art Journal 50*. http://www.ngv.vic.gov.au/essay/devotion-and-idolatry-the-conflicting-purposes-of-a-nineteenth-century-indian-deity/ (accessed September 1, 2016).

Camille, Michael. *The Gothic Idol: Ideology and Image-Making in Medieval Art, Cambridge Studies in New Art History and Criticism*. New York: Cambridge University Press, 1991.

Castells, Manuel, and Cardoso Gustavo, eds. *The Network Society from Knowledge to Policy*. Washington, D.C.: Johns Hopkins Center for Transatlantic Relations, 2005.

Centre for Cultural Resources and Training, Government of India. "Temple Architecture," http://ccrtindia.gov.in/templearchitecture.php (accessed July 1. 2016).

Census Population, Government of India. Swamimalai Population Census 2011. http://www.census2011.co.in/data/town/803698-swamimalai.html (accessed January 1, 2017).

Chakrabarti, Dilip. "The Archaeology of Hinduism," in Timothy Insoll, ed. *Archaeology and World Religion*. Hove, England: Psychology Press, 2001.

Clarke, Kamari Maxine, and Deborah A. Thomas. *Globalization and Race: Transformations in the Cultural Production of Blackness*. Durham, North Carolina: Duke University Press, 2006.

Coe, Michael D., and Donald Swearer. *Angkor and the Khmer Civilization*. New York: Thames and Hudson, 2003.

Cole, Michael Wayne, and Rebecca Zorach, eds. *The Idol in the Age of Art: Objects, Devotions and the Early Modern World*. Aldershot, England: Ashgate, Saint Andrews Studies in Reformation History, 2009.

Collins, Al, and Elaine Molchanov, eds. "Jung and India," *Spring: A Journal of Archetype and Culture* 90 (Fall 2013).

Commaraswamy, Ananda K. *History of Indian and Indonesian Art*. New York: Dover reprint of the 1927 edition by Karl L. Hiersemann, 1965.

Coward, Harold. *Jung and Eastern Thought*. Albany: State University of New York Press, 1985.

"The Creation of "The Public" and the Question of Privilege," (Oakland, California: UC Press e-books collection, 1982–2004), in David West Rudner, *Caste and Capitalism in Colonial India: The Nattukottai Chettiars*. Berkeley: University of California Press, 1994. http://publishing.cdlib.org/ucpressebooks/view?docId=ft88700868&chunk.id=d0e7721&toc.depth=100&brand=ucpress;query=india (accessed July 1, 2016).

Davis, Mike "Traditional Hindu Temple Opening in Robbinsville, Part of BAPS Community," *Times of Trenton*, July 28, 2014.

Davis, Richard H. "Indian Image Worship and Its Discontents," in *Representation in Religion; Studies in Honor of Moshe Barasch*. Jan Assmann and Albert I. Baumgarten, eds. Leiden: Brill, 2001.

______. *Lives of Indian Images*. Princeton: Princeton University Press, 1999.

______. *Ritual in an Oscillating Universe: Worshipping Siva in Medieval India*. Princeton: Princeton University Press, 1991.

Dayanand, Swami. "Satyarth, Prakash," "The Light of Truth," Part 1, Chapter 11, "An examination of the Different; Religions Prevailing in Aryavarta (India)." http://www.aryasamajjamnagar.org/chaptereleven.htm#11 (accessed July 1, 2016).

Desai, Kinnari. Personal interview, Allentown, Pennsylvania. October 25, 2016.

Desai, Shivani. Personal Interview, Allentown, Pennsylvania, Cedar Crest College, 2015.

"Detection of Fakes and Copies," Asian Education. http://education.asianart.org/explore-resources/background-information/detection-fakes-and-copies (accessed June 1, 2016).

Dever, William G. *Did God Have a Wife: Archaeology and Folk Religion in Ancient Israel*. Grand Rapids, Michigan: William B. Eerdmans, 2005.

Dirks, Nicholas B. *Castes of Mind: Colonialism and the Making of Modern India*. Princeton: Princeton University Press, 2001.

Disilver, Drew. "Five Facts About Indian Americans," Pew Research Center. http://www.pewresearch.org/fact-tank/2014/09/30/5-facts-about-indian-americans/ (accessed September 1, 1016).

Doniger, Wendy. "War and Peace in the Bhagavad Gita," *New York Times*, December 4, 2014.

Dubois, Abbe J. A. *Hindu Manners, Customs, and Ceremonies*. Translated by Henry Beauchamp. New York: Oxford, Clarendon Press, 1906, 147.

Durkheim, Emile. *The Elementary Forms of Religious Life*. London: G. Allen & Unwin, 1915.

D-Vasilescu, Elena Ene. "Development of Eastern Christian Iconography," *SAGE Journals. Transformation* 27, no. 3 (2010): 169–185.

East India Company Ships. "The Maritime Service 1600 to 1834." http://www.eicships.info/ (accessed September 1, 2016).

Eaton, Richard M. *Temple Desecration and Muslim States in Medieval India*. Gurgaon, India: Hope India Publications, 2004.

Eck, Diana L. *India: A Sacred Geography*. Bourbon, Indiana: Harmony, 2011.

______. *Darśan: Seeing the Divine Image in India*. New York, Columbia University Press, 1998.

Elliott, Richard, and Kritsadarat Wattanasuwan. "Consumption and the Symbolic Project of the Self," *European Advances in Consumer Research* 3 (1998): 17–20.

Eriksen, Thomas Hylland. *Globalization: The Key Concepts*. Oxford, New York: Berg, 2007.

Faist, T., ed. *Indian Diaspora and Transnationalism*. New Delhi: Rawat Publications, 2012.

Fenton, John Y. *Transplanting Religious Traditions: Asian Indians in America*. New York: Praeger, 1988.

Foreman, Christopher H. "Noted Arts Expert Benjamin Rowland Dies at Age of 67," *Harvard Crimson*, October 5, 1972. http://www.thecrimson.com/article/1972/10/5/noted-arts-expert-benjamin-rowland-d (accessed September 1, 2016).

Friedman, Jonathan. "Globalization, Class and Culture in Global Systems," in *Journal of World-Systems Research* vi, no. 3 (Fall/Winter 2000): 636–656.

Fuller, Christopher John. *The Camphor Flame: Popular Hinduism and Society in India*. Princeton: Princeton University Press, 2004.

Gangoly, O.C. *South Indian Bronzes: A Historical Survey of South Indian Sculpture with Iconographical Notes Based on Original Sources*. Calcutta: Nababharat Publishers, 1915.

Garnett, Jane, and Gervase Rosser. "Miraculous Images and the Sanctification of Urban Neighborhood in Post-Medieval Italy," *Journal of Urban History* 32, no. 5 (July 2006).

Gell, Alfred. *Art and Agency: An Anthropological Theory*. New York: Oxford University Press, 1998.

Goodkind, Herbert K. *Violin Iconography of Antonio Stradivari 1644–1737*. New York: Larchmont, 1972.

Granhoff, Phyllis, and Koichi Shinohara, eds. *Images in Asian Religions: Texts and Contexts*. Vancouver: UBC Press, 2004.

Guha-Thakurta, Tapati. "The Museumised (sic) Relic: Archaeology and the First Museum of Colonial India." *SAGE Journals. The Indian Economic and Social History Review* 34, no. 1 (1997): 21–51.

Haberman, David. *Journey Through the Twelve Forests, My Encounter with Krishna*. New York: Oxford University Press, 1993.

Halbertal, Moshe, and Avishai Margalit. *Idolatry*. Cambridge, Massachusetts: Harvard University Press, 1992.

Hall, S. "Cultural Identity and Diaspora." In Rutherford, J., ed. *Identity, Community, Culture, Difference*. London: Lawrence and Wishart, 1990, 222–237.

Hariray, Goswami. "Hariray Goswami's Blog." https://shriharirayji.com/pushtimarg/ (accessed September 1, 2016).

Harle, J.C. *The Art and Architecture of the Indian Subcontinent*. New York: Penguin, 1986.

Harman, Graham. "Tristan Garcia and the Thing-in-itself." *Parrhesia* 16 (2013): 26–34.

Hawley, John Stratton. *At Play with Krishna: Pilgrimage Dramas from Brindavan*. Delhi: Motilal Banarsidass, 1992 reprint of the 1981 edition by Princeton University Press.

______. *Krishna, The Butter Thief*. Princeton: Princeton University Press, 2014.

Haynes, Douglas E. *Small Town Capitalism in Western India: Artisans, Merchants and the Making of the Informal Economy 1870–1960*. New York: Cambridge University Press, 2012.

Hegel, G.W.F. *Phenomenology of Spirit*. Translated by A.V. Miller. New York: Oxford University Press, 1952.

Heidbrink, Simone, and Nadja Miczek, eds. "Aesthetics and the Dimensions of the Senses." *Heidelberg Journal of Religions on the Internet*, Vol. 4. No. 1 (2010), 151–178. http://nbn-resolving.de/urn:nbn:de:bsz:16-rel-93908 (accessed July 1, 2016).

Heidigger, Martin. *Being and Time, a Translation of Sein and Zeit.* Translated by Joan Stambaugh. Albany: SUNY Press, 1996.

Herman, Phyllis K. "Seeing the Divine Through Windows: Online Puja and Virtual Religious Experience," *Heidelberg Journal of Religions on the Internet* 4, no.1 (2010).

Higgins, Sabrina. "Divine Mothers: The Influence of Isis on the Virgin Mary in Egyptian Lactans-Iconography." *Journal of the Canadian Society for Coptic Studies* 3–4 (2012): 71–90.

Hindu Community and Cultural Center, Livermore, California. "Mahakumbhabhishekam 2010." http://www.livermoretemple.org/hints/MKA2010/index.html (accessed January 1, 2017).

Hindu Janajagruti Samiti, "Hindus' Success: Argentine Exhibit Converting Barbie into Goddess Kali Cancelled," October 2, 2014. https://www.hindujagruti.org/news/25434.html (accessed September 1, 2016).

Hindu Temple Society of North America, Flushing, New York. https://nyganeshtemple.org/ (accessed January 1, 2017).

Hindustan Times. "India, Britain and three waves of migration." https://www.hinduismtoday.com/modules/smartsection/item.php?itemid=1366 (accessed September 1, 2016).

Hinnells, John R. "South Asian Religions in Migration: A Comparative Study of the British, Canadian, and U.S. Experiences," in Howard Coward, John R. Hinnells, and Raymond Brady Williams, *The South Asian Religious Diaspora in Britain, Canada, and the United States.* Albany: State University of New York Press, 2000.

Indian Express, The, July 9, 2016. "Swaminarayan Idol in RSS Dress at Surat School Kicks Up Row." http://indianexpress.com/article/india/india-news-india/gujarat-temple-lord-swaminarayan-rss-sevak-dress-bjp-controversy-2840929/ (accessed September 1, 2016).

Jain, Kajri. *Gods in the Bazaar; the Economies of Indian Calendar Art.* Durham, North Carolina: Duke University Press, 2007.

James, William. *The Varieties of Religious Experience: A Study in Human Nature, Being the Gifford Lectures on Natural Religion Delivered at Edinburgh in 1901–1902.* New York: Longmans, Green and Co., 1902.

Joshi, Khyati Y. *New Roots in America's Sacred Ground: Religion, Race and Ethnicity in Indian America.* New Brunswick, NJ: Rutgers University Press, 2006.

Jung, Carl Gustav, ed. *Man and His Symbols.* New York: Dell, 1968.

_____. *Mandala Symbolism.* Translated by R.F.C. Hull. Princeton: Princeton University. Press, 1972.

Kelly, Robert, and David Thomas. *Archaeology*, 6th ed. Independence, Kentucky: Wadsworth Cengage, 2012.

King, Ursula. *Teilhard de Chardin and Eastern Religions: Spirituality and Mysticism in an Evolutionary World.* Mahwah, New Jersey: Paulist Press, 2011.

Knipe, David. *Hinduism: Experiments in the Sacred.* Long Grove, Illinois: Waveland Press, 1998.

Komaragiri, Narrenaditya. "Amazing Secrets of Tirumala Temple Revealed by Head Priest Ramana Deekshithulu," *Tirumalesa* (October 2, 2016). http://www.tirumalesa.com/amazing-secrets-of-tirumala-temple-revealed-by-head-priest-ramana-deekshithulu/ (accessed October 2, 2016).

Korn, Peter. *Why We Make Things and Why it Matters: The Education of a Craftsman.* Boston: David R. Godine, 2015.

Kramrisch, Stella, and Raymond Burnier. *The Hindu Temple*, 2. New Delhi: Motilal Banarsidass reprint, 1976. https://books.google.com/books?id=8-aS52MgIkMC&pg=PA359&lpg=PA359&dq=hindu+temple+as+living+presence&so, 359 (accessed July 1, 2016).

_____ and _____. *Indian Sculpture.* Delhi: Motilal Banarsidass, 1981 reprint of 1933 Oxford University Press edition.

Kristensen, Troels Myrup. *Making and Breaking the Gods: Christian Responses to Pagan*

Sculpture in Late Antiquity. Langelandsgade, Denmark: Aarhus University Press, Aarhus studies in Mediterranean Antiquity, 2013.

Kumar, Ratnam Krishnamurti Ashok, interview with Rajendran Srinivasan, 2016.

Kumaravadivelu, B. *Cultural Globalization and Language Education*. New Haven: Yale University Press, 2007.

Lahey, Stephen E. "Denying Transubstantiation, Physics, Eucharist, and Apostasy, Oxford Scholarship Online. http://www.oxfordscholarship.com/view/10.1093/acprof:oso/9780195183313.001.0001/acprof-9780195183313-chapter-4 (accessed June 1, 2016).

Layton, Robert. "Art and Agency: A Reassessment," *The Journal of the Royal Anthropological Institute* 9, no. 3 (September 2003): 447–464.

Lazaro, Desmond Peter. *Pichhvai Painting Tradition of Rajasthan: Materials, Methods and Symbolism*. Ahmedabad, India: Mapin, 2006.

Levy, Thomas E., and Alina M. Levy, D. Radhakrishna Sthapathy, D. Srikanda Sthapathy, D. Swaminatha Sthapathy. *Masters of Fire: Hereditary Bronze Casters of South India*. Bochum, India: 2008.

Levy, S.J. "Symbols for Sale," *Harvard Business Review* 37, no. 4 (1959): 117–24.

Locke, John. *Second Treatise*, in Karen Vaughn, *Locke on Property, A Biographical Essay*. Liberty Fund, 2015. http://oll.libertyfund.org/pages/locke-on-property-a-bibliographical-essay-by-karen-vaughn#_ftn22 (accessed June 1, 2016).

Los Angeles County Museum of Art, "Indian Sculpture 700–1800." https://books.google.com/books?id=-fvKVDxcJoUC&pg=PA231&lpg=PA231&dq=characteristics+of+Chola+art&source=bl&ots=CDUtRuQCNX&sig=iCqn6 37 (accessed July 1, 2016).

Lynch, Owen. *Divine Passions: The Social, Construction of Emotion in India*. New York: Oxford University Press, 199.

Marriott, McKim, ed. *Village India: Studies in the Little Community*. (*Comparative Studies of Cultures and Civilizations*, [No. 6]) xi. Chicago: University of Chicago Press, 1955.

McCracken, Grant. *Culture and Consumption: New Approaches to the Symbolic Character of Consumer Goods and Activities*. Bloomington: Indiana University Press, 1988.

McDaniel, June. "Folk Vaishnavism and the Thakur Pancayat," in Guy L. Beck, ed. *Alternative Krishnas: Regional and Vernacular Variations on a Hindu Deity*. Albany: SUNY Press, 2005.

McDonnell, Kilian. "Conclusion," in *John Calvin, the Church and the Eucharist*. Princeton: Princeton University Press, 1967, 363–366. http://www.jstor.org/stable/j.ctt183ph4t.13 (accessed June 1, 2016).

McGrath, Alistar E. *Reformation Thought: An Introduction*. Hoboken, New Jersey: Wiley and Blackwell, 4th ed., 2012.

Medina, Jennifer. "Debate Erupts in California Over Curriculum on India's History," *New York Times*, May 4, 2016.

Meskell, Lynn. *Archaeologies of Social Life: Age, Sex, Class et cetera in Ancient Egypt*. Malden, Massachusetts, Blackwell, 1999.

______. *Object Worlds in Ancient Egypt: Material Biographies Past and Present*. Oxford, England: Berg, 2014.

Metropolitan Museum of Art, Collection Records. "Architectural Ensemble from Jain Meeting Hall." http://www.metmuseum.org/collection/the-collection-online/search/39317 (accessed September 1, 2016).

Milk Miracle. "The Hindu Milk Miracle of Sept 21 1995, August 21st 2006 and September 23rd 2010." http://www.milkmiracle.com/ (accessed January 1, 2017).

Ministry of External Affairs, Government of India. http://moia.gov.in/index.aspx (accessed January 1. 2017).

Misra, P.K. *Studies in Hindu and Buddhist Art*. Chikhli, India: Abhinav Publications, 1999.

Mitchell, George. *The Hindu Temple: An Introduction to Its Meaning and Forms*. Chicago: University of Chicago Press, 1988.

Mitter, Partha. *Much Maligned Monsters*, Oxford, England: Clarendon Press, 1977.

Müller, F. Max, et al. *Sacred Books of the East,* 50 vols. Oxford: Clarendon Press, 1879.

Munoz, Julian Garcia, and Juan Carlos Losada Gonzalez. "Modern Shastras," *Proceedings of the Third International Congress on Construction History.* Cottbus, May 2009.

Nair, Shantha. *Sri Venkateswara: Lord Balaji and His Holy Abode of Tirupathi.* Ahmedabad, India: Jaico, 2013.

Nardi, Isabella. "Re-evaluating the Role of Text in Indian Art: Towards a *Shastric* Analysis of the Image of Shri Nathji in Nathdvara Miniature Painting," *South Asia Research* 29 no. 2 (2009).

New York Times, December 23, 1987. "Barbie: Doll, Icon or Sexist Symbol." http://www.nytimes.com/1987/12/23/garden/barbie-doll-icon-or-sexist-symbol.html (accessed September 1, 2016).

Nongbri, Brent. *Before Religion: A History of a Modern Concept.* New Haven, Connecticut: Yale University Press, 2013.

Oshatz, Molly. "From "Meh" to Amen," *First Things.* http://www.firstthings.com/web-exclusives/2015/06/can-the-nones-go-from-meh-to-amen (accessed April 17, 2016).

Pal, Pratapaditya. "Some Hindu and Buddhist Bronzes from Bangladesh," *Studies in South Asian Heritage, Essays in Memory of M. Harunur Rashid*, Mokammal H. Bhuiyan, ed. Dhaka, Bangladesh: Bangla Academy: 2015. http://www.asianart.com/articles/bangladesh/index.html (accessed September 1, 2016).

Parekh, Bhikhu C., and Gurharpal Singh, Steven Vertovec, eds. *Culture and Economy in the Indian Diaspora.* London: Routledge, 2003.

Parker, Samuel K. "Renovation, Disposal, and Conservation of Hindu Temples and Images: The Institutionalization of Creativity in South Indian and American Art Worlds," *Museum Anthropology Review* 3, no. 2 (Fall 2009).

_____. "Ritual As a Mode of Production: Ethnoarchaeology and Creative Practice in Hindu Temple Arts," in *South Asian Studies* 26, no. 1 (2010): 31–57.

Patel, Shree. Interview with the author, 2015.

Pearce, Susan M. *Museums, Objects and Collections: A Cultural Study.* Washington, D.C.: Smithsonian Institution Press, 1992.

Pew Research Center. *Religion & Public Life,* "Hindus," April 2, 2015. http://www.pewforum.org/2015/04/02/hindus/ (accessed January 1, 2017).

Pillai, R.M., and S.G.K. Pillai, A.D. Damodaran. "The Lost-Wax Casting of Icons, Utensils, Bells, and Other Items in South India," JOM (October 2002). http://www.tms.org/pubs/journals/JOM/0210/Pillai-0210.html (accessed September 1, 2016).

Pillay, K.K. *The Śucīndram Temple.* Adyar Madras: Kalakshetra Publications, 1953.

Pinney, Christopher. *Photos of the Gods: The Printed Image and Political Struggle in India.* London: Reaktion Books, 2004.

Plato, *The Republic*, Book VI: The Allegory of the Cave. http://www.michaelbaur.com/teaching/PlatoCave.pdf (accessed September 1, 2016).

Possehl, Gregory L. *The Indus Civilization; A Contemporary Perspective.* Lanham, Maryland: AltaMira Press, 2002.

Potter, Karl H., ed. *Encyclopedia of Indian Philosophies: Advaita Vedānta up to Samkara and His Pupils.* Princeton: Princeton University Press, 1981.

_____. *Presuppositions of India's Philosophies.* Englewood Cliffs, New Jersey: Prentice-Hall, 1963.

Potter, Simon J. "Webs, Networks, and Systems: Globalization and the Mass Media in the Nineteenth- and Twentieth-Century British Empire," in *Journal of British Studies* 46, no. 3 (July 2007): 621–646.

Purkiss, Diane. *The English Civil War: Papists, Gentlewomen, Soldiers, and Witchfinders in the Birth of Modern Britain.* New York: Basic Books, 2006.

Rajguru, Megha. "From Shrine to Plinth: Studying the Dialectics of Hindu Deities Displayed in the Museum Through Artworks and Their Exhibition." (Ph.D. Dissertation, University of Brighton, 2010).

Rao, T.A. Gopinatha. *Elements of Hindu Iconography.* New York: Garland, 1981.

Redfield, Robert. *Peasant Society and Culture: An Anthropological Approach to Civilization*. Chicago: University of Chicago Press, *1956*.

Reuven Blau. "Hindus Upset Over Brooklyn Museum's Exhibit of Goddess Kali," *New York Daily News*, December 18, 2014. http://www.nydailynews.com/new-york/brooklyn/hindus-upset-brooklyn-museum-exhibit-goddess-kali-article-1.2050474 (accessed September 1, 2016).

Reyna, Ruth. *Introduction to Indian Philosophy: A Simplified Text*. New Delhi: Tata McGraw-Hill, 1971.

Richardson, E. Allen *Seeing Krishna in America; The Hindu Bhakti Tradition of Vallabhacharya in India and Its Movement to the West*. Jefferson, NC: McFarland, 2014.

Rowland, Benjamin. *The Art and Architecture of India: Buddhist, Hindu, Jain*. London: Penguin, 1953.

Saha, Shandip. "Creating a Community of Grace: A History of the Pusti Mārga in Northern and Western India," 1493–1905. Ph.D. dissertation, University of Ottawa, 2004.

Sahoo, Ajaya Kumar, and Johannes G. de Kruijf. *Indian Transnationalism Online: New Perspectives on Diaspora*. Surrey, England: Ashgate, 2014.

Sax, William S. *The Gods at Play: Līlā in South Asia*. New York, Oxford, 1995.

Schiermer, Bjorn. "On the Ageing of Objects in Modern Culture: Ornament and Crime," *SAGE Journals. Theory, Culture & Society* 0, no. 0 (2015): 1–24.

______. "Quasi-Objects, Cult Objects and Fashion Objects: On Two Kinds of Fetishism on Display in Modern Culture," *SAGE Journals. Theory, Culture & Society* 28, no. 1 (2011): 81–102.

Seal, Anil. *The Emergence of Indian Nationalism: Competition and Collaboration in the Later Nineteenth Century*. New York: Cambridge University Press, 1971.

Shah, Bhagwat. Interviews with the author, 2014 -2016.

Sharma, Shital. "A Prestigious Path to Grace: Class, Modernity, and Female Religiosity in Puṣṭimārg Vaiṣṇavism," Montreal: Ph.D. Dissertation, McGill University, 2013.

Shulman, David Dean. *Tamil Temple Myths: Sacrifice and Divine Marriage in the South Indian Saiva Tradition*. Princeton: Princeton University Press, 1980, 48, in Richard M. Eaton, "Temple desecration in pre-modern India. When, where, and why were Hindu temples desecrated in pre-modern history, and how was this connected with the rise of Indo-Muslim states?" *Frontline* (December 22, 2000). http://www.columbia.edu/itc/mealac/pritchett/00islamlinks/txt_eaton_temples1.pdf (accessed July 1, 2016).

Singh, Shruti. "Gujarat Temple Dresses Lord Swaminarayan in RSS Uniform." *India Today*. Ahmedabad, July 8, 2016. http://indiatoday.intoday.in/story/gujarat-temple-dresses-lord-swaminarayan-in-rss-uniform/1/686975.html (accessed September 1, 2016).

Skelton, Robert. *Rajasthani Temple Hangings of the Krishna Cult from the Collection of Karl Mann*, New York: American Federation of Arts, 1973.

Smith, Adam. *An Inquiry into the Nature and Cause of the Wealth of Nations*, 2 vols. London: W. Strahan and T. Cadell, 1776.

Smithsonian Institution. "A Discussion with Young American Hindus," *Puja: Expressions of Hindu devotion*, Guide for Educators. Washington, D.C.: 1997. https://www.asia.si.edu/pujaonline/puja/sitemap_1.html (accessed September 1, 2016).

Sridhar, R. "Right-Trunked Ganesha? Be Careful!" *Mumbai Mirror*, Jan 23, 2009.

Srinivasan, Doris. "The So-Called Proto-Śiva Seal from Mohenjo-Daro: An Iconological Assessment." *Archives of Indian Art* 29 (1975/1976): 47–58.

"Sri Vaisnavam." https://ramanujadasan.wordpress.com/sri-vaishnava-digital-fund/ (accessed September 1, 2016).

Sthapati, V. Ganapati. *Indian Sculpture & Iconography: Forms and Measurement*. Translated by Sashikala Ananth. Ahmedabad, India: Sri Aurobindo Society, Pondicherry in Association with Mapin Publishing, 2002.

Sundaravadivel, S. & Co. http://southindianhandicrafts.co.in/panchalogha_utsava_vigraham (accessed July 1, 2016).

Surdas, Sant. "Krishna Denying He Stole the Butter," *Sant Surdas Poems.* http://vedicilluminations.com/downloads/Bhakti-Vaisnava-Texts/sant_surdas_2004_9.pdf (accessed July 1, 2016).

Talbot, Cynthia. "Temples, Donors, and Gifts: Patterns of Patronage in Thirteenth-Century South India." *Journal of Asian Studies* 50, no. 2 (May 1991): 308.

Taylor, Paul Michael. "Collecting Icons of Power and Identity: Transformation of Indonesian Material Culture in the Museum Context," *SAGE Journals. Cultural Dynamics* 7, no. 1 (1995): 101–124.

Teilhard de Chardin, Pierre. *The Heart of Matter.* New York: Harcourt, Brace, 2017.

Thompson, Michael. *Rubbish Theory: The Creation and Destruction of Value.* Oxford University Press, 1979.

Tinh, V. Tran Tan, and Labrecque, Yvette. *Isis Lactans: Corpus des Monuments, Gréco-Romains d'Isis Allaitant Harpocrate.* Leiden: Brill, 1973. http://www.academia.edu/1954926/Divine_Mothers_The_Influence_of_Isis_on_the_Virgin_Mary_in_Egyptian_Lactans-Iconography_Journal_of_the_Canadian_Society_for_Coptic_Studies_3_4_2012_71–90 (accessed September 1, 2016).

Tilley, Christopher. *Metaphor and Material Culture.* Hoboken, New Jersey: Blackwell, 1999.

Tillich, Paul. *Dynamics of Faith.* New York: HarperCollins, Perennial Classics, 1957.

Timalsina, Sthaneshwar. "Imagining Reality: Image and Visualization in Classical Hinduism." *Southeast Review of Asian Studies* 35 (2013): 50–69.

Toomey, Paul M. *Food from the Mouth of Krishna: Feasts and Festivities in a North Indian Pilgrimage Centre.* Delhi: Hindustan Publishing Company, 1994.

Törzsök, Judit. "Icons of inclusivism: Maṇḍalas in Some Early Śaiva Tantras…" in Gudrun Bühnemann, ed. *Mandalas and Yantras in the Hindu traditions.* Leiden: Koninklyke Brill NV, 2003, 189–190.

Trinidad, Daily Express, September 22, 2010. http://www.trinidadexpress.com/news/Ganesh_murtis_drink_milk_-103591304 (accessed July 1, 2916).

Tucci, Giuseppe. *The Theory and Practice of the Mandala: With Special Reference to the Modern Psychology of the Subconscious.* London: Rider, 1969.

van Eck, Caroline. *Art, Agency and Living Presence: From the Animated Image to the Excessive Object.* Leiden, The Netherlands: De Gruyter, Leiden University Press, 2015.

Vanitha, R., and S. Mayilvaganan. "Organisation (sic) of Metal Icon Production in Swamimalai," *Indian Journal of Applied Research* 3, no. 4 (April, 2013).

Vasquez, Manuel A., and Marie Friedmann Marquardt. *Globalizing the Sacred: Religion Across the Americas.* New Brunswick: Rutgers University Press, 2003.

Veylandswami, Satguru Bodhinatha. "My Friend, Lord Ganesha: Hinduism's Lord of Dharma," *Hinduism Today,* October, November, December 2005. https://www.hinduismtoday.com/modules/smartsection/item.php?itemid=1366 (accessed September 1, 2016).

VYO. http://paroolmodi67.blogspot.com/ (accessed January 1, 2017).

VYO World. http://vyoworld.org/centers/ (accessed January 1, 2017).

Wakin, Daniel J. "Selling a 300-Year-Old Cello," *New York Times Magazine,* January 13, 2012.

Website of the Sanskrit Religions Institute. "Installing a Sacred Image Mūrti Sthapana/Prāṇ Pratiṣṭhā," Devasthanam. http://sanskrit.org/installing-a-sacred-image-murti-sthapanaprana-pratishta/ (accessed September 1, 2016).

Weick, Werner. Director. *Carl Gustav Jung: Artist of the Soul.* New York: Mystic Fire Videos, 1997.

Wenzlhuemer, Roland. *Connecting the Nineteenth-Century World: The Telegraph and Globalization.* Cambridge: Cambridge University Press, 2012.

Williams, Raymond Brady. *Christian Pluralism in the United States: The Indian Immigrant Experience.* Cambridge: Cambridge University Press, 1996.

Wesley, Morgan. "A Dialogue of Connoisseurship and Science in Constructing Authenticity: The Case of the Duke of Buckingham's China." In Aldrich, Meghan and Hackforth-Jones, Jos., eds. *Art and Authenticity.* New York: Sotheby's Institute of Art, 2012.

Wiecek, Matthew Gregory. "South Asian Figurines in the British Museum: Literature Review and Analysis." Master of Arts Thesis, Department of Archaeology, Durham University, 2013.

Yagnik, Bharat. "162-Acre Akshardham Coming Up in New Jersey." *Time of India*, July 22, 2014.

Index

Numbers in ***bold italics*** indicate pages with illustrations

www.ingramcontent.com/pod-product-compliance
Ingram Content Group UK Ltd.
Pitfield, Milton Keynes, MK11 3LW, UK
UKHW041842150726
7214IPUK00015B/122